Postcolonial Counterpoint

Orientalism, France, and the Maghreb

FARID LAROUSSI

UNIVERSITY OF TORONTO PRESS
Toronto Buffalo London

© University of Toronto Press 2016
Toronto Buffalo London
www.utppublishing.com
Printed in the U.S.A.

ISBN 978-1-4426-4891-3 (cloth)

∞ Printed on acid-free, 100% post-consumer recycled paper with vegetable-based inks.

University of Toronto Romance Series

Library and Archives Canada Cataloguing in Publication

Laroussi, Farid, author
Postcolonial counterpoint : orientalism, France, and the Maghreb/
Farid Laroussi.

(University of Toronto romance series)
Includes bibliographical references and index.
ISBN 978-1-4426-4891-3 (cloth)

1. French literature – 20th century – History and criticism.   2. French
literature – North African authors – History and criticism.   3. Orientalism
in literature.   4. Postcolonialism in literature.   5. Gide, André, 1869–1951.
6. Orientalism – France.   7. France – Relations – Africa, North.   8. Africa,
North – Relations – France.   9. Muslims – France.   10. Islam – France.
I. Title.   II. Series: University of Toronto romance series

PQ307.O75L37 2016   840.9'3585   C2015-908025-8

University of Toronto Press acknowledges the financial assistance to its
publishing program of the Canada Council for the Arts and the Ontario Arts
Council, an agency of the Government of Ontario.

Canada Council   Conseil des Arts
for the Arts   du Canada

ONTARIO ARTS COUNCIL
CONSEIL DES ARTS DE L'ONTARIO
an Ontario government agency
un organisme du gouvernement de l'Ontario

Funded by the   Financé par le
Government   gouvernement
of Canada   du Canada

Canadä

For Tahar and Meriem

Contents

Acknowledgments

During the years this book was taking shape, in a very eerie sense, events provided me with powerful illustrations of my ideas and arguments. In particular, the killings in Paris on January 2015 exemplified the historical, cultural, and political undercurrents this study examines. France and the Maghreb had never been brought together this tightly within the postcolonial condition – or in such a dramatic way, one must add.

However, instead of focusing on close readings such events, which would merely generate more interpretations, I have taken the cultural and materialist approach of postcolonial studies, especially as it bears on Orientalism and its mutation(s). In contemporary France and the Maghreb, culture is a site of both interpretation and conflict and is saturated with profound misunderstandings as well as what I refer to as "lingering states of mind."

This book has grown out of a wider conversation with colleagues and students over several years and in diverse venues. For their advice, conversation, consultation, corrections, suggestions, support, and scholarly pointers, I am indebted to Emily Apter, Sandra Berman, Abdelkader Cheref, Tom Conley, Hamid Dabashi, Charles Forsdick, Hafid Gafaiti, Alexandra Gueydan, Fredric Jameson, Michel Laronde, Françoise Lionnet, Achille Mbembe, and Christopher L. Miller. Beyond the academic world, Assia Djebar, whom I met for the last time on Avenue de la République on a beautiful, sad day in May, will always command a special place in my reflections on the riddle of what *Algerianness* might be and entail in the twenty-first century. Also, this book was greatly improved by a superb editor, Richard Ratzlaff of the University of Toronto Press. Institutional support came from the University of British Columbia, and I am deeply grateful to André Lamontagne and Gaby Pailer for their faith and expectations that my work would be completed and published within the time frame I set myself. Most important, I am grateful to Nisa Saadah for her indispensable words and affection.

POSTCOLONIAL COUNTERPOINT

1 States of Postcolonial Reading

N'oublions jamais que nous nous sommes emparés de l'Algérie moins encore par le droit *du plus fort* que par le droit *du plus civilisé*.[1]

Another book on Orientalism cannot reasonably expect a warm reception. Since the appearance of Edward Said's groundbreaking essays on Orientalism and Jacques Derrida's pioneering work on deconstruction nearly forty years ago, criticism of Orientalism and deconstruction has been frequent, often harsh, and, it bears stressing, ill-informed.[2] It seems that our contemporary cross-cultural and transnational visions and experiences, operating under the guise of postcoloniality, have had little effect on how we assess Orientalism – either its epistemology or its historicity. One cannot but be reminded of the words of Allamah Qazvini, one the greatest twentieth-century scholars in Islamic studies, who spent more than twenty years in Europe, most of them in Paris: "In Europe and among the Orientalists the number of fake and would be scholars, and indeed charlatans, is infinitely more than the number of genuine Orientalists and real scholars. [...] These Orientalists then proceed, without the slightest sense of shame or being scandalized, for there is no one to tell, to claim knowledge and authority."[3] My remarks and argument are not intended to single out some Western scholars and native informants, for doing so would only repeat their tendency to glorify global forces (cultural, ideological, economic) while denying the forces that condition the postcolonial local, Muslim, and Other. Yet the latent Orientalist claims are hardly surprising in the context of intellectual and academic traditions that have resisted challenging the foundations of fields of knowledge, especially in the present political climate, which has been catastrophic for emerging minorities, especially those from the Muslim world.[4] One consequence of this is that the truth value of established historical and cultural accounts is unstable, as we will see when we review the challenges faced by francophone literature and when discussing the question of Islam and citizenship in contemporary France. Ideology is like a party crasher in these domains, and this is especially true of ideologies that seek to straddle different levels of civilization. Said's thesis was that the body of theory and practice that Orientalism had become helped forge the intellectual tools that enabled the West to exercise economic and cultural control over the Orient. The key concept for him was *representation*, as opposed to a dualist ideological pattern (West–East). Orientalism, for him, was a universal problem with a discursive flexibility that remains to this day unequalled in its scope and potency: "Orientalism is a school of interpretation whose material happens to be the Orient."[5] Said never claimed that the Orient existed as an objectified or essentialized reality. For him – and this is where there is room to criticize him – Orientalism had drifted away from its humanistic roots. He remained committed to the concept of the sovereign subject, in opposition to the premises of post-structuralism and its questioning of origins and single causes. He was wedded to the old Enlightenment transcendental signifier, and he tried to expand the idea to encompass a broader range of humanistic patterns. Critics were quick to jump on Said's "literary" take on Orientalism's epistemology, and on his superficial understanding of the sociology of what had come to be known as the Orient. In his famous response to Said's *Orientalism*, Bernard Lewis wrote: "Apart from embodying a hitherto unknown theory of knowledge, Mr. Said expresses a contempt for modern Arab scholarly achievement worse than anything that he attributes to his demonic Orientalists."[6] Here Lewis may have a point, but he and his followers should recognize that their critical stance and its archaeology are enshrined in the West and fail to historicize the modes of knowledge of the postcolonial itself. And this is what I intend to do in the particular case of France and the Maghreb.

Said's postcolonial hermeneutic can easily be viewed as a hasty, functionalist reading of Foucault. This is perhaps one dimension that the critical reception of Said has missed and that I want to explore. My argument is not against Said's work, nor is it an apology for his *Orientalism*, which is considered the fountainhead of today's postcolonial studies. Is the situation any different today, as we convince ourselves that the postcolonial era has secured some historical distance from colonial evils? Truth and knowledge, which usually smooth the passage of history into culture, seem ill-suited to size up the relationship between the West and the Islamic world, for reality is always further deconstructed and then reconstructed into representation. Said was correct in this respect; however, we will also underscore the limitations of his methodology when it comes to examining Arab/Muslim cultures. By placing Orientalism at the centre of the legacy of humanism, was he attempting to reframe his aesthetic idea of counterpoint, which is both flexible and inclusive, even while fostering cross-disciplinary and cross-cultural understanding? The Orientalism that Said deals with is not just some scientific and ideological model; rather, it is a way of describing and exploring the world through personal experience, eventually making that experience universal. Said goes so far as to state: "*Orientalism* is a partisan book, not a theoretical machine."[7] Our challenge is to asses to what extent such a commitment still holds currency in the specific postcolonial context between France and the Maghreb. Of course, the fact is that in the twenty-first century the Islamic world is becoming part of the West, even while issues of immigration and *intégration* are being sorted out – in contemporary France, for example. How is it, then, that the postcolonial condition – and we will define what that encapsulates – can be used, especially in the academic world, in these different senses in such a variety of disciplines and backgrounds?

This book is about the inner life of a never-dying ideology, at times called "Orientalism" and at other times "neo-imperialism." It is also an attempt to make sense of cultural practices and historical events by looking beyond their representation and the so-called objective truth of language to reveal how mere speculation is too often turned into settled certainty. Said's main opponent, Bernard Lewis, who focused exclusively on a philological approach to the Islamic East, advocated a single essentialized meaning and ignored calls for interpretation and discussion of the sociohistorical context in which culture and politics foster resistance. We will see that the fraught relations between France and the Maghreb are important not just on historical grounds but also because they will be shaping the new Euro-Mediterranean world of the twenty-first century. The so-called Arab Spring that began in Tunisia in January 2011 demonstrates the extent to which freedom based on universalist agreement is associated with the agency of native cultures and helps articulate new models.[8]

Such a challenging state of relations touches on a question of theory as well as on politics. Even within the emerging nations south of the

Mediterranean Sea, it is often assumed that both universal and relative truths exist that delineate the privileged position of culture in matters of religion, literature, and gender. No wonder the cost of "doing" post-colonial studies has been high. Cultural histories have been ignored or neglected, and as we will see, the discourse itself remains imprisoned in the old imperialistic mode of writing intellectual history, by historicism and post-independence nationalist hagiography. This book – indeed, this amounts to its expanded argument – rejects the confines imposed by standard academic monographs as it seeks a discourse better suited to criticizing latent Orientalism and postcolonial studies from a point of departure between knowledge and hegemonic relationships (as these relate to former colonial states and to today's institutional powers). I am writing from within a postcolonial context, one in which discourse, identity, and memory (for example) tend to be shaped by external forces. For instance, is it possible that key postcolonial terms manufactured by the theoretical machine, such as "hybridity," have created a location that is the same everywhere even while power remains located in the West? I contend that the ideology underpinning the science of Orientalism has had a catalytic effect, so much so that the figure of the Oriental is no longer aesthetically and humanistically comprehensible, while he/she is forced into a secular and historical condition. Examples are many, from the 2003 US military campaign in Iraq in the name of democracy, to the French obsession with Islamic religious symbols, to the entire postcolonial obsession with "locating" the native. The warning came loud and clear more than half a century ago, in *The Wretched of the Earth* (1961), in which Frantz Fanon delineates the differences between cultural (identity, traditions, etc.) and intellectual (revolution, emancipation, etc.) history in terms of specific conventions and particular aims. Present-day attempts to view the postcolonial condition through new eyes have not been very convincing.[9] Yet Foucault explained in *The Order of Things* (1966) how the agency of power – political, economic, and cultural – grounds its own discourse. Seen from this perspective, the performance of postcolonial theory (or theories) invites re-evaluation in order to avoid what Heidegger called "the politics of culture," politics that arise when the essence of culture feeds on itself and thereby risks losing any axiomatic sense.[10] The purpose of this study is to show to what extent the current postcolonial discourse is defined less by a line of demonstration than by the act of communication itself – indeed, by an act of communication about the *Western* self. There must be room to navigate between the monochromatic views of an academic world that is too busy coining "theory," on the one hand, and creative literary endeavours by Maghrebi writers that trawl and recast ideas about "resistance" and "minority voice," too often for Western audiences only, on the other.[11] I will argue in chapter 6 that this strategy of cultural co-optation, which is complicit with neocolonialism, replicates an ideology of identity politics that shares many of the essentialist notions that are implicit in Western views of culture and history. The native informant syndrome has scarcely been addressed; it is as if respectability and admittance to the centres of power have fostered less subversive stances. Or as Anne McClintock put it when postcolonial studies began to gain prominence in North American academe, "colonialism returns at the moment of its disappearance."[12] I will be examining this challenging axiom of postcolonial studies as a means to explore the provocative idea that cultural interests and modes of knowledge have transformed postcolonial studies into a tool that has repoliticized the epistemology of colonialism. By exploring francophone literature and how feminist discourse is mimicked in the Islamic sphere, I will highlight that particular condition as it currently exists between France and the Maghreb. This book also examines latent Orientalism as it relates to the Maghreb – its permanent features, its variants, and its relative absence from mainstream postcolonial discourse. I will consider these questions, among others: What is the postcolonial agency within the contours of the French Orientalist episteme? How does one account for a space that distinguishes between a sovereign postcolonial subject, on the one hand, and France or the West as the principal interlocutor of that subject, on the other? The discussion will also highlight the Western and French "othering" of Islam. What interests me is the tension between the pitfalls of historicism[13] and the production of knowledge about the postcolonial condition; this is part of my effort to bring to the surface the dynamics of othering both Maghrebi and French subjects. If the argument encourages others to grasp the higher cultural stakes in play between France and the Maghreb and to shake off the self-referential universalism at the core of postcolonial discourse, it will have served one of its main purposes. My goal is not to settle accounts with postcolonial studies, for doing so would ultimately reinforce historical determinism; rather, I want to examine the essentializing process that has occurred in the realm of theory, a process that risks turning theory into yet another disposable fiction. The very contemporaneity of Orientalism interests me; so does a sustained argument for repudiating postcolonial metanarratives.

There seem to be at least three ways of conceiving the term "Orientalism." First, it refers to an academic discipline dating back to fifteenth-century Europe, when brilliant scholarly work was carried out that marked the beginning of the fields of philology and religious studies. Second, Orientalism can be viewed as a discourse that seeks to define and understand what the Orient and the Occident truly are in both political and narrative terms. A third approach to Orientalism, and the most polemical one, identifies the Orient as an object of study in order to represent and control it. These three conceptions are linked insofar as they draw distinctions between "us" and "them" and blur the boundary between scientific speculation and systemic discourse. And while they compete on discursive grounds, these conceptions reveal a Western centrism that would have been innocuous or short-lived were it not for its global implications. But I intend to keep my reading clear of the tempting – and misguided – pan-Arabic, pan-Islamic knee-jerk reaction against a West – a reaction that becomes a construct in itself and merely ends up masking the limitations of contemporary Arab/Muslim ideology. Let us be clear: a critique of Orientalism must engage with the discipline and the subject of its scholarship, despite rather than because of any ideological agenda.

In my argument, I pose these questions: What is this conceptual intertextuality that governs the postcolonial relationship between France and the Maghreb? And what are the sources of the loose and sometimes defiant modes of apprehension of the postcolonial condition on the part of the French? French social scientists such as Eric Fassin, Nacira Guénif-Souilamas, Dounia Bouazar, Françoise Gaillard, and Jean Baubérot have in recent years confronted key issues pertaining to French ideas about postcolonial identity, religion, public education, and citizenship. Yet postcolonial theories and critical approaches have not been reformulated (after having been formulated in North America by French theory!) in French academia, especially in the field of literary studies. Is this simply a matter of academic posturing that preserves the boundaries of scholarly knowledge and politics? (Academe is famously insular in both style and content.) Or as Achille Mbembe has put it, is France perhaps still in the grip of its "imperial winter"?[14] Our focus will be on the third way of understanding Orientalism and the mechanisms of power/culture perpetuation. Postcolonial studies will feature significantly in this work, albeit not as a catalogue of the transnational, the diasporic, the exilic, the globalized, the decentred, the hybrid, the politics of difference, and other current theoretical configurations. The latent Orientalist argument is certainly wedded to an evaluation of postcolonial studies, although it will neither secure nor consolidate its supposed academic authority. This book attests to the cultural and ideological perspective of latent Orientalism from an viewpoint predicated on misconceptions of the knowing subject.[15] As I examine the relationship between Orientalism and postcolonialism, I will reflect on what constitutes the (re)production of knowledge about the postcolonial Maghreb and about France. At the same time, no one seriously engaged in this discipline dismisses Orientalism as pseudoscientific or politically driven; it is precisely its cohesiveness and rationalism with respect to other cultures such as Islam that add to Orientalism's amplitude. Let us be clear, this work has no intention of falling into the "Orientalism-bashing" that scholars like Robert Irwin have tried to pin on Said; however, my argument does demonstrate that within the Franco-Maghrebi sphere, one cannot avoid a particular discursive mode of thinking that can be called "Orientalism." And Orientalism is what exemplifies the postcolonial paradigm both in the Maghreb and in France. To dismiss the ideological dimension of postcolonial studies is to attempt to sanitize the academic discourse of the humanities while providing an alibi for complicity with neocolonialism.[16] It is evident that the recent Arab revolutions in Tunisia, Egypt, Libya, Yemen, Bahrain, and Syria have overthrown long-standing failed forms of nationalism – forms based either on the legacy of the Enlightenment and its fanciful notions of nationhood, or on a socialist model of government with no genuine working class in which to ground its Marxist principles.[17] In the twenty-first century the much-vaunted Western institutional models seem to have generated a global dilemma, one that rears up when this question is posed: Are the "Arabs" ready for democracy?[18] Think for a moment what the term "Arab democracy" signifies when applied to countries with diverse histories, contrasting demographic profiles, distinctive social structures (with regard to public education, models of government, the political visibility of women, the role of the media in society, etc.), and varying degrees of economic development (in terms of unemployment rates, the ambiguous benefits of oil revenues, and the strength or weakness of tourism, and of agriculture), and when we summarily lump those countries together and judge them according to some democracy "index" (see, for example, the annual *Arab Human Development Reports* of the UN Development Program), the lofty standards of which strangely do not apply to other nations, such as Russia, which two decades after the fall of the Berlin Wall finds itself again in the grip of an authoritarian and corrupt regime bordering on the grotesque.[19]

Colonial occupation differed in its forms across continents and over the centuries, but in broad terms, it started for the same hegemonic reasons, which revolved around war or trade, and ended up drowning in an idealism tenuously associated with democracy. In the case of France, we now understand that a republic that blends democratic and egalitarian virtues with economic pragmatism and the energetic pursuit of geopolitical interests is capable of countenancing the morally dubious enterprise of colonialism, along with all the suffering and exploitation that are its foreseeable consequences within the frame of global capitalism. The former colonial overlords, after granting independence to the colonies, felt the need to develop an economic and cultural apparatus that was capable of orchestrating globalization, a phenomenon emblematic of the dissolution of ideologies and of nation-states. In postcolonial discourse, with its connecting threads of "hybridity," "third space," and "cultural fetishism," we hear echoes of past attempts to rewrite the Other's world. Taking Said's definition of Orientalism and his theoretical premises as my starting point, this book will analyse how the postcolonial theory "industry" (for lack of a better word) has been ridden to its logical conclusion by the Western academy and its fantasy of universalism and sovereign subject, as well as by the cohorts of native informants and intellectual fellow-travellers who have proven themselves incapable of disavowing the centre of globality. Lastly, one critical question stands out in the representation exercise that postcolonial discourse constitutes: Is theory ever independent of the historical forces that produce it?

An examination of Orientalism and postcolonial studies allows me to approach my subject from a number of different entry points, including those of history, religion, and literature. The goal is not historical reconstruction; rather, my argument will question the foundational form of knowledge that has arisen in tandem with with the postcolonial condition. In the case of the francophone writers, we will see, for example, how the concept of nationalism has been embraced by the first generation and rejected by contemporary authors, as if the redrawn picture of nationhood – especially Algeria's – could bypass the epistemic texture and leave the postcolonial subject unaffected. In other words, the concept of postcolonial does not always apply (e.g., within the dichotomy of nativism and Enlightenment) simply because of a given colonial legacy or the logic behind the homogenization of the world. Perhaps this reflects the fundamental dialectical question that revolves around identity and power. It is evident that the current postcolonial condition does not provide a coherent amalgam of practices that depend on class and location. We will examine the problematic instance of upper-class Maghrebi female intellectuals in France, who dabble in Western as opposed to Islamic feminism, who declare themselves "emancipated," and who brand as socially inferior and culturally illiterate their fellow female natives, be they at home or in the underprivileged French suburbs. A striking consequence of this destructive ideological position is that it turns the "native" into an outsider in his/her own home, demonstrating again how knowledge is historically produced.

Whose views am I indicting, then? Perhaps those of people who posit that postcolonial studies has become a new discourse with a limited note of dissonance in polite academic society.[20] In France the postcolonial critique has essentially operated within chronological markers set around the Algerian War of Independence, branching out to include its sociocultural ramifications such as the practice of torture, the fate of the *pieds-noirs*, the founding of the Fifth Republic, new waves of immigration, and the heightened profile of Islam. Expressions such as "colonial impasse," "integration sequel," "war of memories," and *"la repentance nationale"* have taken over the debate. Yet despite the seminal works of French intellectuals such as Balibar, Césaire, Fanon, Deleuze, Glissant, and Memmi, the postcolonial critique remains barely alluded to in the field of inquiry. One worn-out justification for this lack of concern among French academics (George Balandier and Jean-François Bayard, for example) – a justification that suggests insecurity – is that postcolonial studies is merely an Anglo-Saxon import, that it is cultural studies under another paradigm (i.e., multiculturalism). This is also how I will situate my argument within the critical landscape: that the postcolonial remains overlooked perhaps because the colonial repressed has returned to nest on its native ground. In overcoming this French aversion to postcolonial studies, the challenge is to understand how France imagines itself. The final chapter of this book will examine this particular "historical unconscious," to use Bourdieu's terminology. I find this evaluative distinction against French academia problematic: there have been plenty of studies, books, and colloquia dealing with immigration or questioning France's colonial metanarrative. That is why it will prove worthwhile to examine the overlapping syncretisms that frame today's sense of Frenchness, as well as how latent Orientalism plays into a false idea of Eurocentrism.[21] I am interested in this buried epistemology that permeates intellectual and social representations.

Exceptions abound among scholars outside France, whose works have contributed to the fracturing of historiographical constructs and epistemological models. It comes as no surprise that the leading academic figures of postcolonial critique – Appiah, Bhabha, Dabashi, Dirlik, Khatibi, Said, and Spivak, to name the most visible – hail from the so-called emerging nations. Their discourse, whatever approaches and theories they employ, continues to feed intellectual conversation on the world scene, and this has conferred a corresponding legitimacy on the native Other. It suddenly appears that in a Foucauldian sense, the Western humanities hold a meaning beyond their power centres and beyond the sites of their internal operations. This potent combination of postcolonial origins and the linear projection of Western humanities informs the particular and fascinating intellectual model of postcolonial studies. And postcolonial studies has certainly morphed into different species, according to the languages, locations, cultural areas, historical praxes, and narrative performances of the natives, and sometimes also according to the ideological bent of scholars in the field. We understand that postcolonial studies is predicated on a manifold hermeneutics. And while it may seem unfair to paint postcolonial studies with the broad brush of anti-Western posturing, the metaphorical condition remains the one discourse reconstructing Oriental subjects, be they intellectual exiles (e.g., most writers) or a commodified culture (as represented by Muslim women, for example), with that same sense of dissonance typical of the colonial era. And the silence that hangs over this critical state becomes even more uncomfortable when Islam is historicized in terms of its resistance to traumatic events of the colonial and postcolonial periods. Of course, there is more to faith, both as culture and as praxis, than any critical discourse can capture. That said, Islam always seems to go somehow unheard in the West. To illustrate: after the 9/11 attacks, a notion of the "moderate Muslim" arose in Western discourse that tended to elide and ignore the conditions in which political extremism arose in Muslim lands. Not surprisingly, Islam has become, on etymological grounds, an object of theory – that is, of observation. The signs, structures, and claims about the native culture(s) – all of which resembled the old colonial project of splitting the subject between discourse and history, between materialization and symbolization – helped smooth out the Western fantasy of the Orient and turn it into an experienced reality. My point is that when faced with historical movements, discourses of power – Orientalism one among many – tend to transmute rather than break down. Orientalism in Voltaire's plays cannot compare with Orientalism in Hollywood movies, yet it continues to operate as a mode of selling an ideology of representation. By the same token, the French convinced themselves for more than a century that Algeria was part of France, just as much as Lorraine or Gascony; the shift of locations was held not to affect the mode of knowledge production, called the French Republic. In colonial times, Islam was rarely viewed with any sense of urgency and was apprehended through fractured empirical sources. Yet nowadays, with the proliferation of inevitable if somewhat artificial contact zones between French citizens of different ethnic backgrounds, Islam appears to be displacing new anxieties at a time when Europeans of all backgrounds supposedly share identical values. But of course the new European nationalists would be hard-pressed to explain away their own record of centuries of land grabs, religious conflicts, and shredded treaties, not to mention two world wars. Today, the presence of the Islamic headscarf in the French public space is feeding an exclusivist ideological discourse based more on the stereotype of Islam's resistance to modernity than on the sacrosanct principle of French *laïcité*, as we will see in the last chapter.

France, as a result of its historical denial and shrinking sense of citizenship, is making it more and more difficult to assess its legacy of human rights and representative governance. A lack of coherent selfhood looms between French institutions and the postcolonial subject, who mourns the growing gap between identity and citizenship. The difficulty in choosing between forms of being French can prove overwhelming, and this difficulty relates not to the choice itself, but rather to what one must find out. For example, French political discourse has demonstrated since colonial times how this particular culture has thought of itself in relation to the the Islamic Other. The ideological root of this matter, from the *infidèle* to the *immigré*, poses one question – "How many?" – and creates its own reality by postulating how cultures can be "mutually incompatible." Basically, I want to demonstrate that the French postcolonial condition is inherently incapable of stabilizing itself, not just because of current conflicts, but also because it shapes its own forms of resistance. I will elaborate on this in chapter 7.

It is in light of the conception of a still dominant Orientalist logic that French assimilation, or elements of postcolonial resistance, can be identified, measured, and questioned. The chapters of this book are linked by a series of motifs attributed to the Islamic Other as cultural and political references between France and the Maghreb have been gradually reinforced. Most significantly, it is the place of the Islamic Orient that, in my argument, sustains a critique of French and Western postmodernity. A hotly debated question in academia is how the postcolonial condition has inherited, in subtle ways, many Orientalist tropes. The recent revolts in the Arab world have demonstrated that Islam has taken a new road, one that is different from the radical concepts proposed by Sayid Qutb in the 1960s, for example. Islam is now more diffused, less centralized, and less ideological; it is also more attuned to political affairs, especially to the issue of representative governance, which newly elected governments are slowly learning.[22] This historic moment in the development of a post-ideological Islam has somehow escaped the West, which seems stuck in the old Orientalist representations of authoritarianism, fanaticism, corruption, and so on. In July 2014, the founding by a transnational jihadist movement of an Islamic State straddling Syria and Iraq elicited guarded reactions in the Arab world, when this entity was not viewed as out-and-out heresy. Discourses that fail to transcend a single culture must be questioned carefully. To what extent do the ideologies of the Atlantic world continue to shape the encounter between the West and the Islamic world? This book revisits critical engagement with the legacy of Orientalism, notably through the French colonial experience in the Maghreb. I will also be asking what the postcolonial condition provokes in both national and academic contexts. How does the epistemological valence travel and perhaps end up out of place?

As we attempt to reconceptualize notions such as Orientalism and postcolonial studies, which themselves are theoretically unstable, we must define anew the discourse itself. We need to examine the displacement and relocation of colonial patterns and how their intellectual moorings have become in some ways weaker but in other ways stronger. For example, the narratives of French-speaking writers of the Maghreb enshrine themselves in a discursive experience of loss located in language performance and a remapping of the nation, mostly from the perspective of the exile. The unstable relationship between France and the Maghreb is a consequence of how each has imagined the other. While Edward Said made sense of Orientalism from within the confines of Western discourse, especially Foucault's critique of humanism, I would like to think that Orientalism, just like the colour purple, does not exist in real life and is processed or elaborated in our brains only. The notion is that Orientalism has cleared a space between the humanities and politics, a space that allows us to explore new discourses, yet with a continual return to the *topos* of representation of the Other. This Orientalist ideology is not simply an exhibition of power

– to represent the Other; it has been an attempt at full disclosure of the Western self, where faith, politics, economics, and culture are forced to coexist and to pre-empt a world of alterity. For example, both spheres, Judeo-Christian and Islamic, become comprehensible in a distinctive and singular yet elusive unification. A theoretical *unum* emerges with a single, simple tenet: monotheism. So long as they remain apart, both spheres are doomed to cultural entropy. It seems that people know that only collective intelligence needs to be updated.[23] Even leaving aside the consistency of difference within perception, it is clear that disputes over the postcolonial condition, be they over citizenship, national identity, or the place of Islam in the West, have in recent years become more common, and more deep-seated, rather than less so. Social unrest in the suburbs of French cities over the past twenty years, the civil war in Algeria in the 1990s, and the recent and ongoing Arab uprisings have prompted politicians and academics to examine arguments for an ethos of pluralization based on common bonds of citizenship, nationhood, and promises of social equality. Too often, the colonial legacy has been left out of the equation, as if the history of the colonial period seemed already to have been swept up into a larger narrative. The uncertain status of the colonial legacy has had unfortunate consequences, such as forgetting Maghrebi immigration and its contribution to France's economic boom from the mid-1950s to the mid-1970s. My work, echoing Said's view of the lasting impact of Orientalism on the West's political culture, strives to locate the reasons for the enduring problem of latent Orientalism. An unflinching scrutiny of discourses concerning the Arab/Muslim sphere easily convinces the observer that the emergence of postcolonial theories has too often gone hand in hand with revisionist intellectual history. It is true that postcolonial studies has reached global significance as it has branched out to create multiple critical positions and debates. Yet the tradition of Manichean binaries that conceives of cultures in terms of their differences rather than in terms of their differences *and* similarities is never far from the surface. For example, the inchoate state of francophone studies in French academia draws attention to the weaknesses of a critique of representation that has France at its centre as well as to the weaknesses in the disciplinary project itself, in which facts are not allowed to speak for themselves but require a politically acceptable narrative, as we will see in the case of literature in French by Maghrebi writers. By focusing on France and the Maghreb, I will be seeking those parts of the postcolonial discourse that are determined by political and cultural circumstances alone, and

where communication actually occurs and develops. My personal reflections and the diverse resources presented in my work support my
endeavour to shed light on the cultures of the Maghreb and France –
which are linked by their common colonial experience – and how they
might grow in the new century. I also want to showcase the ideological nuances of the newfound power of postcolonial studies and their
reverberations. My aim is to illuminate important aspects of this piv-
otal region, connected by the Mediterranean, and to underscore what
could be either the agony of identity conflict, both in the Maghreb and
in France,[24] or a successful cultural movement in which transnational
authority develops the capacity to hold itself accountable.

Communication – as opposed to mere interaction – between communities with different histories and world views is more than a challenge
of everyday life. It is also a world-historical necessity, for otherwise we
will never answer questions such as these: How do we grapple with the
complex relationship between culture and domestic imperialism? To
what extent is the ban on Islamic headscarves in French public schools
part of a new nationalism that claims to uphold "freedom and dignity" but fails to promote inclusive citizenship? Does France really need
a universalist vocabulary in order to perceive its unique relationship
with the nations and cultures of the Maghreb?

One possible explanation for the limited responsibility the French
have felt for their colonial history has to do with the ambivalence
and permanent deferral of tension arising from the recognition of racial oppression in a culture steeped in the tenets of humanism and the
Enlightenment. There is a logic in this recognition that disrupts the
Occidental ontology. This feature has not yet been related to the signifying, cultural Other that the immigrant, just like the colonized native,
has become. With the arrival of the postcolonial condition in France, a
split of another order now looms, one in which "identity" and "secularism" have drawn a metaphorical border within the Republic. These
two worn-out concepts in current French political and media discourse,
with their putatively universal application, serve as an ideal gateway
into the cultural domain of French exceptionalism and the intellectual
domain of hexagonal entropy.

In this respect, the "counterpoint" of my title takes on a certain
meaning, understood both as investigative in nature and as exposing
cultural misreadings. I believe that Orientalism is very much an active,
natural, and thereby nameless construct, but I realize, too, that it also
sets up a progressive dialectic of repetition with emerging identities.

It is not just that millions of postcolonial citizens live in contemporary France, but that the country is slowly divorcing itself from its old national, republican self, hence the unrest and manifold challenges it faces. Of course, the fact that France is struggling with its postcolonial (as well as European) identity is not of primary significance. The validity of the French position flows out of its politics. For example, turning the far-right *Front National* into a foil for discourse on national affairs only demonstrates that when a theory is wrong, putting it at the centre of discussion won't make it come out right. Extremism, even from the safe, reassuring distance of a voting booth, remains false, fraudulent, and sometimes frightening. Contrary to the claims of the old colonial ideology, the ideology of current right-wing extremism avoids any exploration of Western hegemony.[25] This type of ideological parochialism accounts for the emergence of a national history that is incapable of looking forward, either within a European frame or within its historical postcolonial narrative. This political reality underscores the importance of Orientalism today. And it is not limited to the history of aesthetics, because in order to maintain discursive superiority, latent Orientalism needs to travel outside traditional ideological domains, such as the humanities.

A core aim of my argument is to forge a relational method for charting the intellectual movement known as Orientalism and what was actually anticipated from the time of the original encounter with Oriental culture up to contemporary theoretical constructs developed in the fields of postcolonial studies, subaltern studies, transnational studies, diaspora studies, trauma studies, and so on. Thus my analysis will avoid using a single *logos* that might confuse critical positions rather than be transformed by them. I have also taken care to avoid developing any sequencing or variegated account, from humanism to postcolonial studies, for doing so would amount to creating an exact copy of Western ideologies and their narrativized historicism. Instead, I trace the affective, imaginative tropes that underwrite latent Orientalism, hoping to emphasize the evolution of the concepts of citizenship and nationhood, in a sort of double-strategy of storytelling from each side of the Mediterranean. What modes of representation were generated before they became reified? Why does a rights-conferring nation-state such as France codify its citizenship in words that both recognize and defy the truth of Otherness? Beyond a study of latent Orientalism proper, I examine how exclusion from critical discourse operates by, for example, dismantling the discursive constitution of the postcolonial subject.

As it turns out, the narrative discourse on citizenship is sustained by a racialized view of the subject. So, how does our much vaunted transnational space collapse citizenship into essentializing categories?

This study has eight chapters. It starts with a focus on the Orient and the Oriental. My intention here is to demonstrate the nature of radical mimesis, a process by which those possessing colonial power end up believing the representations of the colonial subject they created in the first place in order to validate and make sense of the colonial undertaking. From this fallacy onwards, meaning is bare and worthless, with almost no connection to any coherent set of interpretations related to scholarly independence and political objectivity.[26] This partly explains why colonialism was more than an act of appropriation; it also produced markedly twisted discourses, from the most racist to the most paternalistic. I follow up with a case study: the relationship between André Gide and Algeria. Beyond Gide's well-known homoerotic fetishism, the important point is that I present his works as a transhistorical, universal language, one that is loaded with all the trappings of cultural castration within French *bourgeois* constructs. In this regard, Algeria is elevated to the status of a mirror reflecting French self-desire back to itself. Whatever Gide's own premises, he never calls into question French cultural universalism. The Arab body helps enact the condition of domination that is inscribed in the traveller's subjectivity and ontological quest. Chapter 6 continues with a discussion of nationhood from the perspective of the colonized Maghrebi. I am interested in how political thinking developed by establishing its own brand of nationalism against the backdrop of colonial nationalism. I argue that the colonized peoples of Morocco, Algeria, and Tunisia had to fight not just to claim their independence; the nexus of the struggles was about national myths more than about recapturing one's own history. It is no wonder that to this day, democracy has been slow to flourish throughout the Maghreb. The later chapters concern themselves with the consequences and functions of latent Orientalism in contemporary France. This brand of Orientalism does not vary a great deal from the foregrounding movement of the nineteenth century. I begin with a study of *Beur* literature, that is, literature written by French authors of Maghrebi descent. My goal is to demonstrate how these texts, saturated with historical and sociological provenance, have failed to occupy the conceptual space of French postcolonial identity. Then I move on to explore Orientalism and the subtle strategy of violence among fellow-citizens.[27] One case in point is the debate about a brand of feminism that targets French

Muslim women. I examine the tensions between universal principles and the solidarity within racial and religious groups. Because I want to reclaim the importance of identity as a politically necessary source of knowledge, I turn to the place of Islam in present-day France. As it happens, there is more than the headscarf at issue in the debate about Muslim women in France today. Classifying French citizens on the basis of their foreignness – on the basis of their faith, for example – not only creates an ambivalent genealogy but also, in the case of women, creates a deterministic construct that postcolonial studies find it challenging to move beyond. And beyond the Foucauldian critique of the ubiquitous violence of power lies a complex dynamic of resistance that neither Said nor the French postmodern thinkers have truly addressed. If we acknowledge the weakness of mainstream epistemologies (the postmodern mantra!), where is the locus of feminism to be found within the French brand of universalism? Once again, the postcolonial critique of belonging, identity, and location becomes instrumental in denouncing the normative violence exerted in the name of rationality and democracy. Just as it is important to research this type of colonial continuum imposed on Muslim women, my analysis will challenge the discourse on victimization and other forms of romanticization of the immigrant's experience.

What is unique about Orientalism is that it creates hierarchies even while sacrificing meaning; it thrives on representations even while eschewing referentiality and turns historical violence into experience that overrides authentic cultural encounters.

2 The Orient in Question

More than ten years after Edward Said's death, and without any implicit celebration of a truly dissenting intellectual, his work continues to be the basis of an extended reflection across the humanities he was so fond of, against an ideology that manufactured Otherness. But the truth is that Said did not single-handedly create postcolonial studies. The *Négritude* movement in the 1930s in Paris, and the founding of subaltern studies in India in the 1960s, are two reminders that postcolonial studies is a complex and multifaceted apparatus that at the very least cannot be separated from the colonial experience itself. It is inaccurate also to claim, for example, that Said blindly borrowed Foucault's paradigm of power. For Said, power was deeply personal, something bearing on intention and whose consequences were either alienating or liberating.[1] Whereas for Foucault, power grew in a rather unremarkable – yet all the more threatening – manner, largely through institutions and their histories. In that sense, Said adhered to a humanistic, Cartesian model, whereas a thinker like Fanon clearly established power as a set of relations within the colonial ideological machine when he theorized racism (its various codifications) as the pillar of imperial ideology. Lastly, if Said postulated exile as the condition of dissent, it was Adorno who foregrounded such expectations against the tragedy of uprootedness and the subsequent need to create new worlds, new rules. Benhabib, a more contemporary critical theorist, has put forward the view that "we are facing today a disaggregation of citizenship."[2] It may be that ontological considerations and cultural imagination are both on the receiving end of the logic of globalization and have grown obsolete. At the same time, postcolonial agency and subjectivity are contesting the boundaries of the *polis* through a new normative grid that Said did not have to confront and elucidate. Yet if one is to embark on a comprehensive, critical argument concerning Orientalism and postcolonial studies today, one must hold on to Said's tenacious uncovering of world-historical forms of culture that hail from the old combination of science, arts, and empire. It must be clear that my use of Said's work harks back to the critical tools he has provided us to negotiate the subtle disenfranchisement of both native informants and postcolonial subjects. Drawing on Said's work, my argument will cast into relief the place where the relationship between France and the Maghreb clashes with circumstantial historical and cultural conditions, as well as the consequences today for intellectuals and postcolonial citizens. This chapter examines Said's theoretical framework; later chapters will explore the influence that *Orientalism* has exerted in academe, as well as a postcolonial sense of culture.

Why is Edward Said a literary critic who cannot be ignored in a world where globalization demands that theories and ideas be disposable? How did he put the longevity of humanism to the test while steering clear of the Eurocentric trap? And how is this relevant to a critique of the contemporary postcolonial condition? As Emily Apter suggests: "Saidian humanism, defined with the Orientalist critique at its crux, pointed to urgent issues in the field of language politics."[3] This is one example of why Said continues to matter, and the core of my argument is that his critical approach can be employed to develop new perspectives on the larger question of representation and its origins and politics, as in the case of the Maghreb. But again, this is neither a blank cheque for Said nor a vindication of Saidian discourse. Because we must look rather carefully at such a thetic figure in postcolonial studies, this chapter will elaborate on the archaeology of Orientalism and its advent between the Christian and Muslim spheres; the next chapter will then focus on Said's groundbreaking book itself. It is important to bear in mind that the two chapters inform and consolidate each other.

The key criticisms directed at Said's *Orientalism* have been that in it, he fails to historicize colonial representations; at the same time, its historical scope is too wide, so that he often falls into sweeping generalizations, thereby trivializing his subject matter. Among many thoughtful and relevant readers of Said, Daniel M. Varisco underscores the extent to which Said remained unmoved by scholarly views that impugned his anti-Orientalist dogma and that failed to engage with the rapidly changing perspectives in postwar Islamic studies, which Varisco tells us amounted to "a hermeneutic shift from what Islam 'is' to what Islam 'means.'"[3] But whether or not the limits of a *longue durée* genealogy of Orientalism tend to set aside the finer points of a robust, manifold discourse across several academic disciplines, it is clear that Orientalism's temporal trajectory travels from the Crusades to the postcolonial era. Naturally, the timeline pauses with individual nations, as the density of detail increases. Another criticism of Said is that to contextualize Orientalism in terms of the end of European colonialism, as he did, may appear to entail no more than a modern scholarly frame of reference, but it could also amount to an attempt at a circular return to the golden age of Western cultural hegemony, with its ethnocentric bias. Most of the Islam bashing that fed into Orientalism over the centuries is barely recognizable as scientific discourse today, yet this abundant body of scholarly work can still tell us much about past perceptions of Islamic culture and the epistemological shackles that continue to impede the formulation of objective, nuanced approaches to the Islamic world. The simplistic and hackneyed generalizations about the Middle East found in the Western media, for example, are probably the clearest example of the legacy of the Orientalist body of beliefs. What is most striking about the latent Orientalism in discussions of the Arab/Muslim world is the guise of neutrality assumed by Western commentators, their self-righteous claims to be conducting objective intellectual inquiry. At the height of the "Arab Spring," for example, the most prestigious newspaper in the United States, the *New York Times*, provided this striking illustration of its position: "Our instinct is to search for the clarity we saw in last winter's televised celebrations. However, what Egyptians, and Americans, need is something murkier – not a victory, but an accommodation."[4] Democracy in Egypt can wait – is this what we are to surmise? – unless the Americans require it to happen sooner. But of course the military coup of July 2013 showed the world that democracy was not coming to Egypt any time soon and that the United States could live with yet another authoritarian Arab regime. The positions taken in international relations and diplomacy are by no means mere inconsequential wordplay: there is a legacy of "othering" the archetypal Oriental, who, as usual, cannot claim any agency in the narrative. How did we come to this?

The word "Orient" carries so many meanings in both classical and contemporary Western culture that disciplines as divergent as anthropology and political science have created their own definitions. The projections, interpretations, and tendencies resulting from this panoply of definitions have often turned both the concept and the reality of the

Orient into a perception that largely fails to question Western sources, as we will see in the case of the Maghreb.

In representations of the Orient, truth and falsehood matter less than the responses they elicit, with the result that perceptions create their own reality. Most of these representations, which Said tells us can be traced back to Euripides or Dante, have been by-products of the process of European self-affirmation.[5] The consolidation of Europe as a single cultural and geohistorical entity stemmed from the expansion of trade in the transatlantic triangle that reached its apogee in the eighteenth and nineteenth centuries with the full flower of colonialism. The essentialist view of the Orient also grew from ontological distinctions. As early as the twelfth century, the various European perceptions of the Orient coalesced into labels that contributed to polarizing the Christian and Islamic worlds, although other factors came into play as well, such as the rise in the fifteenth century of the Ottoman Empire, which came to control most of the trade routes in the Mediterranean. Clearly, these narratives about the Orient were teleological in structure: the politics behind Europe–Orient interactions were goal-driven. And they led to something probably unique in Western culture – a hybrid discourse that blended inclusion in the Judeo-Christian world with exclusion from the utopian world of the Islamic Other. Now the Orient, having been contacted through trade, needed not to be not just represented, but organized in the imagination.[6] Non-European worlds came to be experienced through fantastic medieval stories and elaborately illustrated maps that created categories of thought that served to unify a European sphere in search of its own historical destiny. Once the belief set in that everything could be historicized, the idea of universal applicability was not far off. Cultural legitimacy was planted with the help of what Paul Gilroy referred to, with respect to slavery, as "the tragic popularity of ideas about the integrity and purity of cultures."[7] Illustrations on manuscripts and maps featured allegories that fed into the evolving constructs that comprised the Orient in the European imagination. In France, the Orientalist construct was shaped by three forces: humanism and academic achievements beginning in the Renaissance,[8] ethnographic studies and research in other social sciences, and colonial rhetoric derived from a racial or religious typology. It seems that at this junction of knowledge and power, Foucault misread the historical evidence about control (or confinement, as he liked to put it) by completely excluding struggles and resistance from his totalizing theory.[9] It is easy to see how one can fall into such a trap, when history comes to be formulated as text rather than textualized, as began to happen in Europe during its modern era, that is, with little room for counter-hegemony, particularly in the colonial context. Moreover, the nascent ideologies of control (extending the idea of European sovereign power) articulated promises of a profitable future. Early on, Orientalism grew out of these characteristics of dominating systems – systems that turned out to be circular, antagonistic, and self-fulfilling. As Albert Hourani noted in his now classic *Islam in European Thought*: "Separated by conflict but held together by ties of different kinds, Christians and Muslims presented a religious and intellectual challenge to each other."[10] The emphasis on relationship *and* conflict suggests that Orientalism, as science and as discourse, arose out of "doing" culture from a point of view grounded not in the needs and expectations of the Other but rather in the needs of the dominant powers.

The legend of Prester John, which proliferated in multiple versions throughout Europe from the sixth century to the fifteenth, epitomizes the deep-rooted stereotype of the Orient that emerged from a European world view that was presumed to be objective. Depending on the version of the narrative consulted, Prester John was either a king or a priest who ruled over a magnificent Christian kingdom somewhere in either Ethiopia or the Far East. In this equation of religion and power, Prester John stood out as a redeeming figure, one whose inspiring example had political implications. Popes and kings dreamed of meeting him.[11] His kingdom supposedly contained the Garden of Paradise and other wonders from the lives of saints, tales of which stimulated religious inspiration in Europe and a desire to explore this fabled land. Both the Pope and the King of Portugal launched expeditions to meet and help this Christian king living in his land of gold and honey. Some of the apocryphal materials that fed into the myth suggested that Prester John was surrounded by barbarians and infidels. Christian expeditions and voyages to Abyssinia and other exotic lands found no trace of the kingdom.[12] The legend of Prester John is an early clue as to how history and literature, both oral and written, would continue to inform each other in Western culture and stimulate interest in the sources of Christianity. Most importantly, this legend enacted a performative ideology based on the domination of one civilization over another – an ideology that provided a justification for the Crusades, and, later on, for European colonialism. By claiming an ancient origin for itself in the Middle East, Europe prepared the ground for history and representation to accommodate the continent's expansion of influence around the world over the coming centuries.

It was no coincidence that between Prester John's kingdom and Europe lay the vast Muslim world – a world that would play a significant role in the shaping of both national self-images and Otherness in modern times. Europeans had to make sense of an Islamic civilization that was rapidly expanding, not just as an empire but as a functioning world-system devoid of everything that Europe cherished: church, nationalism, and a pre-capitalist economy.[13]

Discourse on Otherness originated with the ancients. Whether in Heracles's battles with monsters, in the travels of Odysseus, or in their descriptions of the barbarians, the Greeks defined the "Others" as terrible races living at the edge of known lands, who possessed no rational faculties and who were spiritually, socially, and technologically backward. The ancients, though, did not base any of this on race or ethnicity; rather, what defined the condition of the object of cultural domination was the speech act and its meaning. As Said pointed out, one text that strikes us in this regard is Aeschylus's *The Persians*, a play told from the point of view of the Persians after the their navy was crushed at the Battle of Salamis in 480 BCE. In this tragedy with no hero, the Greeks, with their high rhetorical style and sense of a higher calling, symbolize reason and democracy, while the Persians are depicted as savages who shout and moan and find themselves caught up in emotional posturing and despotic arrogance. Is there is a continuum between ancient Greece's literature and Orientalism as science and as discourse? What is the historical reach of lumping together as the "West" ancient Greece and modern-day Europe? Said does not address these questions; it is as if he has been swept up in symbols that require less analytical information. By choosing Western myths as the norm, Said reduces the scope of his examination to an epistemic perspective that does not distinguish between ancient and modern and that remains captive to binary assessments. No wonder he fails to underscore that figures like Darius and Cassandra, even though they are Oriental, display the same virtues as their Greek counterparts (if not superior ones).[14] Could it be that Said was ensnared by the inescapability of relations of power? True, this kind of archaeology of Orientalism, set in ancient Greece, was predicated on its power to represent the "uncivilized" as doomed to be either defeated or assimilated into the *logos*. Tragedies like Aeschylus's taught their audiences how to look at the world and benefit from experiencing this paradigm of Otherness. Said, in his cursory examination and commentary on *The Persians*, emphasizes the "virtue of European imagination,"[15] when in fact that play offers a new model for generic othering: the Greeks versus the Orient (Persians, Trojans, Egyptians, Ethiopians, etc.).[16]

This pattern of tethering one's cultural perspective to one's own self-perception has endured in the Western psyche, not only among cultural zealots but also (and especially) in the discourses of educated, post-Enlightenment people of letters. Little could be salvaged when intellectual beacons of Reason dabbled in cultural essentialism. Kant's idea of the sovereign subject, for example, was a person who was European, who presided over the world, and who was fully in charge of historical agency.[17] The knowing subject and the knowable world were exclusively European concepts. This mindset helped enact European hegemony in the non-European world, in the form of slavery and colonialism; it also erased all notions that these latter civilizations had a culture, any body of ideas and institutions that defined them. In this way, it invalidated them either by force or, in a more subtle manner, by freezing the Oriental in naturalized, romanticized constructs. For example, Johann G. Herder, a student of Kant and a forefather of European nationalism based on language and culture, wrote about "the noble legacy of the Arabic language" without any suggestion that that language was embedded in a civilization.[18] But rather than an exercise in plain Orientalism, the problem of the Enlightenment was that of self-representation – its world view lacked any conception that the subject was centred, could speak for itself, and had an authentic voice.

The framework used to complete the figure of Otherness in the European mind contained elements from the Greek heritage, the Biblical tradition, and a post-Enlightenment undertheorized Other. The Christian tradition influenced the construction of Otherness with imagery of a permanent struggle with the Other, from Adam's expulsion from Eden to Moses's confrontation with the Pharaoh, and it included the omnipresent "temptation" facing all mortals. Christological debate contributed by celebrating the division between nature and religion, body and soul. This dichotomy would became a crucial element in the yardstick the Christian West wielded when measuring the possibility of civilizing individuals. Also, the possibility of the saviour's return underscored for the West that it had a spiritual and historical mission to save or convert. The messianic content of Christianity was awkwardly superimposed on that mission. In post-Revolution France, for example, where the gap between temporal and spiritual authority was always narrow, the much vaunted *mission civilisatrice* coincided, at least in part, with messianic expectations, notwithstanding the heritage of a secular revolution. What the French monarchy made possible by virtue of its alleged divine attributes, the Republic saw as vital to legitimizing its place in history. Orientalism operated along this chain of substitutions by displacing other cultural values and historical systems – something Renan called "the genius of nations."[19]

The idea of the state-sponsored redemption of Others took root in Europe with the establishment of a normative faith back in the fifteenth century, when expansionism and mercantile capitalism first intersected. The concept of blind, unquestioning faith became uncomfortable to many and gave rise to scepticism – which led to the founding of the Anglican Church, the Inquisitions in Spain and Portugal, religious wars in France, and the Reformation in the Holy Roman Empire, and even to revolutions of another sort in the figurative arts when *bourgeois* characters began to replace Christian figures in Dutch paintings. The narratives of religion and cultural heritage had provided Europe with a triumphant self-image that was to set the mould for its concept of national sovereignty as well as its framework for foreign policy. Especially after the colonization of the Americas, Europe's new image in the world was premised on the belief that it could shape reality by negotiating a place for itself. In a sense, Europe came together by reducing the Others to their distinct forms, their tribes, their religious denominations, their places of origin, and any number of other misapplied concepts of cultural encounter. The Others were kept in a state of perennial reinvention – and of approval, too, within Western historical teleology. The problem was not that an exclusive, hegemonic ideology was being manufactured; rather, it was that ideology's pretension that it corresponded to reality. And Europe's perception of Others became more garbled as cultural and geographical distance increased. The politics of representation seemed to follow the patterns of Copernican geocentric postulations, but with Europe as the new cultural and political sun. The famous Psalter map, an English work of the thirteenth century that supposedly represents Africa and India, shows people depicted with the heads of dogs or with eyes on their torsos; others are shown feasting on human limbs. Similarly, maps from the sixteenth century offered monstrous representations of the peoples of the New World. This is not surprising, given the misstated expectations and naively boosterish pathology of colonialism. How else could Europeans have represented Others – given their powerful tendency to view them in sharp contrast to their own goodness – except in terms of crude fetishism? From this point on, conceptions of liberty and modernity would be of no concern to the subjected peoples; it was as if Europe had dumped on them discourses of identity while choosing narratives of power for themselves. But of course the ideological performance of silencing the Other never truly caught up with all of this. The subalterns continued to speak their languages (which were also the languages of their literatures) and escaped the expectant gaze: colonialism came with critical demarcations that, over time, it proved unable to overcome. The colonial powers failed to heed the diverse contexts and forms of subordination and resistance, whether in the Americas or in the Orient. It is this very dichotomy of Western idealism that Said tries to undercut in *Orientalism* in order to eliminate the newly (post–seventeenth century) fabricated peripheries. He astutely points out that "to say that Orientalism was a rationalization of colonial rule is to ignore the extent to which colonial rule was justified in advance by Orientalism, rather than after the fact."[20] Again, all power stems from the West in intentionality, shape, and application, and a pernicious consequence of this is to deny the possibility of reciprocity by the Oriental in his/her own historical agency: to represent is to make powerless. In the case of the Maghreb, we will see how even "resistance" and "anticolonial struggle" were structured from within the colonial centre.

The heuristic notion of "difference" – which developed in its own logical way vis-à-vis peoples perceived as barbarians and savages – led to the idea of possession through slavery and colonization. The *oculus mundi* of the Renaissance, first expressed by the Flemish cartographer Mercator in 1585, was that very eye whose glance symbolized Western power in all geographical areas and spheres of human activities. Conquests in the sixteenth century, and colonization throughout the nineteenth century, merely confirmed the knowledge created by Europeans. The drive towards empire did accompany an increase in knowledge, but rarely was the impact of non-Western cultures recognized or assessed. Over many centuries, Western expansion to all corners of the planet metastasized as self-righteous ambition; but in reality, European travellers, military, missionaries, traders, and intellectuals remained ill-equipped to understand the faiths and cultures of other peoples. The paradigm of Western modernity based on difference, however, was less a matter of trans-European narcissism than of collective activism against a supposedly passive *terra incognita*. This principle would survive until the twentieth century, when confrontations with non-Western peoples brought about the questioning and transformation of historical conceptions and of cultural patterns. Naturally, the self-understanding of Western nations was impacted from the outset by the encounter with the Other. By the eighteenth century, international trade was acquiring global reach, putting Western culture into broad circulation. In this regard, Christopher Miller notes that "slave merchants were 'cultivated' people ... In Nantes, the négriers established six *chambres de lecture* and helped to establish the music academy."[21] Perhaps this implausible cultural injunction to become "cultured" allowed for a canny borrowing of structural power that could eventually posit the Other as a transcultural subject. Christian ethics as well as prejudices were co-opted by Enlightenment cultural superiority;[22] they then seeped in, which set the stage for a genuine appeal for moral guidance with universalist overtones. The traumatic caesura of slavery and colonialism fractured the linear history of the colonized cultures, but it also helped problematize the Other's narrative(s) of progress. But this "progress" would not take place overnight.

Ironically, the requisites for Reason – the lack of which was perceived as the Others' major flaw – were ultimately identified as non-European attributes. After centuries of philosophical discourse on the subject, Western academics had come to realize that rationality (that which gives knowledge in the first place) is an unstable notion, especially in the realm of morality. As in the case of physics, Western cultures lacked appropriate paradigms to represent Others *per causas* – that is, as they really were. Instead they relied on Western constructs with limited ability to comprehend identities outside the European sphere. Orientalism's purpose was to distinguish the significant (languages, faiths, literature, histories, etc.) from the commonplace (essential foreignness), in the guise of scholarly study. Yet this often amounted to banding together in epistemic assaults on the foundations of the "Oriental" subject by, for example, obfuscating cultural singularities and the merits of their truth claims. In the field of philology, for example, it was widely accepted, from Sir William Jones to Ernest Renan,[23] that Hebrew and Arabic were the languages of monotheism, spoken by cultures that had failed to produce myths, higher literature, and science.[24] At the same time, Sanskrit, Greek, and Latin were tied together as a group, which ushered in the endemic metaphysics of Western superiority, with its Aryan myth.[25] Nineteenth-century Orientalist scholars eagerly sensationalized history by linking it to contemporary events, the colonial undertaking being one of them. The project of Orientalist ideologies can be summarized as an effort to merge the past with cultural inquiry and thereby accord Western discourse legitimacy for its own ethnocentric sake. By operating outside the principle of dialogue, Orientalism produced its own repressed material; it abandoned contextualization and cultural reciprocity and eventually turned history and science into mere opinions masquerading as knowledge. And knowledge operated as part of a network of power whose key purpose was to cancel out the power of Others to be read and understood. Said perfectly deconstructs this critical agency, which not only produced knowledge but also created a crisis for the subject, be he the Oriental Other or the colonial subject. And it was mainly through language that the illusion of the Western sovereign and knowing subject sustained itself, as Said demonstrates in his parsing of famous Orientalists' works (Sucy, Renan, all the way to Massignon). The more it grasped textuality (philology, theology, history, anthropology, etc.) for itself, the more Orientalism helped govern the production of culture by, for example, ensuring both the subjugation of its colonial subjects and a welcoming place for historical determinism in cultural discourse about them. That said, Orientalists were not colonialists. Among European Orientalist academics, there were repeated attempts to move beyond uniform and reductive interpretations of "native" cultures.

But Said targeted the wrong people with his wholesale attack on Orientalist scholars. The greatest authority on India in the nineteenth century, Friedrich Maximillian Müller, who taught philology and comparative religion at Oxford, also happened to be the most committed advocate for a comprehensive recognition of India's languages and faiths. Orientalists were not shy in assailing the colonialist mentality; they even denounced the armchair linguistics or history work that was initially aimed at propping up the political elite and advancing careers in academia or in the diplomatic corps. In twentieth-century France, Louis Massignon claimed to be the greatest expert on Shiism and mystic Islam, but unlike his friend Paul Claudel, he never managed to land an ambassadorial appointment. One may also wonder whether a state of confusion stands between Orientalism and the culture of the post–eighteenth century capitalist world, more precisely between an ideology and a historical reality. What are we to make of the subversive truth that while Orientalist scholars were studying and classifying Oriental languages, Europe was consolidating its knowledge of its own national languages? And this touches on the very postcolonial issue of the ties between language and national identity, as we will see in the chapter on francophone and *Beur* writers. The need, therefore, to nuance Said's attractive yet too radical views on Orientalism, construed as both a set of sciences and a discourse, has never been more urgent, because the Other's voice risks being essentialized and challenged in its very identity.

Throughout the prolonged contact between Europe and the rest of the world, the geographical or cultural distance from Others has had little to do with misconceptions and *a priori* assertions. Rather, it was Europeans' injection of self-identity into the process that inevitably created comparisons with Others. Loaded as they were with rational exculpation, these comparisons provided European cultures with narcissistic self-gratification; it also socially conditioned them. Above all, they encouraged the West to embrace the belief that domination was historically inevitable, with the result that its relationships with Others were based on that perception rather than on historical fact. With this attitude towards history, superiority took the form of authority rather than being rooted in speculation and inquiry. The asymmetries between codified discourses and the fascination with alien, "exotic" cultures resulted in a blindness towards other cultures because Orientalism relied fundamentally on logocentric representations. This heralded a twentieth-century *realpolitik* whereby borders and national interests conjured up an ever-greater role for themselves over that played by cultural paradigms. Scholars and artists played along with this, offering themselves up as useful platforms for illuminating the singularity of Western culture. In France, Diderot, Montesquieu, and Voltaire found that there was indeed a history they could talk about, and that it was not theirs but that of Persia, Tahiti, Zadig, Zaïre, the Great Turk, and Mahomet, although their depictions were not to be taken literally. They argued that political power was not needed to control the population, and they set out to debunk anything fixed and singular; but in doing so, they only created their own variety of universalism. These philosophical elisions generated a project to consolidate natural rights as a Western prerogative. It is no wonder that while the forces of the French Revolution transformed one another, the flow of political power quickly became both cyclical and alienating, especially during the overseas expansion of the nineteenth century. Capitalizing on its Orientalist momentum, the colonial undertaking pioneered a negativity posturing, converging into everything Europe was *not*, thereby shedding its authenticity.[26]

The degree to which Others could be known was limited both by religious prejudices and by the subsequent opaqueness of those prejudices. As long as Others were ontologically missing, the Western self was safe and, in academic and political spheres, deemed to dwell on a higher plane. In a sense, the metaphorical and literal obliteration of the Other safeguarded Europeans against self-doubt and upheld their cultural continuity. Said talks about the formidable "power to narrate, or to block other narratives from forming and emerging."[27] Closer to the issue of France and the Maghreb, one need only recall Alexis de Tocqueville's argument in his *Seconde lettre sur l'Algérie* that Algerians were killed for their own good.[28] Indeed, the European identity bore a dual origin, Greek and Judeo-Christian, and developed in a continuous evolution, which in the post-Enlightenment age would be dubbed "progess" by scholars and politicians alike.[29] More often than not, Europeans proved themselves unable to read different cultures *against* their own self-styled civilization. For example, mosques in the Levant (a geographic term equivalent to the Arabic *Mashriq*, meaning "land where the sun rises") were described as "Infidel churches"; medicine men in the New World were simply "sorcerers"; even China, despite being called a land of wisdom, could never become a truly civilized nation ruled by laws because it did not belong to the course of history, according to scholars such as Vico and Bacon.

Even as foreign encounters inevitably increased, Europeans insisted on living by "true" knowledge alone – that is, the knowledge they were able to fabricate. This cultural/political creativity reached a certain level of complexity in the religious, technological, and aesthetic character of what we, in the West, now call the modern age. And this "modernity" had little to do with a conflict between the past and the present, or the old and the new; rather, it was determined largely within a character shaped by selfhood and otherness. It took a long time and many missteps to grasp that relations to/with the world were mediated through representation. By extension those relations were tentative, contingent, and open in their very structure: on the one hand, the Enlightenment and its genuine knowledge (liberty, progress, Reason, political representation, etc.), and on the other, power that became a discipline in itself. No wonder the cultural perceptions, and then the political solutions, came to a full stop with the twentieth-century ideological crises, especially those that revolved around nationalism and racism. But of course a study of the scope and influence of Europe, from the Renaissance to the first half of the twentieth century, cannot be lumped together around problematics of historicism and universalism. Such a passive intellectual orthodoxy can only lead to theoretical dead ends, as we often see, for example, among those who eschew issues of cross-fertilization.[30]

The West did not create foreign geography, languages, and religions out of nothing; however, Western culture did rework them so that they could be viewed through the lens of a knowledge that conformed to already known patterns of European thinking. It did not take long to apply this narrowly created vision of knowledge to the tenets of what was considered universal human experience. For example, in the thought world of *The Merchant of Venice*, *Les lettres persanes*, *Les fleurs du mal*, and *Vanity Fair*, a "good" European would never behave as a Jew, a Moor, or a black. Later on, the humanistic, anthropocentric form of knowledge would be related to the very idea of Reason, which was then extended to administrative perfection and the civilizing process, applied first at home and then throughout the empire. The principle of consensus (in ethics, science, the law, and so forth) became the hallmark of Western universalism, through language and signs dressed as natural and timeless in order to conceal their own historicism.

There is more to this elusive or flawed understanding than simply throwing one's own civilization into sharp relief against other peoples' ways. Although Western knowledge, based on the simulacra of its own metaphysics (as Nietzsche tried to spell out in his *Gay Science* [1882]), was essentially faulty, Europeans could not do without it because it was the only system they possessed for interpreting other cultures. Colonial enterprises throughout the Mediterranean and the Americas were, in a very literal sense, experiments in reproducing a model of enslavement that had worked in Africa, and earlier still in the Roman Empire. In Spain, the new idea of a "motherland" was superimposed on the world as it existed. After the fall of Granada in 1492, King Ferdinand and Queen Isabella decided to bring to an end the multiculturalism that had been the hallmark of Spanish civilization: Jews and Muslims were expelled, killed, or forced to convert to Catholicism. Spain rose as a nation-state, but one doomed to decline under the weight of its own religious fundamentalism and by its failed economic policies, despite the vast fortunes the Spaniards plundered from the Americas. Spain became a self-confirming example of a predictable, disengaged cultural critical system, and in the nineteenth century the country morphed into a duplicating representation of the European subaltern, even while slowly being painted as an appendix of the Orient.[31]

With the arrival of the European nation-state came the concept of authenticity, reflected in various stages as historicism or ethnocentrism. This concept of authenticity emphasized the "true" (i.e., unique) features of a nation and its culture. It likewise rejected attributes that were shared, or mixed – or worse, *imitated* – as in the case of the Orthodox Christians in Greece and Syria, or the Armenians, who were slaughtered by their fellow Christians during the Crusades and were later conveniently ignored when they fell under the rule of the Ottoman Empire. At this nexus between political reality and moral choice lay a presumption of cultural identity that was constantly being reshaped to account for changing expectations and legitimacies. The "us versus them" distinction was extremely useful and valuable for Europeans. Its value, however, remained the product of prejudice and misconception that proved unable to accommodate dissent and negotiation until later in the twentieth century. Yet it is true that many Orientalist scholars fought back against any racialized view of European superiority. The concept of race did not come into existence until the advent of anthropology in the eighteenth century; that said, it was a famous nineteenth-century anthropologist, Johann F. Blumenbach, who claimed that racism had no scientific validity – that it was a historical construct that required a historical treatment.[32] Note here that both Britain and France abolished slavery before their golden age of colonial rule, so race was a moot item in the expansion and domination machine. Only the rhetorical tangent remained untouched, with the imaginary and Destiny woven into its narrative. Europeans understood too that the rest of the world could not be reduced to an object. One may even suggest that Orientalist scholars knew that what distinguished the modern age was its capactiy to recognize the Other as an objective truth. By then, religion had been swept away by the French Revolution. An excellent example of how the European fascination for the Arab/Muslim world was framed is that of Jean-Joseph Marcel, a printer-engineer with Bonaparte's expedition to Egypt. In October 1798, when the French leader embarked on a "defensive" move against the al-Azhar university in Cairo, Marcel was able to save ninth-century copies of the Quran from fire and destruction. Later on, in France, he became an Arabic scholar (he taught at the *Collège de France* from 1808 to 1811) and established an extensive library of Islamic culture.

However, no relationship has prompted such challenging cultural and political stances as the one between the West and the so-called Orient. For this reason, we must follow three principles as we tackle the concept of "Orient." First, we need to distinguish the whole (the abstract idea of "colonial enterprise") from the part (one particular undertaking, e.g., France in Algeria) in myths and representations that set the Oriental as a subject already analysed and solved. Second, once the "Orient" appears in this fashion, we must not essentialize it, for it creates its own counterpoints and counter-discourses, as was shown in the struggle of post–First World War India against British colonial institutions, demonstrating that there have always been alternatives to hegemonic power in the fabric of a colonized nation and throughout the cultural contact zone between colonized and colonizers. Third, the *topos* of "Orient" varies across different historical moments and geographic areas, and this premise runs against time-flattening approaches. France's policies in Algeria and Indochina varied greatly, even though both colonial lands were viewed as the global "Orient."

The word "Orient" calls to our attention its dual etymological root – from the Latin *oriri*, to arise, and the Greek *οροϛ*, mountain. Thus its origin is both a verb and a noun: action and description. The transition from Greek into Latin and then into modern European languages may best explain its meaning, which is discontinuous, as well as that of its counterpart term, "Occident," which long ago came to suggest stability and progress. The various names that stood for parts of the "Orient" (the Sublime Gate for the Ottoman Empire, the Barbary Coast for the Maghreb, the Levant for the lands stretching from Palestine to Syria, Golkonda for southern India, the Middle Empire for China, Cipango for Japan) enjoyed widespread use as long as they presupposed a plurality, compelling Western powers to acknowledge degrees of difference among the cultures of Others.

What the sociocultural world view of Europeans demonstrated more than anything else was that they were unable to view their own positions as subjective; they considered their relationships with the Other in the Orient to be objective, rational, and unilateral. As a result, representation took on a new meaning: it became the index of reduction of the vast majority of the world to a cultural prototype. From these roots, the relentless narrative of "progress" – the staple of objectivity and rationality – was born. This narrative has segregated the exterior of the Oriental construct from the deep reality of Western defining values. Thus, a striking contradiction in the European colonial structure of power can be found within the paradigms of nation-building and the role assigned to native languages. These two paradigms contradict the tenets of Western humanism and the realities of national independence and cultural autonomy. Yet they eventually became neutral tools of transmission for indigenous communities.

When Columbus embarked on his first voyage to India, he took with him scholars who could speak Hebrew and Aramaic, for he and his crew believed they were going to meet tribes and nations closer to the peoples of the days of the Creation. They seemed not to distinguish between an elusive object and one that was imaginary, albeit expected to generate real economic benefits.[33] On his third journey, Columbus even mistook the mouth of the Orinoco River for the entrance to Paradise. Again, India as a bounded territory with its own history and peoples remained completely ideational. While some may consider this *näiveté* on a grand scale, the fact remains that these misapplied characteristics and inaccurate attributes served to define Columbus's Orient and render it intelligible to him. The quandary of the para-geographical metaphor (India and the East as the Americas and the West) served to dismantle the location of the Oriental as well as the epistemic and theoretical binary positions that defined it. The Other morphed into a structuring character in the West's narrative quest, in contradistinction to Europe at a specific time and place, until that Occidental figure collapsed because its own ideologies, cultures, and institutions created an antihegemonic hegemony, demonstrated throughout the twentieth century in two world wars and many successful colonial struggles for independence. In an irreversible development over several centuries, Europe combined a subjective view of the individual as self-moulder with a conception of history as a perpetual intentional activity culminating in the exclusion and domination of anything non-Western. This, and the fact that European power was based on the authority of the state and sometimes the church, meant that the Orient had to reinvent itself – both before and after achieving independence, as we will see in the case of the Maghreb.

Distinctions between "Orient" and "Occident," however, may mislead us by failing to support the notion of a multidimensional Orient. Western distinctions tend to overlook an important fact: both the idea and the reality of the Orient are mobile, changeable, and deceptive. The Muslim Orient, for example, is rooted in shifting soil: new cultural paradigms arise that become sources of rival ethical, political, economic, and cultural traditions. Persia, the Arab world, and the Ottoman Empire are all Muslim, yet they are highly distinct in their traditions and in their political relations with the Christian West. Islam did not generate a cultural totality. The term "Orient" developed within an open field of ideologies and modes of intellectual inquiry, without resistance from the "subaltern,"[34] as it was later called. The subaltern evolved as both a figurative entity and a representation. Through the former, the Orient became a spatial concept, created to preserve the absolute centrality of the Occident. The Orient became a form of discourse so distant from any definitive meaning that its essence lost all direction. And because the very existence of Oriental discourse remained unacknowledged, it was generally accepted that the Orient under Western rule was silent. To set aside this preposterous claim, we need only remind ourselves that the Orient is the birthplace of the scriptures on which all monotheistic faiths are based, as well as many poetic, philosophical, and scientific works now viewed as landmarks in world culture. The value of these works, however, was long negated by the Western notion that economic and cultural products were valid only to the extent that they had a utilitarian function. The dialectical dimension of Orientalism and colonialism confronted a broader crisis in European consciousness: for it to rule, Europe could no longer take the Orient out of itself. It is not surprising that to this day, for most scholars trained in the West, the post-independence literature of the Third World amounts to no more than national allegories of failed Western models; so we shall see in the chapter devoted to postcolonial studies. Very early on, however, culture became the logical and rhetorical paradigm for the political. The subaltern, through traditions of language, faith, literature, and music, drew critical demarcations with the white interlocutor. One proof of it is that, while the subaltern may be using the (former) imperial language, English or French, he/she is not talking *to* the white interlocutor. Thus it can be argued that both the old hegemonic and the new globalized approach desperately lack historical awareness, including deep insight into the various spheres of the Muslim world.

Wherever this collective construction holds sway, at least two conspicuous and conflicting conceptions of the word "Orient" appear. The first entails "marking out," or designating as familiar and identifiable. The other entails "showing or exhibiting," or withholding real meaning by offering an image in lieu of the actual object. The first conception applies to the Western construct of the Other, formed in the absence of any direct contact. For example, it is perplexing that within the colonial endeavours throughout North Africa, a comprehensive sense of superiority was legitimized as a civilizing tool; yet Islamic studies gathered momentum only in the late nineteenth and early twentieth centuries, with the work of towering Orientalism scholars such as Jacques Berque, Henri Corbin, the Marçais brothers, Louis Massignon, and Maxime Rodinson. What was morally contestable was also empirically false: no culture, Arab or otherwise, needed Western civilization. The second conception falls within the province of experience, cued by the presence of the Other. To scholars of the postcolonial condition, the Orient remains at the core of the unfulfilled promise of Western universalism. This is echoed in political debate in contemporary France, where politicians and the media conflate issues suchas immigration, crime, feminism, Islam, and transnationalism (also connected to national misgivings about the European Union, which is perceived as under siege). Put more simply, the claim is made that postcolonial France may be seeing the erosion of its Republican tenets, and therefore its history, because Oriental elements in its midst have failed to become assimilated. Immigrants – the claim continues – are fundamentally incapable of bridging the gap that separates them from the colonial state of mind, and in this way, they and the mythology of the Oriental have fallen into a perverse dialectic: the West created the Oriental, yet it is the Oriental who is responsible for the perceived cultural discontinuity, exemplified by the overinflated issue of *intégration* in France. One can easily see that discussion of how couscous came to be served in Parisian restaurants is a substitute for confronting the challenge of riots in the suburbs: the postcolonial subject is essentialized by something he no longer is or never was – a couscous eater – while suffering alienation as a consequence of socio-economic problems such as failed public schools and high unemployment.[35] After each suburban uprising, debates and national discussions have been many, yet these have been essentially misdirected because they have merely given rise to a renewed awareness of France's untouchable identity, with both the left and the right – through their own agendas – appealing to *intégration*. This state of affairs could be dubbed "the political reality of the museum effect" – an effect becomes visible when the nation itself looks back on a past that it does not know or own but that it deems unique and authentic. It may be that such a complacent national position stems not so much from nationhood but from the discourse on nationhood, a bit like painting that could not exist without contemplation of painting.

During colonial times, murky references to a Christian Algeria predating Islam were often considered by French policy-makers sufficient to render the "Orient" recognizable to the Western eye. The ability to interpret as one chooses becomes key to this sort of recognition. The word and the object appear to lack a fundamental unity, perhaps because both are stripped of their concreteness in Europe's co-option of Islamic cultures. To that extent, the "Orient" becomes a metaphor that lacks a proper referent – perhaps it does not even require one. This is true, for example, of Europe's anti-Islam discourse, which is not based on documented knowledge; rather, it permeates the Western psyche, by absorption, through the biographies of individuals (travellers, scientists, soldiers, writers, missionaries, diplomats) as well as through the collective experience of groups (Western colonial enterprises, scientific expeditions, the European postcolonial encounter with Muslim minorities). Words such as "Arab," "Moor," "Saracen," "Infidel," and *Mahométan*[36] helped shift the Judeo-Christian logic of identity and strategies of identification towards essentialism, which became one foundation for Orientalism. This, in turn, motivated the attacks against the Other's faith, land, and heterogeneity of culture. A striking feature of Bonaparte's campaign in Egypt (1798–1801) was that the country's contemporary Arab and Muslim culture was bypassed, dismissed in favour of a single (scientific) focus on a long-dead Pharaonic empire.[37] Egypt's political invisibility actually helped increase the prestige of a country like France, which by then was deep in its own historical revolutionary present. The trick to dismissing Egypt's Islamic legacy was to transfer the cultural capital of the pyramids to the domain of Europe's political modernity, an exercise in civilizational translation. Despite this sleight of hand, which has fed back into Western cultural and political self-esteem, very little has changed. Nowadays, literature, ideologies, and the mainstream media in Europe and North America are perpetuating the same old misconceptions and untruths: (1) that Islam is a perversion of Judeo-Christian truth, (2) that Islam advocates violence, (3) that Islam is fixated on vice and characterized by intolerance, and (4) that the Prophet Muhammad was a charlatan. Communication between the West and the Orient – and, above all, *within* the West – has rarely occurred outside the litany of these unchallenged fallacies, and the end result has been cultural obscurantism. It was Said's achievement to partly dismantle the ideological agency of Orientalism, specifically its organic link between knowledge and power whereby one essentialized the other in a stubborn post-Enlightenment age. Unfortunately, the moral (and capitalistic) vagaries of Europe's colonial and neocolonial undertakings came at a high price for the Muslim Other. This kind of substitution of violence for reason had actually been theorized early in the twentieth century, during the peak years of capitalism and colonialism, by French philosopher Georges Sorel in his *Réflexions sur la violence* (1908), an essay that greatly impressed Frantz Fanon, who proceeded to theorize violence as a liberating force offering escape from the colonial paradigm: "From birth it is clear to him [the native] that this narrow world, strewn with prohibitions, can only be called in question by absolute violence."[38]

Representations of the Muslim Orient have also led to an astonishing annihilation of linguistic, historical, and psychological distinctions between the borrowers and the borrowed-from. A striking example was the use of French by politicians and writers from the Maghreb – because they were never educated in classical Arabic – as they were struggling against France to bring about independence for their native lands. For Europeans, cultures are objects to be possessed, and are consumed with little or no acknowledgment of their origins and developmental histories. What has emerged clearly in the challenging and conflicting relationship between the Judeo-Christian West and the Muslim world over the centuries is that the latter ended up being domesticated within the contours of cultures (British, French, Spanish, Dutch, American) that remained both foreign and restrictive. Even concepts such as the "nation-state" were normative and operative only so long as they bore the West's imprimatur. As a result, there was no pre-existing national community in the post-independence age for the individual to be reconciled to. The colonial habitat, so to speak, had been contaminated by an emphatic alienation.[39]

The point was – and remains – that history, as an ideological category, keeps the conditions of national identity in the West undisturbed. This explains, for example, why conservative and far-right political parties in Europe are organized around fetishized constructions of citizenship. The epistemic violence of Orientalism, slavery, and colonialism no longer deals with the postcolonial subject as an economic instrument of production, but rather as a political actor. The postcolonial condition thereby illuminates the fundamentally dysfunctional relationships between identity, citizenship, ethnicity, and faith – especially in France, which has dismissed its own Christian roots while simultaneously denying its colonial accountability. Perhaps France is unable to acknowledge its postcolonial condition because to do so would highlight the centrality of the colonial narrative. It is safe to say that French nationalism, centred on an obsession with laïcité and the tenets of republicanism, grows in the shadow of Orientalism with the aim of asserting identity rather than of standing witness to the trauma.

Western representations of "I" as subject – from the Cartesian era to the death of the contemporary subject – presuppose that his or her moral law and technological advance are meaningful and smoothly accommodate a succession of political platforms and cultural institutions. The Oriental Other, by contrast, is cast as a figure of opposition and reversal, and as largely disposable as formerly colonized people and later on as immigrants. The difference nowadays with the Oriental postcolonial subject is that instead of functioning in an allegorical sense

– in paintings, or during the colonial exhibitions, for instance – he is defined as pure immediacy, at levels both political (citizen) and ethical (non–Judeo-Christian values). There is nothing new here. Thus it was believed for a long time that northern Europe developed rapidly during the early fifteenth century even while southern Europe was being ruined by Arab/Muslim threats and influences.[40] Similarly, it was acknowledged that Arabs introduced Europeans to neo-Aristotelian philosophy, architecture, and new sciences such as algebra, optics, and chemistry, even while it was supposed that Arab culture and progress had been corrupted by the inherent contradictions in their faith and their ethnicity.[41] This gave flesh to the contrast between the supposedly unstable Arab/Muslim world and a West whose essence was, by comparison, permanent and incorruptible. This image has scarcely changed since the Enlightenment.

As colonialism set the standard for a moral consciousness whereby two incompatible humanisms cancelled each other out, the contrast between the Arab/Muslim world and the West was reinforced or modified. One brand of humanism, specific to the French and imbued with post-Revolutionary values as well as a discourse of origins and interests, was unable to accommodate cultural tensions, even though a revolution of ideology had replaced that of the soul, greatly undermining the validity of Christian theology. This type of humanism, emblematic of a typically French paradigm, posits an inclusive approach to understanding cultural values that, because it is absolute, serves to validate the figure of the Orient. This figure even becomes the foil to history and literature (as will be discussed in later chapters). The second brand of humanism can be defined by its capacity for both replication and isolation. This is the Anglo-American model, the only one to survive nineteenth-century colonialism. Its current iteration allows the figure of the Orient to align itself with Western culture, even though capitalism, democracy, and social equality are not taken fully to heart; put more simply, modern democracy is reduced to manufacturing economic advancement and second-hand human rights. In this specific case, the Orientalist logic of a binary opposition between East and West, Christian and Muslim, the industrial and the traditional, the democratic and the despotic, is deemed irrelevant. At the same time, the fluidity of this logic folds the foreignness of the Orient back inside the West itself.

Returning to the theme of the Orient as a figure of oneself, the concept evolves in time and space, operating on two levels of rationality. The first level assesses a sense of being against a historically changing perception. This was true in the case of the Arabs, who were perceived as a threat to Europe from the eighth century to the fifteenth. Yet after the Mongol invasion of the Middle East in the thirteenth century and the beginning of the Ottoman Empire's spread around the Mediterranean by the late fourteenth, Arab civilization became a prime target for colonization. Colonialism, in fact, allowed Orientalism to resume its course, and to rethink its ideology along the way as a token of modernity. It is no coincidence that France's military campaigns in Algeria in the 1830s coincided with the painting of the Hall of the Crusades at Versailles, a project begun in 1834 and completed in 1843. King Louis-Philippe, deemed at that time to be too close to the bourgeoisie and its revolutionary aspirations, needed to make peace with the Catholic Church as well as with the old nobility. The Crusades offered a highly useful theme for promoting reconciliation at a time of renewed war with Muslims in Algeria. It is no surprise that in the Hall of the Crusades, one painting stands out, that of Algerian leader Emir Abdelkader's surrender to French troops on 16 May 1843. This was a time of deeply felt nostalgia that saw the French indulging in their fetishistic fascination for the Middle Ages while attempting to absorb the reality of an imperial expansion that still lacked political content. In a perverse manner, the military conquest helped foreground the episteme of Orientalism. The French king was personally involved in this campaign, sending three of his sons (the Duke of Orleans, Duke of Aumale, and Duke of Nemours) to ensure the legitimacy of imperial conquest on the battlefields of Algeria. Delacroix contributed to the painting of the Crusades scenes, which played an important role (alongside the violence of the colonial wars) in the political formation of a nation that was still reeling from Napoleonic rule and that more than half a century after 1789 had failed to live up to its own revolutionary democratic ideals. Conflating the Crusades with the conquest of Algeria probably helped crystallize a memory construed as glorious, besides conveying historical continuity. Said's argument conflates that agency with, for example, the dogma of realism in nineteenth-century literature: "In practical meaning and operating ideology [...] Europe led the way and was the main subject of interest. [...] At a still deeper level, it is from the Christian Incarnation that Western realistic literature as we know it emerges."[42] Even literature could not distance itself from presumed representation, whether in the case of the "savage natives" in Conrad's novels or, as we will see, in Gide's North Africa.

The second level implicit in the concept of the Orient as a figure sym-
bolically debunks Westerners' constructions, which tend to span all
cultural and civil contexts, including those of their own origin. On this
level, the rationality of the Orient along with the excess of representations of it verging on stereotyping – those focused on faith, language,
and gender issues, for example – set a limit on Western reason because
they require stability and self-awareness. Western universalism thus
falls victim to cultural and political relativism by casting aside the need
for limits. For example, more than a century after the French occupation
of Algeria, Algerian writers such as Jean Amrouche and Kateb Yacine
demonstrated clearly that French literature signified different things on
different sides of the Mediterranean. Even such a figure as Camus could
not find his own "limit," being the Other among both the European
French (as a half-Spaniard *pied-noir*) and the Algerians (as a symbol of
the patronizing European, especially during the War of Independence).
In the specific case of Camus, there was a fleshing out of the distinction
between homeland and nation because of the ideological mystification
brought about by colonialism. In the final and decisive test of his allegiance, the War of Independence, his identity failed to find roots in its
historical conditions, due to a lack of immanent political critique: the
Other's freedom entailed Camus's own alienation.[43] In a sense, Camus
was hardwired to respond to humanistic values that worked wonders
in metropolitan France but that failed to grasp the colonial ideological
reality of Algeria. Authenticity (historical, ethnic, faith-based, and so
forth) had turned freedom into a categorical imperative. The irony that
escaped Camus and like-minded French intellectuals was that colonialism forces the colonized to become free.[44]

As I will discuss in a later chapter, there have been many theories that
attempt to single out historical problems as well as contemporary critical discourses regarding the Other and Orientalism.[45] Scholarly attention has focused largely on the issues of multivalence and relativism,
rather than dwelling on the subject's surface. It is also fascinating to note
that, while the experience of colonial rule heightened European self-
awareness and influence, most academic voices in the West today are
still keen to produce a discourse about the Other against a background
of growing global cultural misunderstandings. The Arab world's in-
dignant reactions to the American "war on terror" demonstrate how
much remains to be done in terms of developing political programs
and dovetailing cultural mechanisms. Relations in the academic and

political spheres, viewed from afar, point less to a legacy of anti-Islam prejudices than to Europeans' deep-seated sense of superiority in all aspects of culture and identity. Yet for any explanation to be valid – as Said offered in the archaeology of Orientalism – it must address its own origins, in terms of either mission or contingency.

Organic links unite the various approaches to identity-seeking, be they religious, historical, linguistic, or literary. Consider the birth and stage-by-stage development in Europe of the Orient concept. Its purpose was not to lay the groundwork for cultural imperialism; rather, it grew out of Europe's irrationality, selfishness, ignorance, religious rivalries, and unbalanced sociological mechanisms. Europe had long cultivated its own perspective on deviancy, its targets being Jews, lepers, heretics, homosexuals, New World cannibals, and even syphilitics. Yet Muslims were exempted from this dialectic of identification and repression. At the onset of the Crusades, Europe condemned Muslims as infidels; then Europe's own history, ambitions, and cultural certainties began to overstate its own singularity. Later on, the values of liberty and self-determination, so crucial in European societies, received only local, limited awakening within the anticolonial discourse. Thus in the 1950s, Fanon advocated violent revolutions of the colonized because the colonized were unable to assimilate their past in its totality. They needed to work from a blank slate, bypassing their own colonial history. But one need not be a Marxist to grasp the importance of how both Algeria and France were transformed by the colonial experience and how economic conditions that were both significant and interrelated – immigration on one hand, fossil fuels on the other – kept Algeria and France interconnected. Furthermore, violence was connected to a transnational movement on the African continent itself and, to some extent, to what would later be dubbed the Non-Aligned Movement. So the goal for Algerian revolutionaries was to contextualize their own national history in terms of new dynamics that were simultaneously un-Western and un-Oriental, just as it was for their Vietnamese counterparts of the 1950s. Yet the Marxist option failed to bow to the logic of postcolonial modernization.

Although the figure of the Orient developed differently in different European countries, its various concepts and representations competed with a single Western notion, arrived at as the fulfilment of prophecy. Note here that the French grasped the Islamic sphere as a subject of encyclopedic and artistic inquiry, while for the British the Islamic sphere amounted to a diplomatic and economic challenge. As it evolved from metaphor to direct designation, the Arab/Muslim figure became formative for European nationalism.[46] It literally prefigured the vitality and depth of identities and identifications. Under the auspices of the rising nation-state, the European self-image became corrupted by speculations about political agency: ideologies became cross-essentializing tools. One example is the relevance of French universalism in the colonies.[47] At the time, universalism was a strategic term, one, however, that continues to derive its compelling force from the sole accepted view of history and its discourse in the face of the postcolonial situation.[48] The oriental Other became "a figure of ourself," as it were, but stripped of his or her normative character and reduced to a shadow status, albeit a useful one. This condition reinforced every form of colonial utilitarianism, largely dependent on a paradigm of pleasure by way of death and sex: eliminating the threat and possessing the subject. The point is that the Oriental Other was made mute not so much by the absolute effectiveness of imperial discourse – which is far from true[49] – but rather by the power of representation that seeped deep into intellectual constructs until the mid-twentieth century. Even Simone de Beauvoir, in her much vaunted *The Second Sex* (1949), seems to have fallen prey to a facile pattern of gender distribution across civilizational lines: "The Oriental, careless of his own fate, is content with a female who is his; but the dream of the Occidental, once he rises to the consciousness of his uniqueness, is to be taken cognizance of by another free being, at once strange and docile."[50] Beauvoir fought hard against any sort of cultural determinism, yet she seemed unwilling to apply her budding feminist concepts to the Oriental Other, whom she depicted as wearing the shackles of a long-standing essentialism: as doomed never to play a prominent role along the path of progress or in the course of human history – a prevalent statement in the golden age of colonial France that elided the narrative of capital on which colonialism had been built.

The construction of the Oriental Other allowed Europeans to pass from the pathological to the status of super-being: white, Christian, knowledgeable, wealthy, and so on.[51] At the same time, the status of the colonized was essentially that of a symbolic fiction: the more he or she was dominated, the stronger the justification for colonial power. The perpetual and provisional condition of Oriental Otherness in the West cuts across traditional Cartesian subjectivity, especially its prescriptive content. It is no surprise to uncover, in contemporary anti-Arab racism and Islamophobia in France, the same discourse found in nineteenth-century anti-Semitism. For example, writers such as

Proust (whose mother was Jewish) and Ben Jelloun (who proclaims his Moroccan identity in French) articulate, in their respective works, selective judgments of Frenchness.[52] Jews and Arabs and Muslims in France are blamed for presumably having two different homelands, for mismanaging the national credo and faith, and, above all, for resisting assimilation into the melting pot of the French Republic. The identity of the Oriental Other thereby collapses into this: the West exists as long as its cultural and political utopias flourish anywhere, including at home. To that extent, colonialism – or historical preemption – was an experiment that both fulfilled and cancelled out the systemic perception of the Orient. In other words, Orientalism continued to thrive on a psychosis of the Common Good that was excluded from the realm of ethics. But what was it that gave rise in the first place to the chasm between politics and ethics?

This idea of separation and psychosis was advanced by Freud in *Civilization and Its Discontents*. Freud highlighted the importance of awareness that comes when civilization leaves the subject no choice but to become alienated in the face of a have-it-all ideology. By living in a world of biddable values and principles, citizen-subjects find themselves domesticated within the community and caught in the upside-down world of ethical acts. Domination, exploitation, and other pathological symptoms of hegemonic ideologies are not just gratuitous additions to intercultural exchanges – they have become their very foundation. Freud puts the claim in quite striking terms: "When people came to know about the mechanism of the neuroses, which threaten to undermine the modicum of happiness enjoyed by civilized men [...] It was discovered that a person becomes neurotic because he cannot tolerate the amount of frustration which society imposes on him in the service of its cultural ideals."[53] By vindicating such an intuition within the postcolonial condition, one risk is to set into a clash of authenticity. Simply put, what was lost in sensationalist representations of the Orient was not gained in national histories and individual activity. Even after the wars of national liberation, for example, Europeans continued to regard African nations as former colonies, as deprived of the impetus of their own histories. These new countries, especially their economies, were branded uncompetitive and poorly managed; at the core of this denunciation was the suggestion that the formerly colonized had missed out on modernity despite now living in independent states. Their political and military elites had been trained in France, within a safe distance of the source of cultural continuity. It is no wonder that peoples who had been narrated out of their own histories during the colonial era were unable to find a site of contestation and resistance on becoming independent. By eradicating true nationhood, Orientalism had produced its own brand of futile idealism.[54] In most cases, French remained the official language of these countries;[55] the currency for some West African nations is still the CFA franc even though the French franc has ceased to exist. Although Europe and Africa were separated in political time, they remained part of the same historical stream, except that now Orientalism expressed itself not as representation but rather as self-perception. In short, even as their lands gained national independence, the African and Maghrebi elites participated in their own Orientalizing; meanwhile, it was unclear whether the masses had been converted.[56]

All of this points to why the paradigm of "us versus them" seems so off-target and must be re-examined in the postcolonial political order. Wasn't decolonization, after all, an assertion of the independence seekers' identity? In fact, decolonization and the migration of the formerly colonized to Europe gave way to an entirely new configuration, one in which the paradigm of the local and the global has come to the rescue of the subject. Yet the fashionable (postmodern) notion of "subject" remains as valid as the concept of national authenticity.[57] In any culture, authenticity places self-recognition at centre stage. That was true, for example, of the old Chinese Empire, which based its authenticity on the notion that it was the centre of the world.[58] But for this process to be fully grasped with respect to Europe, one must presuppose that universalism, as it has flowed out of the Enlightenment, rests on the idea that the Other must take on the attributes of the West in order to belong to the universal community. This has inverted the relationship between East and West: as the Oriental Other became more concrete, the West became more allegorical in the broadest sense, in both its sign and in what it signified. It was Rousseau, after all, who suggested that Europeans had the capacity to struggle out of themselves in order to become free, while the "savage" (the people of the New World and of Africa) was essentially enslaved from within.[59] In the modern era, postcolonial Europe seems to have been outmatched by its own "Europeanness." Indeed, the paradox is such that, if the West were to disappear completely, this Western "Europeanness" would survive in the rest of the world. In a sense, Shanghai, Singapore, and Dubai are as Western as Paris, London, and Vancouver are Eastern. So it seems that Western virtues, institutions, and so forth are defined less in their full historicity than in a figurative extension. This acknowledgment of shifting powers, if only in economic terms, complicates national myths. As borders have become an issue for both the European Union and the United States, insecure nations have spawned a new kind of racism, one that is not focused on hatred of the Other but rather that is eager to foster or preserve an ideal community. This is a kind of reverse segregation that works like a fiction within the grand narrative of Western nations.[60]

The extrapolitical interpretation of the relationship between Occident and Orient is rooted in what imperial history has either denied or eschewed. This is true in part because arts and ideologies have stripped Europe of its concrete reality. By means as various as the ontological projection of the Renaissance onto the Enlightenment (drawing on the past to build a new future) and the fleshing out of the global figure of the Occident, Europe has not so much shaped its own Orient once and for all as it has continued to re-create it. From the seventeenth century to the twentieth, France reflected itself in its own Oriental fantasies: *turqueries* in music and literature, *arabesques* in dance, *chinoiseries* and *japonaiseries* in art, the psychological attributes of *espagnolisme* in literature,[61] and *art nègre* in painting and sculpture. The key to understanding this cultural process lies in the idea of re-creation, not by starting afresh, but after fully grasping the preceding fundamental truths. What is most striking about the lineage of Western thinking about the Orient is that, while it is omnipresent, it is never officially acknowledged or even identified as such. An example is the racialization of issues of sex and gender along with the conception of social history that was derived from this. In attempting to explain "polygamy and homosexuality" in Eastern cultures, Montesquieu pointed the finger at the warm climates, which helped weave debauchery and perversion into the fabric of Oriental despotism.[62] Of course, Louis XIV, with his fifty-two children born out of wedlock in the mild climate of France, remained unaffected by this climatic disorder.

The re-creative process grew more obscure as Europe spread its presence in the real Orient through colonial occupation. Within the forced conversation of colonialism, the Oriental subjects converted a culture to its plurality. That may be why universalism stood no real chance of being adopted as the dominant principle in Eastern culture. In a sense, the colonial experience outed the universalist imaginary, as if ideologues of all stripes – academics, writers, missionaries, and diplomats among them – had realized that their "world-hypotheses"[63] were long on speculation and short on fact. This reality eventually cohered into self-revelation for the colonized and their anticolonial political and cultural movements – which tends to disprove Said's argument concerning the absolute hegemony of colonialism. Even the modern separation of discourses – between the hard sciences and the arts, for example – was rescinded in Orientalism through narration of its culture, knowledge, and methodologies. So one could speak of a dual presence of the Orient – one inside the Western paradigms, and one outside, but always lacking a point of origin, or rather expelled from its origin. Thus it is not surprising that behind the colonial ideology was the demand for both permanence and change. In the case of Algeria, the land itself was dubbed French, because it had supposedly been Christian since the time of Augustine; yet at the same time, this Algerian colonial possession needed to be brought into the fold of societies embracing technological modernity. This type of thinking amounted to a misguided strategy that consisted of putting down roots in lands where the French would always remain outsiders. The issue of origin only resulted in cultural incompatibility.[64] Frenchness could never become the precondition for constructing Algerian identity and subsequent nationhood.

The violent culmination of colonial occupation meant that Europe needed to produce some sort of political and cultural tradition in order to be present in and contained by its own discourse. And it is, in fact, in relation to Islam, and not to the fall of the Roman Empire or to that of Chinese civilization, that Europe came to exist as a purposive and creative whole. Even the decolonization of the Americas (the United States, Haiti, Spanish America) remained marginal within the European construct of history because of the radical opposition between nation-building in the Americas and colonial expansion in Europe, while the Muslim world evinced a general complacency and lack of methodology in responding to Orientalism. Underlying the discourse's articulated purposes, however, were unspoken attitudes of superiority.[65] What matters most here is that the rationale for maintaining coherence and meaning is often derived from what is kept silent within what is being said. A famous early literary example is found in Rabelais's *Gargantua* (1534), where, in chapter 33, Pichrocole travels to the Maghreb and meets with pilgrims bound for Mecca. There is something provisional and incomplete about the protagonist-hero that suddenly makes sense in the heart of the feared Orient. He points to the Muslim world as a perverted incarnation against which his own self can be revealed and saved from the barbarism of the Others. Once identified, the Muslim

Oriental source needs to be cancelled out. This literary illustration recalls the erasure from memory of how the Arab/Muslim world passed
the Greek legacy to Western Europe, as well as attempts to forget that
the Muslim civilization achieved vital breakthroughs in astronomy,
chemistry, medicine, and mathematics. The nostalgia for, or invention
of, non-Muslim origins has always plagued the West. The West's Arab/
Muslim paradigm is not a matter of interpretation or correction; rather,
the paradigm is all about locating oneself in a world of absolute al-
terability and hegemony. It is easy to grasp how such a construction
moved from fantasy to imperial epic.

There is no need to view the Middle Ages as an era that fore-
shadowed the Muslim–Christian misunderstanding of later centuries,
although twentieth-century authors did delve into the ancient propa-
gandistic effort.[66] Just as there had been "a Jewish question" in Europe,
the "problem of Islam" needed to be circumscribed and dealt with. It
took a foundational discourse, largely based on polemics and misrepresentations, to shape Europeans' sense of a prevailing identity. It turned
out that Islam, like Christianity, had formalized a spiritual monotheistic principle with little vested interest in other faiths. At the peak
of their civilization, Arabs and Muslims were preoccupied with self-
critique. Rhetoric and theology slowly took over the hard sciences, especially after the split between Sunnis and Shias.[67] The Other remained
for Muslims a non-proposition until after the Crusades and, later on,
during the various Western colonial enterprises in Muslim lands. The
religious and epistemic principles elaborated in the Islamic world between the eighth and fourteenth centuries validated a true and exem-
plary universalism. This was universalism at its apex: Islam was global,
while cultures remained local. The expansion of the Muslim world,
and the triumphalist attitude that surely accompanied it, have always
posed a challenge to Christian civilization. No one can forget the image
of the Caliph Umar, dressed in a simple camel-hair garment, entering
Jerusalem (still called by its Roman name, Aelia) without bloodshed,
in 638 (year 16 in the Muslim calendar) and going straight to the
Temple mount to clean it with his own hands because local Christians
had turned the sacred place into a garbage dump.[68] By contrast, when
Jerusalem fell to marauding Frankish armies in July 1099, signs of the
massacre remained visible throughout the city at Christmas. At the
al-Aqsa Mosque, also known as Solomon's Temple, more than 70,000
Muslim scholars and other civilians were slaughtered in a matter of

days.[69] When the Christians refused to touch the Muslim dead, deemed "unbelievers," the Jews were left to do the cleaning up. Afterwards, the Jews were sold into slavery or held, together with their sacred books, for ransom.[70] Thus the Orient – the Muslim one at least – represented a threat that needed to be rendered powerless, but not before its usefulness was exploited.

From this perspective, it makes sense that the figure of the Oriental was conceived as an ideal literary subject. The narrative of Western will-to-power, couched in the ideologies of humanism and the Enlightenment, is now understood as intellectual and theological defensiveness. From the outset, the projection of Orientalism has presupposed a special bond between the validity of European culture – which rests more on contingency than on absolutes – and the ongoing process of historical integration. While the French Revolution replaced the *Ancien Régime*, for example, it did not put an end to French civilization per se. A relationship existed, but it needed a new narrative.

Underlying the Western ideological/political work is a concept of law based on a subversive reading of Islam. From the "Infidels" of the Middle Ages to the "jihadists" of the twenty-first century, Muslims have found themselves cut off from the spectrum that encompasses reason, ethics, law, politics, and science. Yet within this vision, lines are blurred. Indeed, as Christianity has continued to lose its bearings in Europe, it needs more and more to find a different set of absolutes with which to define itself. That is why, for example, the industrial and technological revolutions corroborate the Christian notion of being reborn, yet reborn in a centreless world. It is no wonder that these revolutions first took place in Anglo-Saxon nations, where the original model of Christianity had been reshaped into a personal connection with God – just as has always been the case in Islam. Interestingly, it is also in England that the word "Orientalism" was first coined and acknowledged as such by academic institutions, in mid-sixteenth century. The word appeared in France much later, in a journal, *Magasin Encyclopédique* XXV (November 1810), 122, in reference to Father Paulinus, a scholar in Oriental languages.

In the hands of ideologues, enlightened thinkers, and colonialists, Europe's perception of itself turned out to be parochial, if not simplistic. The dichotomies produced by efforts to fathom the Orient are reminiscent of exclusivist categorizations perpetuated in old empires or modern totalitarian regimes. For example, a Maghrebi immigrant in contemporary France remains very much the Other, while a Korean or Canadian worker does not. According to Johan Galtung, this attitude is determined by specific factors: (1) space: the West is the centre of the world; (2) time: any process, including a crisis, is unidirectional; (3) knowledge: the world is better understood by the lowest common denominators; (4) man–nature: man necessarily rules over nature; (5) man–God: there is a fundamental principle that rules over man; and (6) man–man: equality cannot be achieved and has no bearing on the historical process.[71] It comes as no surprise that Western nations have been vying with one another over the blurred vision they still have of themselves and the Orient, especially the Muslim one. What is most fascinating is that, early on, travels and expeditions to the Orient were deemed to be essentially homecomings, mainly on Biblical grounds.

In the field of literature, this false universalism might be attributed to an untamed imagination. In all types of literature (literary, historical, religious, diplomatic, etc.), Arab characters have always appeared untrustworthy, sectarian, cowardly, and oversexed. Sometimes they are simply invisible, as in Albert Camus's works of fiction where the name "Algerian" never appears in stories taking place in Algeria.[72] Western writing is reactive and tends to focus on reinforcing a sense of both historical and material identity, especially in a post–French Revolution culture that slowly became profane and secularized. That sense is usually stronger still when the writer has extensive contact with the Orient. Even those who held favourable views of the Muslim world, such as André Gide and Jean Genet, underlined incompatibilities between Islam and the humanistic, enlightened intellectual legacies of their own culture.[73] Rana Kabbani, in her monograph *Europe's Myths of Orient*, writes about what could be dubbed a metafiction: "In the European narration of the Orient, there was a deliberate stress on those qualities that made the East different from the West, exiled into an irretrievable 'otherness.'"[74] It is as if collective identity, be it Christian, nationalistic, or capitalist-driven, could only be fulfilled in an arena of conflict or domination. Yet what is fascinating here is that the conflict itself becomes a form of socialization. It brings cohesion to a culture best described by its technological achievements as well as by its gift for destroying itself and its surroundings. Part of the fascination with the Orient was a rejection of how Europe was transforming itself. In such a crisis of antagonistic cultures, it is in the field of literature that one may best trace the misperceptions related to the "Other" as well as world views that explain the objectivity of Orientalism. One result was that the perceptions around power and sex, in French literature at least, integrated their own legacies to form a distinct genre. From the first translation of *The Arabian Nights*[75] to the recent academic disputes concerning who is an "arabologue" (Arabologist) and who is an "arabisant" (Arabist),[76] French culture never got over the measure of its Orientalist identity. The great movement of Western culture was redrawn – not necessarily questioned – by Edward Said when he tackled humanism and it bourgeois selfhood and tried to link aesthetics with politics. Said dropped the category of the Oriental, and its deconstructive questions, so that he could dramatize rather than resolve what Orientalism continues to be.

3 Orientalism and Postcolonial Studies

My aim in this chapter is to pursue my conversation with Orientalism by demonstrating more specifically how Edward Said made manifest the political and cultural practices of Arab and Muslim representation, as well as by examining the impact of his ideas on postcolonial studies. The formation of knowledge in the West about the Muslim East came to the forefront with Said's *Orientalism* (1978). Of course, Arab accounts and criticisms of Orientalism[1] had long been present in Near Eastern intellectual debate – in the work of the Egyptian reformer Muhammad Haykal in the early twentieth century, for example, and more recently in that of Syrian philosopher Sadik al Azm. In my view, Said's book belongs to a genre of Arab authorship that is time-specific – rooted in the 1970s, when Arab identity and representation were still seeking stability on the world scene as well as at home. The humiliating Syrian–Egyptian defeat of October 1973, the headlong rush towards terrorism among Palestinian leaders, the reality of Arab puppet regimes caught up in the proxy politics of the Cold War, and an Islamic revolution in a non-Arab nation all became structuring motifs in cultural criticism. Much has been written about the extent to which *Orientalism* was somehow tendentious. Said was accused of romanticizing Oriental victims of Western ideologies and colonial enterprises, of being "selective" with his sources, of ignoring issues of social class and glossing over ethnicity and faith, of simplifying the intellectual relationship between discourse and domination, of overlooking the disjunctive configuration of the "Oriental" intellectual who lives in the West, and of omitting Eastern intellectuals from his analysis and thereby perpetuating the stereotype that Orientals cannot speak for themselves. All of these comments are valid and help open up new readings of the West–East dialectic beyond the arguments proposed by Said. Yet this perhaps ignores the fact that Said, as a critic of imperialism, was a minority voice (a Christian Arab born in Jerusalem) who struggled to transform the Western academic world from within. His scholarship was indeed an intrusion, one that rejected the postmodern premise that all knowledge is tainted and complicit. Whether his achievement remains undiminished is irrelevant: he succeeded in initiating an "irritative process of critique."[2] *Orientalism* generated a great deal of blowback. A different side of the story was being told, and the book's thesis upset people in all walks of academic life. Initially, the harshest reactions came from a Western scholar, Bernard Lewis, and an Eastern scholar, Aijaz Ahmad: the full spectrum of academic and ethnic commentary was reacting to Said's writing. Regardless of the book's many shortcomings, what the critics failed to grasp was that Said was writing from *within* the Western academic tradition and was bringing together humanistic values in an effort to replay the deconstructionist battle on the native terrain of Orientalism.

Guilt and various destabilizing factors factored heavily in the critical reception of *Orientalism*. Setting aside any anti-Western posturing, Said's premise was clear enough: knowledge cannot be dissociated from the exercise of power. He actually took Foucault's critique a step further by questioning the centrality of the sovereign subject. But Said left this question unanswered: What was the epistemic root that led to the manufacturing of the Orient? What worked with respect to the Industrial Revolution in Europe, and the rise of the bourgeois class at the expense of the working class, disappeared in the blind spot of self-representation of the Oriental. Western powers manufactured history into historicism. For example, for the French throughout the Maghreb, understanding Islamic codes of law helped them administer their subjects in ways that seemed fair to the colonial power. Critics who excoriated Said for his vertical analysis of the historical complicity of political establishments and academics were probably struggling with current issues relating to their own complicity with global oppression, especially in the Middle East. It is hardly surprising that Bernard Lewis, whose Zionist position informs his work,[3] underscored the contrast between Said's pronounced pro-Palestinian discourse and his own.[4] According to Lewis, Said's anti-Western dogmas reflected a very weak grasp of Orientalist science. Likewise Aijaz Ahmad, taking a Marxist perspective, tended to relate Said's argument to a discourse descriptive of cultural hegemony (much along the lines of Gramsci's "dominant culture" paradigm) emanating from the elite institutions of American academe. According to Aijaz, Said was an intellectual comprador operating within an unabashed Western cultural ideology. One lesson to be learned from the fallout from Said's work is that conflict is a valuable asset in a world too prone to recycling its own truths. Since Said's work, a conventional reading of Western epistemology has been impossible, although he acknowledged that his thesis was derived from Foucault's analyses developed in *L'archéologie du savoir*.[5] Said avoided categories, reasoning that they would amount to dogmas, and in doing so he laid the groundwork for his own indictment. For example, the Australian philosopher Arran Gare underscores that Said "has virtually presupposed that there is no such thing as the understanding of cultures, that statements or representations can be nothing but exercises of power as parts of discursive formations."[6] The charge that Said's argument applies to his own book is weak at best, given that most Orientalist literature had been written earlier, while the colonial enterprise was ongoing. Orientalist misrepresentations thus echoed into the present day, becoming mechanisms of self-referentiality. By definition the Orientalist ideology could not understand other cultures as such, because that approach was grounded in the praxis of occupation itself. Knowledge was a product of local interactions and – to some extent – of determined measures of understanding. For example, Montesquieu's and Voltaire's old theme of Oriental despotism re-emerged during the nineteenth century within the framework of alleged Islamic fanaticism. After all, in Algeria, India, and Sudan, jihad had been fought against the French and British Christian "infidels."[7] This provided sufficient material for politicians and the media in Europe to elaborate on the "essential" violence of Islam. Yet by tracing the supposed weaknesses of North African cultures with regard to religion, the French revealed their own brand of cultural imperialism. Said emphasized this particular point: "To have such knowledge of such a thing is to dominate it, to have authority over it. And authority here means for 'us' to deny autonomy to 'it' – the Oriental country – since we know it and it exists in a sense *as* we know it."[8] In this respect the Western powers were able to confirm that they were rational, developed, humane, and democratic, while the Orient was the exact opposite. The Orient was described as unchanging, uniform, and impervious to political evolution. Most importantly, the Orient was able to assess itself only through Western input. It is interesting, and rather ironic, that all of these passive and belittling representations paralleled a weak socio-political situation at home. Even while the French were engaging in a full-out military campaign to "pacify" all of Algeria, they were defeated in the Franco-Prussian War of 1870, losing the provinces of Alsace and Lorraine in the process; the following year, the Paris Commune nearly overthrew the entire regime and its institutions, and was only suppressed after widespread carnage. So it seemed that colonialism was providing correctives to a debilitated French democracy.

Of course, examined from Said's perspective on epistemic violence, colonialism and Orientalism together overturned the assumptions of humanist discourse. His critique emphasizes the contingency of a totalizing and capitalistic paradigm, as in this famous passage: "It is therefore correct that every European, in what he could say about the Orient, was consequently a racist, an imperialist, and almost totally ethnocentric."[9] Orientals were left to restore some kind of historical agency by jeopardizing their own history and traditions, as well as by appropriating the colonizers' models – a phenomenon analysed by Albert Memmi half a century ago.[10] Yet the colonial condition left the colonized with one asset – they were able to identify and challenge Western world values from within, thus exemplifying the Marxist view that economic exploitation fuels historical conflict. The Orientals shaped their resistance – dramatically so – with Western tools. This historical evidence, this workable truth, escaped Said, as if he preferred to dwell on the idea that the Orient blindly followed everything Western, whether under duress or not. It was not just a matter of mimicry.[11] Resistance seeks to counterbalance the dynamics of oppression; it also operates like a categorical imperative that shapes Otherness. What merits attention here is the fact of collective awareness, or the Maghrebi community's capacity to reinvent itself when confronted with the fiction of Orientalism. This was no easy feat, if only because the French language buttressed colonial nationalism. The Arabic language, meanwhile, collapsed into a problematic *topos* riven by the fault lines of religion – Arabic was the language of the Islamic faith – and ethnicity – it was seen as valid to ask to what extent Maghrebi peoples were Arabs. North African intellectuals were left to struggle for symbolic order, and this included disseminating Western truths (they were educated in French schools and published by Parisian publishing houses) as well as challenging Western self-entitlement by bearing witness to historical discrimination and exploitation. Their no longer "Oriental" identity relied on the very object they were trying to expel. No wonder a leading Algerian writer, Jean Amrouche, developed the myth of the *éternel Jugurtha* (eternal

Jugurtha),[12] in direct opposition to Albert Camus's *éternelle Méditerranée* (eternal Mediterranean).[13] Both positions encapsulate the idea of purity that stemmed from Orientalism. These labels consolidated principles as if they were ideological straitjackets. That is why Maghrebi intellectuals and political leaders – most of whom were Marxists – argued for a rethinking of selfhood and national identity. But was it truly a course they had chosen, or had they been hurled down that path by Orientalist knowledge production? Said sought to demonstrate that the national histories of formerly colonized cultures and countries could not be grasped outside the Orientalist context in which they had been produced: "The boundary notion of East and West, the varying degrees of projected inferiority and strength, the range of work done, the kinds of characteristic features ascribed to the Orient: all these testify to a willed imaginative and geographic division made between East and West, and lived through during many centuries."[14]

In a sense, the postcolonial condition brings to light the repercussions of unities that are separate but not distinct, mostly in relation to Maghrebi immigration to the former *métropole* and the economic neocolonial bonds that have joined France to its former colonies. The role of the Orientalist legacy in the construction of knowledge stands at the core of the power dynamic. Orientalism was essentially directed at the conquest and occupation of the Muslim East; today's postcolonial discourse maintains the record of knowledge, but in a state of crisis both for the Maghrebi intellectual and for France. Borrowing from Marxist rhetoric, Gayatri Chakravorty Spivak talks of "surrender to the controlling power of neo-capitalism."[15] Postcolonial writers are not soulless, nor are they commodified subjects, and above all they do not need to uphold liberal humanism as it exists in contemporary Europe. Indeed it is France that is preoccupied with mapping its own cultural contours and pinning down its political principles.[16] Orientalism is effective insofar as its intended result is to resolve contradictions between lived realities and representation. Now that both France and the Maghreb are trying to come to terms with their cultural differences, the past is proving to be an unreliable resource when it is not complicating their narratives outright. Self-absorbed cultural practices find themselves drawn into question by the language itself. Indeed, representation exposes the limitations of the subject matter. If French literature sought to define itself as canonical – that is, as a key source of ideas and values – then Maghrebi writers in French would perpetuate this. But what is called francophone literature is still largely fuelled by a resistance that calls for new interpretations. Postcolonial identity itself is beset with issues of displacement and alternative understanding. It comes as no surprise that in the twenty-first century, French universalism has yet to extend itself to all groups in the French-speaking world, including French citizens who belong to ethnic minorities.

If it is true that recapturing the language of the former colonial power reflects cultural dislocation, one can add that there is something utopian in the very idea of writing and thinking in a non-native culture. Maghrebi intellectuals, because they are critical of homogenizing practices derived from a colonial excursus, ask their readers to pay attention to national identity, not so much as a token of their anticolonial credentials, but rather as a reorientation and as a transformative force. To understand this particular utopian paradigm, one must first understand the role that Orientalism played in the nineteenth-century Western landscape. John MacKenzie argues that Orientalism developed as a reaction to the Industrial Revolution and to the many counter-discourses (mainly in the arts) that stemmed from it.[17] Europe's cultural uniformity had been shattered, and the Orient proved an outlet for emerging dreams of unity and meaning.[18] Meanwhile, the twin scourges of racism and economic exploitation in the colonies helped mask the twin failures of French republicanism in the *métropole* and universalism across the empire. It seems that Orientalism had been designed in terms of limits as well as fiction. Normative French history, which relied for its authority on the (eminently exportable) ideals of the *Révolution* and the fervour of French culture's *mission civilisatrice*, found itself outmatched by the new possibilities brought about by the ideological shift. In a quite paradoxical fashion, the Orient became the centre of what was missing in the West. This may be how colonialism eventually shaped French national identity. Almost no one belonging to France's political and intellectual establishments questioned that Algeria was an unconditional part of the fatherland. In this regard, Algeria was both the real and the allegorical locus where nation and empire intersected. Like drama, which has the power to make present rather than just narrate, Orientalism throughout the Maghreb took the place of the missing object, the repressed representation of stability and unified identity. Like a mirror, postcolonial literature enacts its trauma in a semiotic relationship between history and text, life and story. But does putting the past into words do justice to the colonial reality and its cultural and social impact? It is safe to say that Orientalism required of non-Westerners (called the "minority" in the empire) that they forget who they were and aspire to the norms contained in someone else's history. In 1925, during the golden age of French colonialism, Paul Valéry pointed out that "the Greeks and the Romans showed us how to deal with the monsters of Asia, how to treat them by analysis, how to extract from them their quintessence."[19] The idea of reclaiming the Other's cultures illuminates a fundamentally disjunctive perception of race, language, religion, and nationality. The modern manner in which Orientalism operates assumes that one myth supports another in an infinite chain. Thus, the violent postcolonial inscription that the Oriental lacks a mother tongue derives from the fact that, as Said put it, "[he's] *written* about."[20] It seems, then, that Orientalism can be symbolized by a fable, one that replaces remembrance of language with a social order based on symbolic power. All that Maghrebi writers can then do is speak the historical outrage that touches both memory and identity.

Postcolonial literature has become the tool that allows the metonymic perception of continuity by and through language, and by agency rather than passive victimization. The racist premises of Orientalism, combined with the crude logic of capitalism, have been turned into a meaningless commodity as a result of the essentialist position that postcolonial writers must take. They must free themselves from the mesmerizing stare of Western subjectivity, if only to rethink the limitations of European aesthetic norms. In a quite phenomenological way, language engages human consciousness, not just human identity. In that sense the colonial language becomes the experience of home; the whole postcolonial self is that which synthesizes the past and the present. The francophone author writes against the imperialist's belittlement (based on an axiomatics of inferiority) and does so in precisely the field of interpolation that shapes French culture: literature. It must be understood that in France, one of the many purposes of literature is to continue the imperialist project; in this regard, the contemporary political concept of *francophonie* (the French-speaking world) has supplied Jacobinic France with the narcissistic illusion of transnational cultural exchanges. Most of all, the genealogy of Orientalism that posits that Orientals have achieved little culturally pursues its own narrative course, which informs the myth of origin, or rather revises it by turning language and fiction into emancipatory concepts. Unlike postmodern literature, postcolonial literature does not simply problematize itself here and now; it also seeks to tear down Western cultural benevolence. For example, there are hardly any breakaway or avant-garde writers from the Maghreb in the postcolonial movement. They must always consider their own location and dig through the strata of ideology deposited by the colonial period before they can find their own literary voice. In a sense, the creative and aesthetic endeavour must make a specific contribution to an emerging literature as a distillation of pure experience, opposed to what I dub the second nature of revisiting history. As a parallel, this reminds us that Wittgenstein was able to *do* philosophy without ever quoting philosophers. In a perfect world, the postcolonial writer would be able to rid himself/herself of the garments of the postcolonial condition. And it is this challenge that feeds the conflict between what the postcolonial is and what culture is. Essentially, culture draws its legitimacy from historicism rather than from history.[21]

This reminds us that Orientalism was truly modern because it was mainly about self-discovery, even while it recast old terminology into a translation of *différence*. Orientalism's challenge was to enclose humanistic values within its configuration of discourse formation, if only because philologists viewed the Orient as the cradle of all languages. As for the Orientals themselves, they were simply obliterated as a negative deconstruction (the difference of *différence*) and were often perceived as either subservient or uncontrollable. After independence, they found themselves in transition, or what falls under the term "hybridity," and French became the language in which the knowledge of Maghreb cultures was produced.[22] *Francophonie*, hybridity, and *métissage* are not happy coinages, because even though the transcoding is useful, it still points to unequal encounters. Even so, these terms gained academic currency, mainly because they entailed a realignment of literary epistemic grids. The centrality of France in North American and British universities has lost some of its conceptual grip; French postcolonial studies themselves bear on the alien and remain a phantom category. Why do the boundaries of the national paradigm not apply to so-called francophone literature? The intent here is not so much to contextualize literature in terms of ethnic dynamics as it is to question the identity taxonomy itself. In short, if literature is an expression of national identity, why are Algerians, Moroccans, Tunisians, Senegalese, Congolese, Ivoiriens, Haitians, and Québécois all lumped together under the francophone banner? Is it because a true literary reinscription cannot flourish within the colonial fracture? Probably not, because of the historical disjunction between France and the Anglo-Saxon world, as well as the misleading implied assertion that what is analysed is and will remain the same always and everywhere. Comparative approaches provide a relevant gloss on the problematics, which in theory do not exhaust the postcolonial world of representations. The challenge is to reopen the wounds without succumbing to a nostalgia that dwells on origins, archives, languages, *différence*, technological advances, and so on. Still, this moment of transcultural crisis folds into a narrative of identity and authority. For example, the contemporary global paradigm fails to disrupt colonial patterns, not just in terms of economic policies but in terms of cultural productions as well. It is not surprising that postcolonial analytical strategies work better in the West than in the "rest." It is also accepted that the transition from the colonial to the postcolonial has never indicated, directly or by allusion, greater autonomy, sustainable academe, or any normalization of the curricular space. What is called "postcolonial" at universities in Birmingham (England) and Los Angeles is astonishingly "national" in Algiers, Delhi, Nairobi, and Port-au-Prince. By failing to distinguish between the various shades of native cultures, does postcolonial theory function as a retroactive tool of ideological correctness? Does postcolonial studies perform the trick of scrubbing prejudice and propaganda from history while leaving the stain of cultural domination untouched? Any doubt left in one's mind serves as further evidence that the asymmetrical and limited range of postcolonial theory simply does not address the configuration of power. Once postcolonial literature is read as "resisting," "subversive," "transgressive," "polyphonic," "eccentric," "transnational," and so on, the political and intellectual threads of inquiry snap.[23] Said suggested that Orientalism taught us more about the Orientalists' own cultures (i.e., British, French, German) than about the "Orientals"; it is nearly as puzzling to note that postcolonial studies has, to some extent, become a discourse centred on the crisis in humanities in Western academe. The blanks of oppression are never filled in completely, as if literary interpretation were fuelling the too familiar cultural cycles. The native's "discursive resistance" endorses the theory's central tenets and manages them in a fashion reminiscent of the historical outrage that made the articulation of identity and memory impossible. More than thirty years after the founding of postcolonial studies, it can be safely argued that critical discourse has failed to take to task the ahistorical posturing and the idealization of texuality, as if the postcolonial condition did not include the political here and now, as if narratives overrode facts. In short, postcolonial studies has sent us back to a world of representation.[24] A minority academic in North America does not enjoy something "extra" thanks to the position he or she is speaking from; his or her position implies, rather, that whiteness is the default. Simply put, are not minority academics othering themselves because their race and history are marked out for special notice? Africans, Arabs, Asians, Caribbean people, and so on strive to make their historical narrative more important relative to what remains dominant and evident and requires no explanation. Spivak is more straightforward when she writes that "we cannot 'learn about' the subaltern only by reading literary texts, or *mutatis mutandis*, sociohistorical documents."[25]

With latent Orientalism spanning politics and culture, it was necessary to remain vigilant against strategies of disenfranchisement. The Orientalist discourse had a strong tendency to reduce meaning and intentions. Also, Orientalism could accommodate the illusion that the colonial undertaking involved more than political domination and cultural erasure. Metaphors of "reason," "principle," and "responsibility" only highlighted the West's compromised value system, which in the twentieth century spawned two world wars and a Cold War that held mankind's fate in the balance. Interpretation was bound by the reach of Western self-absorption, especially after post-structuralists read our post-Marxist world in terms of categories of culture and desire. The old non-capitalist lands, which stretched from Africa to Asia, found themselves split into subverted representations of themselves; then through independence they exported wave after wave of emigrants along the political and cultural fault lines leading to the *métropole*. Conversely, in Western academe, postcolonial theory functions as a vehicle that affects the text as much as it is affected by it. The vehicle of meaning that is a book works to maintain dominant interests (in terms of the market) and to express cultural sedimentations (in terms of nation formation). Aspiring to be more than a set of representations, the theory ends up being subverted by the ontological gap between hierarchies and divisions. The "subaltern" does not need to be "saved," and the rational, enlightened principles of Western academe can be shown to be counter-intuitive, especially when Maghrebi literature in French finds itself awaiting completion – translation on the French cultural scene, and legitimacy in the Maghreb.

The end of empire, just like that of hegemonic theoretical discourse, is never merely a national affair, or at least not one set in a particular cultural frame.[26] Orientalism used to be concerned with narrow, unwarranted assumptions. Uncannily, the postcolonial discourse tends to focus on a small assemblage of literary texts that rarely represent the people of the land. The most powerful cultural statements are often made by diasporic authors. The issue of truth and its complicity or randomness vis-à-vis the question of origins or nativeness is best illustrated by the case of Salman Rushdie. Can his fiction "truly" portray what India is today? Or Islam? The prestige and authority granted to exiled writers at the expense of native writers amounts to a restriction of the critique. Because of this, postcolonial theory leads to the realization that there cannot be any truth-claim in the figuration of the Oriental Other. Just as Orientalism used to proclaim that the Orient was "an entirely coherent phenomenon,"[27] contemporary academic discourse in the West finds itself shored up by strategies of unwitting exclusions. The postcolonial discourse, in its many guises (Marxist, feminist, deconstructionist, transnational, etc.), is called upon to homogenize itself into a single signifier of dissenting voices penned as modern chronicles of displacement. Yet the theory expands on hackneyed political positions based on a model of assimilation that is unruffled by its own deficient knowledge of the Other's cultures. And meanwhile, the postcolonial condition projects itself in worlds of interactions, mainly against the foreclosure of political and economic hegemonies. If, as Rushdie puts it, "to see things plainly, you have to cross a frontier,"[28] why is it that the ruling ideas come from a West at peace with itself? Are we not faced with a collective Third World *bildungsroman* that perpetuates the West's literary machine? One could argue that the Oriental or native culture was transformed by transnationalism and by cosmopolitan schools of thought but that the "inferior," "marginal," or "eccentric" positions of natives have remained untouched. This is the core of the critical discourse of a scholar like Spivak regarding the condition of women in contemporary India, for example. Reason in postcolonial public life is deployed in a different manner, and this needs to be addressed as a legitimate issue rather than simply in terms of what Kant, in discussing non-European peoples, called human "immaturity." Intellectuals like Bourdieu, Cixous, Derrida, and Lyotard, all of whom enjoyed a strong bond with Algeria, did break away from the conservative French continental theoretical machine, but did they advocate a critique of narratives of identity? Derrida and Cixous were too busy "locating" their autonomous subjectivity, mainly from an exilic perspective. Cixous believes that women have their own story to tell, and she rightly assumes that there are many ways of being in the world (as a woman, as Jewish, as Algerian, as French, as a lesbian, for example.) with one's own voice. Yet she, too, falls for the universalist brand of feminism that bypasses the natives and thereby historicizes them as a permanent minority in their own condition. Strangely, it seems that for Cixous, Algeria is the name for a non-home, even while it is also the core of her creativity. See, for example, how she has associated Algeria with a dead past: "When I walked with my brother on the hot trails of Oran, I felt the sole of my body caressed by the welcoming palms of the country's ancient dead, and the torment of my soul was assuaged."[29] This is probably how the pendulum swings back to historical determinations that draw out systems of values and meanings: colonial guilt on the one hand, cultural capital on the other. Those closer to the postcolonial condition – Derrida, for example, or Cixous – remain firmly bound to overarching narratives: they continue to assert their authority over Algeria. Basically, they never left Algeria because they never *arrived* there: place and people are at best empirical in their writings. Cixous toys with the question of nationality, mourning "her" Algeria even while calling it not-home. But she also steers clear of the hard political questions – the impact of colonialism on the colonized's identity – and all the while her poetical writing embellishes a strictly individual experience of a woman and her career. Cixous even dwells on some providential Arab–Jewish enmity, resorting to an archaic type of Orientalism that reinforces both dualism (time and language) and the temporality of repetition (at best, the two peoples are supposedly doomed to ignore each other).[30] This sort of Orientalism prevents any postcolonial postulate of modernity from arising. Where is that third culture that might mediate the dialogue between the colonial and the postcolonial? By this account, postcolonial theory closely resembles an ideology, a force that need not be proven true or false but simply lived out like a constant tautology. Past or recent struggles of race, gender, and social class in the Maghreb account for little in the dynamics of Western theory. Writers find themselves aligned with established critical orientations: Assia Djebar is anticolonial by historical design, Abdelkebir Khatibi is a Moroccan secular deconstructionist, Boualem Sansal is an Algerian Céline, and Malika Mokeddem is a self-appointed rational, anti-Islam feminist. It is as though the Oriental Other has been turned again into a cultural fetish, newly arrived at through a discursive mindset ordered by the unabashed practice of theory that corresponds to no real-world doxa. Where does the postcolonial subject fit in this picture? Likely, as a defined formal position within latent Orientalism representation. The most glaring instances do not even lay claim to questioning: the Muslim woman is a permanent victim (a reading that proliferates among francophone/postcolonial writers). In the views of these writers, Africans cannot escape poverty by themselves, the French language is a democratic asset, and pre-colonial history constitutes the "romantic era" of the formerly colonized[31] (when the former *métropole* and the former colonies are not both deemed postcolonial). Surprisingly, the postcolonial discourse has flattened the heterogeneity of its subject matter, thereby diminishing the impact of theory. The critical narratives fabricate cultural explanations at the expense of culture and geopolitical history. It is astounding, for example, that present-day fundamentalists throughout North Africa and the Middle East, both religious and ethnic, are keen on recycling postcolonial rhetoric by raising issues of identity, history, colonization, native language, mystical actuality, and the like; they rethink history without any dialectics because zones of exchange no longer exist. Could it be that the postcolonial discourse, just like that of Orientalism itself, is caught in the double-bind of power analysis? The condemnation of repression emerges from a collaboration with repression (if only intellectual), which is why postcolonial discourse refers to violence while failing to bring it to the point of crisis. A case in point is the painful silence of academics throughout the United States (apart from the usual suspects: Edward Said, Noam Chomsky, Juan Cole, Rashid Khalidi, etc.) vis-à-vis that country's disastrous Middle East foreign policy – not just the war in Iraq, but also the support for authoritarian and grossly incompetent regimes throughout the Muslim world, and continuous lobbying against a viable Palestinian state.[32]

In Western institutions, both political and academic, Orientalism is still at work, fuelled by Arab chaos and collective religious failures. The mechanism of postcolonialism is thus directed not towards recognition but rather towards repetition. The old ethnocentrism of Western science has superseded the critical vigilance that arose after the Second World War and the era of independence. The "programmatic anti-humanism" of postcolonial theory fails to stand the test of cultural relativism. It is not surprising that the key concept of hybridity is always applied by the formerly colonized to the West, not among peoples formerly under Western rule. One illustration of how hybridity truly works is Frantz Fanon, a black Martiniquan French citizen who chose to become an Algerian nationalist. Even now, one can only wonder whether there is such a thing as a fixed self or a fixed culture outside the Western frame. How can human rights and macroeconomics be applied to the emergent Muslim world? This would assume that we have no reason to invest postcolonial theory with the privileges of radical explanation. The battle between latent Orientalism and postcolonial theory has boiled down to amicable encounters on the terrain of rebound conservatism and cosmopolitan window-dressing.[33]

Once again, the Orient becomes a multifaceted *topos* that hinges on the impossibility of representing the unrepresentable. This is what Said was alluding to when he referred to "the Muslim as a native informant for the Orientalist."[34] The order of history and ideas remains Western; the former coercive structures have been replaced by symbolic power. For example, Maghrebi intellectuals are expected to embrace Western democratic values, but they cannot be perceived as critical of Zionism[35] or as calling into question secularism and how it is played against Islam throughout Europe. In that sense, their literary production is bound to feed on both cultural expectations and the sensational.[36] Concerted criticism of postcolonial studies is nothing new;[37] what makes it a challenge within the problematics of Orientalism is that it has failed to escape history's reflexivity, especially with regard to the mystique of nation and race. The tricky problem with postcolonial scholarship in North America is that one cannot indict a specific author or school of thought: the whole discipline conforms to the protocol of the "good" discourse rather than the subversive one. And by "good" I mean one that allows for an ability to retell a story (about a minority, a subaltern, an immigrant, etc.) in such a way that it becomes a political act. It is not surprising that postcolonial scholars dabble in history, religion, law, and perhaps literature at the same time, and in the name of the post-colonial subject. The scholarship taps into a never-ending narrative of trauma, loss, infantilization, and so on, and all the while this hydra-like discipline feeds on a methodological and epistemological challenge. The postcolonial paradigm has indeed been inspiring, but only up to a point. One crucial question remains: Can one truly grasp how global culture works? No one is calling for reformed theorists, although this would be an original way to begin. Nor are graduate students expected to produce classroom ethnography on the lived lives of the postcolonial Other. The irony of most postcolonial scholarship is that it is not just politically correct – and thereby fails to address the entanglements and compromises of postcolonial reality – but culturally inert as well. In its mature and ideal forms, the postcolonial discourse has created its own pantheon of idols with the power to enable the recycling of narratives, thus denying the construct of the identity of the Orient. Rushdie's *The Satanic Verses* (1988), for example, does not read as a subversive novel: the author's skill was in trivializing the imaginary of Indian peasants in order to cater – with a hefty dose of magic realism – to the tastes of the London intelligentsia.

In the end, it becomes a dogmatic untertaking for writers to place identity, hybridity, and religion at the centre of their writing, as if they were merely engaged in a cross-cultural endeavour. Because these agendas come together, Maghrebi authors are subject to cultural reconstitution, just as in the case of the much-disputed process of Orientalism. In a challenging reality, multiplicity, notwithstanding *différence*, is forged into tools of expansion. It is not just that books are published and read in the West; this spectacular reality of cultural consolidation also takes the form of hyperbolic prejudice. Even Gareth Griffith, a pioneer and advocate of postcolonial studies, recognizes, following in Fanon's footsteps, that "it is this world in its newly mythicised and essentialized form which becomes the specific appropriated terrain of the new colonial elite in projects of self-justification and self-aggrandisement."[38] More than in any other scholarly endeavour, working through the frame of postcolonial theory obliges one to operate with abstractions and with experiments with the materiality of textuality. It is probably not fair to ask Western academics to retreat unusual distances when thinking about an Arab or Muslim presence in North African and Middle Eastern fiction. A similar pattern manifests itself in what Toni Morrison wrote about the resistance to difference within American culture: "What became transparent were the self-evident ways that Americans choose to talk about themselves through and within a sometimes allegorical, sometimes metaphorical, but always choked representation of Africanist presence."[39] These prejudices coalesce to support the thrust of performative interpretations in a way that sublimates the minority – African, Arab, Muslim, Asian – into an already there (*déjà là*) deciphered script. Orientalism related to imperialism in the sense that it rethought the dominant narratives of Western histories. The fundamental strategy was to represent not so much the Other as the Other in his place. For example, Orientalism in its core ideology could never have conceived of mass immigration, or of individualism, which was perceived as the private domain of the Western political and cultural establishment. The Other was robbed of its identity, then turned into an allegory and left without any mediating function. By recasting Maghrebi intellectuals as voices of hybridity, multiculturalism, diaspora, transnationalism, or the instability of the "cultural sign," postcolonial theory has in more recent times enacted a debate presided over by the universalistic terms of Western literature. Maghrebi authors, should they stand their ground, avoiding poses and prejudices, could be expected to discard the fetish at work between the narrative of the individual and the fable of the nation. So what their writing summons up here is the question of legitimacy in the field of world literature, against an occultation that masquerades as analysis and admiration.

Considering its scope, postcolonial theory should speculate on the dissonant process of total history. It should confront such questions as "Are such concepts as East and West, centre and margins, valid any longer?" instead of concentrating on transnational approaches in which, for example, intellectual codependency (of subjects, areas, attributes, linguistics, etc.) arises and blurs the critical focus. Postcolonial theory dawned against the backdrop of collapsing ideologies and national narratives, yet it still draws from dualistic assumptions and paradigms. For example, it is astonishing that the concept of empire is deemed Western both as historical representation and as essence. Confronted with the pernicious benevolence of unthinking homogenization (of colonized and colonizers, Muslims and Christians, the traditional and the advanced, the oral and the written, and so on), Western academic consciousness[40] must keep away from both political correctness and patronage systems, as well as from hidden discourses that predicate history in a repetitive mode.[41] Across the political spectrum in France, for example, transformative identities, the utopia of representation, and static aesthetic viewpoints have long hardened into ideological positions. Nothing is axiomatically assumed so long as cultures continue to engage in an itinerary of recognition, more specifically of heuristic operations that postulate the Orient as a liminal space where everything starts again – democracy, civilization, human rights, capital ventures, military campaigns, and the many narratives of Scheherazade. This may not happen until theory and political discourse more generally have ceased being illuminated by Orientalist protocols. The give-and-take of former colonial regimes, often intended to obtain mutual consent, cannot lay the groundwork for an operative theoretical model. Calling Maghrebi writers "metropolitan hybrids," for example, denies them access to authorship.[42] The literary and paradigmatic fields become so overdetermined that diverse cultural inscriptions cannot occupy a continuous narrative space. In Rachid Boudjedra's La Répudiation (1969), the main female character is not the abused mother but rather Céline, a nurse who is also the narrator's abused French lover. Interestingly, Boudjedra wrote his doctoral dissertation on the French writer Céline, which generates these questions: Whose repudiation is it? Is it that of backward Algerian family traditions, or of French canonical literature? In gaining the French language, Maghrebi postcolonial literature seems to have lost something. It seems that in contemporary postcolonial theory, any stringent oppositionality has been domesticated, if not neutralized. The problem is deeper than that of merely conjuring up the scapegoat figure of the Third World (renamed by the West "emerging nations") subject. Maghrebi authors cannot undo the exoticist dramatization of their *différence*. The core thesis of the postcolonial discourse would present a more compelling case if it made an argument in the name of truth against collective fantasy – that the Christian West is saving Muslim women from Muslim men, for example, or that Maghrebi authors cannot escape the aesthetic *illusio*[43] of consecration in the West. Assia Djebar became a major writer overnight after being elected to the *Académie française* even though she had never been awarded a major French literary prize in her more than forty-year career. In a theory in which memory, subjectivity, essence, language, and location are privileged as the origins of culture, writers are left with no option but to produce countermyths and to plot narratives against the rather functionalist frame of postcolonial discourse. In that sense, postcolonial theory, like Orientalism, enjoys a material existence through its institutional apparatus (universities, publishing houses, international institutions, etc.) and its practices (codes of knowledge, course syllabi, semiotics, readership, etc.). It should not be surprising that joining together theory with sociohistorical developments turns out to be a trite combination that portrays the Other once more as an outsider. In France, Maghrebi writers are considered "francophone," whereas in American academe, they are "postcolonial subjects." By keeping authors in the circle of postcolonial arguments and epistemic priorities in this way, are we not reviving the old Orientalist assumption that Arab/Muslim culture is confined to colonial negotiations and thus plagiaristic by definition?[44] For example, the past is perceived as constitutive of the speaking subject, and this sleight of hand allows a revisionary use of origin as hybrid or impure: the Maghreb amounts to the sum total of its various colonial invasions.[45] Yet what remains non-negotiable in Maghrebi literature written in French is the French ingredient itself. Thus, the subaltern can speak indeed, and what he tries to articulate is that "Maghrebi" cannot be simply equated with "postcolonial." Postcolonial narratives do more than speak to forms of "good" story/history: they signal the irreducible plurality of voices.

4 Unfinished (Literary) Business: Orientalism and the Maghreb

Central to my concept and approach to latent Orientalism are the overlapping layers and oppositions produced in the specific relations between France and the Maghreb, a matter that has received little coverage in postcolonial studies. The difference between postcolonial studies and francophone studies is a question to which I will return when I address the works of Maghrebi writers. Without wishing to indict it, on close examination I find this literature problematic. From earlier examples we will see how francophone literature from the Maghreb has engaged in a dialogue even while failing to anticipate the ideological unification of French hegemony since independence. What interests me is the establishment and development of these relations and the extent to which they have shaped space and agency for peoples and cultures. Arjun Appadurai's notion of "ethnoscape" is a useful point of departure for such an inquiry, provided we take into account the strong cultural and historical forces that have shaped the landscape of French–Maghrebi relations over the centuries. We have seen that, although postcolonial theory never ceases to challenge us, it remains somehow hollow in terms of essence.[1] Because it tackles too many issues, postcolonial studies finds itself laden with an inchoative value or gummed up with subcategories. But the real danger does not stem from this type of academic dilettantism; rather, this is the ideological object that looms large within the discourse.[2] One risk has been what could be called, for want of a better term, "canonical consolidation," the situation that results when one particular work casts a theoretical shadow over a discipline. A case in point is Joseph Conrad's *Heart of Darkness*, a novel that has been parsed inside and out by great scholars (by Said in *Orientalism*, Jameson in *Postmodernism, or, the Cultural Logic of Late Capitalism*, and Bhabha in *The Location of Culture*), becoming what Bhabha calls "a symptom of pedagogical anxiety" (213). It comes as no surprise that the initial notion of displacement turns into a single continuous reality – or does it surprise?

This ambivalence is best understood if one examines Maghreb writing itself. This will keep us away from Said's monolithic Orientalism, in terms of poetics and aesthetics, and help us avoid the pitfalls of theoretical homogenization (i.e., bringing together under the same tent everything that is not the West). In postcolonial literature, time, place, language, and imagination work together, not so much to recapture something universal as to be discovered and deemed unique. We know, for example, that European literary realism does not and cannot apply to African postcolonial literature because the imaginative creative process in Africa is caught between the demands for rationalized modernity (in terms of politics, aesthetics, etc.) and a return to tradition that helps legitimize a certain idea of the nation. History still weighs heavily on the output and exilic condition of most Maghrebi writers, yet in their hands, the laws of traditional French literature are warped by imagined narratives and pointed investigations into a recalled past. Furthermore, one wonders to what extent the assumptions of the critic of postcolonial theory corrupt the postcolonial author's integrity. Today, for Maghrebi writers in particular, the motivation to write resides in answering this question: "What is it that remains unclaimed until it is worked through?"

Academics are so caught up in the ideological dimension of postcolonial literature (e.g., in striving to signify the cultural in-between) and its transgressive powers that they barely trouble themselves to understand other vital elements of the corpus. When pieced together patiently, the evidence reveals that the real condition of Maghrebi writing in French is staged not by ideology but by the non-representability of cultural trauma. Postcolonial studies tends to eschew timelines and the rhythms of history that "Oriental" subjects have produced from within themselves. One aspect of the literary issue has to do with the function and use of Orientalism. When discourses are dominated by political visions and by paradigms of cultural enunciation, empirical facts are sometimes overlooked. The postcolonial or Oriental writer is treated as a signifier within a subject/object relationship – the publication/readership paradigm, for example – while critical value is driven by political agendas that are postnationalist in content. A more valid if not fully accurate critique must take into account the dominant forces at work in the Western humanities. For example, it is taken for granted that postcolonial literature must either inspire or reflect national ideologies that have come into existence since the end of colonialism. But literature is not just an index of a given world – it is, most often, a product of that world. Postcolonial writers cannot be essentialized in a set of values or identities, in the way that Jane Austen is considered essentially British and Marcel Proust essentially French. Within the confines of Orientalism, consistently engaged in negating the identity of the Other (whether Black, Arab, Muslim, or female), contemporary Maghrebi literature remains trapped in old modes of representing a still dominant culture. Assia Djebar rightly points out the dilemma when she writes: "Let's agree that regarding the linguistic landscape of so-called *francophonie* I, for one, stand at the borders."[3]

Maghrebi literature in French is by no means monolithic, though it has been, for the most part, organized by an intelligentsia trained in the Western logic of resisting and countering dominant discourses. We know how novels written by male and female authors, of both younger and older generations, blend the themes and *topoi* of Maghrebi cultures with concepts common to European, and specifically French, thought. For example, as early as the 1950s in Mouloud Feraoun's *Le fils du pauvre* or more recently in Malika Mokeddem's *N'zid* (2002), literary projects have met the narrative of a history and entity called "Algeria," although Algeria as such did not exist before French colonization. The timeline from the blossoming of Maghrebi literature of the late 1950s to today does not reflect the diversity of voices. Yet Maghrebi literature is nonetheless operative in the theoretical discourse, with for example the denial of subjective content compensated for by the historical and social material. Therein lies one of the conflicts between literature and nationalism: Europe supposedly succeeded in claiming and merging both, whereas authors from formerly colonized countries are supposedly still figuring out which language is theirs and from which place they are speaking and writing. Most writers attempt to flaunt their historical interpretations along nationalist lines or against the dismaying post-independence condition of their homeland, yet they seem to lack the insight and authority that would counteract, if not end, the pervasive neocolonial logic evident in books published, stamped, approved, distributed, and read in the West. Maghrebi writers in French with any success in the Western-dominated global marketplace find themselves dispatchers of cultural products; Maghrebi readers have become outsiders to their own literature. And no matter how successful book fairs in Algiers or Casablanca appear to be, they tend to express a bold line of thinking out the domestic political reality more than a subdued aesthetic behest. State censorship provides another reminder of the plural and unstable identity status of francophone literature in the Maghreb. Francophone readers in the Maghreb – a statistical minority – read books that explain the universe in fantastic or realistic terms, but they also reclaim the French language to read about the minutiae of everyday life. Even if these two are connected, both readings cannot be right. When we confront this cultural conundrum, it becomes clear that Orientalism is far from a mere discursive fiction: it continues to operate as a grafting of oppositional representations. Only this time it is working among Orientals themselves. The Orientalist ideology was based on the notion that the colonized is fixed, even quasi-universal. This false assumption has affected the arts as much as it has the policies constituting the foundation of human laws on both sides of the colonial divide, as demonstrated by Albert Memmi in his *Portrait du colonisé*. But in literature, which is as nuanced and unpredictable as the real people who write it, there is no such thing as a static nucleus of values or an unalterable world view. In Maghrebi novels, perceptions of coming to birth and of the archetypal quest for wholeness should, and do, override the Orientalist *topos*. Yet cultural accommodations of any kind on the part of the Western establishment have remained token efforts (e.g., welcoming Algerian bourgeois women "writers" during the civil war of the 1990s, publishing critical essays only after dictator King Hassan II of Morocco died, organizing literary conferences in Tunisia at a time when it was a police state), and these efforts have rarely been validated by reciprocal projects. At the heart of the matter, we need not look for a Maghrebi Marguerite Duras or Claude Simon; rather, we need to point out the heterogeneous cultural and aesthetic expressions of the chorus of Maghrebi voices. Is it not the main challenge for postcolonial Maghrebi authors to escape that universalism, which has faded among Western postmodern writers?

The story of Edmond Laforest, a Haitian writer, who on 17 October 1915 tied a thick Larousse dictionary around his neck and jumped off a bridge to his death, is well known. Laforest's action symbolizes the impossibility of assuming both the legacy of a minority culture (including its religion) and the language of the former master. Fortunately, no Maghrebi writers have yet been led to this kind of existential "indenture."[4] However, francophone writings indicate that both culture and nation fail to provide homogeneous and reliable systems of expression.

And the exilic condition has clearly undermined the coherence of national identity, at least in construing literature historically. There is a great deal worth saying about this disconnect – a disconnect in the literal, historical sense – but one example strikes a chord: Mohamed Dib, after settling permanently outside Algeria in the mid-1960s, stopped writing about his homeland's history. To this extent, fictional works of the Maghreb are experiments in postmodernity, with its emergent fragmentary voices, even as they break away from strictly Western literary codes. We notice in works by Moroccan poets Abdellatif Laâbi and Mohammed Khaïr-Eddine, for example, that writing is intended as an exploratory practice, an ongoing discourse between the identity of the individual and the identity of the nation around issues of the father figure, the mother tongue, freedom of expression, religious taboos, exile, and so on. In this context, these poems reveal the distinction between the French language and the Oriental condition, placing Maghrebi cultures and peoples into categories, not just of acknowledgment but of existence and non-existence. The postcolonial ambivalent use of "I" in French enforces the empathic value of literature itself, even in cases of borrowed subjectivity when Arabic or a Berber dialect is the native tongue. As they compete, the syntactical, aesthetic, and ideological paradigms at work reveal the artificiality of so-called francophone literature. Once the French literary model as a universal organizing unit is set aside by Maghrebi writers, they must tackle the persistent myth of being a defined nation, not just in terms of imaginaries and ethnicities, but most of all in terms of loyalty. Each nation of the Maghreb is thus reified into a fact of nature, a process that, painfully enough, was the rationale for the Orientalist ideology, in what Edward Said called a "discipline of detail."[5] Most often, writers find themselves entertaining a monocultural conversation scrutinizing the past, as in the references to archives in Assia Djebar's work, or the function of tribal memory in Rachid Mimouni's novels. By telling a story, the postcolonial writer brings history alive, and this illustrative power does not historicize the former colonized because the narrative possibilities do not depend on Otherness.

Literature becomes irrelevant when the fact of cultural difference is itself the defining core of discourses. It comes as no surprise that Marxism, cultural studies, deconstructionism, and new historicism weigh heavily in textual interpretations of works by postcolonial writers. Such an affiliation with Western theory draws into question the quasi-silence of postcolonial voices, who can be tempted to break away from that silence and representation so as to encourage a fundamental national revival. In the specific case of the Maghreb, authors who write in Arabic operate outside both the sphere of *francophonie* and cultural pan-Arabism are still locked in a colonial experience by the mere fact that they seek to differentiate themselves as Algerians, Moroccans, or Tunisians. In the twenty-first century, the main concern of francophone counterparts in these various countries has been to move beyond concepts like hybridity in their writing.[6] The resulting configuration of knowledge gives the illusion of engaging writers and readers in "border thinking"[7] even as it encourages further intellectual stereotyping. For example, novels by Tahar Ben Jelloun still unintentionally privilege a kind of belated but comprehensive Orientalism. Nation and history are rendered obsolete in these works. What, then, is the epistemology of literature written in French by Maghrebi authors?

Heidegger linked knowledge to meaning in a way that articulates an inflation of narratives or, more precisely, an investment in textuality.[8] Yet this proves true only so long as systems of thought, the cultural subconscious, and what Barthes called *le plaisir du texte* are the conditions for knowledge and not mere tools used for creating disciplined boundaries and differences between the dominant and the subaltern. Centuries ago, Muslim theologians, while eschewing any distinction between the spiritual and temporal worlds, anticipated the consequences of mapping history onto a cultural order, with its subsequent stifling hegemony.[9] This insight is paralleled by the enthusiasm of Western critics for categorizing and dividing. Of course, any such Islamic theory would have had maximum impact in any language other than one from Europe. Now, in the context of voice versus authority, what makes Said's work and public stances so seminal is that he managed to take hold of the discourse of cultural appropriation still pervasive in Western humanities as well as to hold a mirror to the debilitating binary oppositions underlying the Orientalist construct. In his postulate for the Orientalist praxis, knowledge and meaning are indeed two different realities. In an essay predating *Orientalism* (1978), Said stated that "what is possible to do is to analyze the structure of thought for which such a phrase as 'Arab society' is a kind of reality – and this structure as we shall soon see, is a myth, with its codes, discourse, and tropes."[10] To this day in the current mix of geopolitics and Western media frenzy, there is talk of "the Arab street" when referring to the national mood in Arab countries, yet we continue to point to "public opinion" for peoples in the West. Potentially liberating theoretical discourse appears to be locked in a never-ending representation of Western subjectivity. Call it latent Orientalism when it comes to splitting the global Muslim Other (from North Africa to Central Asia).

Maghrebi literature in French denotes to what extent knowledge considered interesting in the Oriental world – in this context, the Arab/Muslim world – is from then on considered marginal by a self-proclaimed "advanced" culture such as that of France. In this regard, it is striking to note that autobiography remains a minor genre for Maghrebi writers, whose approach fails to reinforce the centrality of a subjective voice. Rather, they turn autobiography into something that speaks for the nation, to which all powers of identification must be turned. In *L'amour, la fantasia*, Assia Djebar acknowledges that "my fiction is this autobiography in progress."[11] One's own life is rarely the subject of art, as though it were paramount to evade personal and factual history and to keep the traces of cultural imperialism and neocolonialism on individuals as abstract as possible. Nonetheless, something important emerges from the anxious desire to keep a lid on the personal: a refusal to play intermediary between an underdeveloped homeland and a welcoming yet intrusive West. It can be said that the near absence of autobiographies in and from the Maghreb accentuates the inherent ambivalence of adapting to a new community that, although freely chosen, still keeps its exotic guests as tokens of both xenophilia and xenophobia. Autobiography as a literary genre is trumped by whatever might be imagined for the nation. The creative distance does not flow from a literary ruse played on readers, as in Sartre's autobiography, or Robbe-Grillet's. It is rather a matter of playing around with myths and representations that are bigger than the self and that too often remain taboo. In reference to one of the favourite *topoi* of Orientalist discourse, one may surmise that Maghrebi literature in French claims for itself the dialectic of veiling and unveiling.

The parochial and sometimes narcissistic dimensions of contemporary French literature place limits on effective criticism, but this constraint does not delegitimize canonic literature as a point of reference for contemporary literary endeavours in French. At the same time, the terms *"francophone,"* "hybrid," and "postcolonial," although quite popular in the Western humanities, undo the assumptions underlying the other terms. This is why Maghrebi literature in French is typically understood as embedded in broader cultural and political forces, with any national meaning only provisionally established. The literary approach of postcolonial writers from the Maghreb resembles a continual exercise in demystifying the Oriental subject. It is clear that from the inception of Maghreb postcolonial literature in the 1950s, when the French colonial empire was beginning to crumble, Sisyphus has been its defining figure. There is a fault in the Western literary critique of literature from the Maghreb, a critique that attempts to objectively categorize the Maghrebi subject. Writers are both de facto exiles and postcolonials; they are also extraterritorial figures in any vein of orthodoxy or criticism they might choose to adopt. While literary and narrative representation only corresponds to a discursive object, the Orientalist *topos* is rarely taken to task for exploiting the failures of the post-independence condition because it is, structurally, a copy of European colonial ideology. When Rachid Boudjedra deconstructs the madness of post-independence Algeria in three of his first four novels, the project is essentially an inventory of knowledge concerning politics, sexuality, religion, and the social order that tows the line of liberal humanism. At the same time, postcolonial selfhood remains an assumption, a stand-in for the clean conscience of the French.[12] In the name of legitimacy, nationalism strives to make political and "cultural" power timeless and natural; for its part, Orientalism pushes into indefiniteness its own brand of superiority when advocating the privilege of Western literature – for example, over that of the Arab/Muslim world. Literature bears the residues of old struggles. It is impossible not to think of the history of Algeria as the history of a colony, of the power of French and the Western humanities, and of the market forces that turn books into ideological and theoretical commodities, especially in North American academe.

For the Maghrebi intellectual, writing back can mean deconstructing and exposing the cultural patterns that make literary theories applicable to postcolonial writers. Kateb Yacine and Abdelkebir Khatibi have developed a discourse of resistance within the corpus of Maghrebi literary production. Concepts such as "legitimacy" (a replacement for the broken postcolonial identity) and "natural laws" (as justified in the academic world for ideological purposes or for career ambitions) find themselves exposed to critical examination. It is remarkable that these two Maghrebi writers have rejected the theoretical name-giving that is, in essence, an act of power. When francophone literature rejects name-giving, it dislocates an order that is repressing its own imaginative and discursive structures. In this regard, Kateb's first novel, *Nedjma* (1956), is indeed a narrative of interruptions. History in this novel is mixed with myths concerning genealogies, an original language, identities,

and so on, and those myths give way to metaphors. For Kateb, any conventional use of language must coincide with the growing awareness
that history is a purely aesthetic experience that creates and destroys
both ideas and individuals.[13] Under the systemic and descriptive pro-
cedures of Orientalism, which are informed by colonialism, culture and
civilization cancel each other out. Most remarkably, in Kateb's novel
there is no such place as "home."[14] Instead there is a force – *Nedjma*
("star" in Arabic) – that guides a people struggling for independence to
an unknown place where they might transcend their condition. But because Kateb rejects a narrow concept of nationhood, his heroes lack historical validity. The dynamic of Western historical change is rendered
idle by a new poetic phase that is able to penetrate the truth behind the
colonial experience. Khatibi is another writer who, by advocating cultural fragmentation, delivers a concrete, historical Otherness. Whereas
Orientalism tends to crystallize the event or fact of domination, Khatibi
builds a system of thought predicated on true dialogue that counters
the neocolonial patterns in French culture and cultural policies. In his
first text, *La mémoire tatouée* (1971), the loss of a reality defined by the
old colonial presence and the importation of the novel and autobiography genres into the Arab/Muslim literary world become themselves
the defining concepts of post-independence nationhood. The Western
metropolis as a seat of power has been dislodged but has not yet been
replaced by another location of power somewhere in the East. In the
works of these seminal authors, the ideological stakes are spread thin,
as if to downplay both the centrality of the Western position and the
idea of a possible multiplicity of locations and temporalities between
Europe and the Maghreb.

In a sense, the works of Kateb and Khatibi help reconcile two kinds
of Orientalism – historical, and ideological. In this context, one must
pay attention to the rationales for cultural openings offered by the established powers, be they political, economic, or academic. Applying
this to the intellectual life of exiles and migrants, Arif Dirlik states:
"Postcoloniality is designed to *avoid* making sense of the current crisis,
and in the process, to cover up the origins of postcolonial intellectuals
in global capitalism of which they are not so much victims as beneficia-
ries."[15] Dirlik's accusation underscores the permanent discontinuities
among power, knowledge, and action. In francophone literature and
studies, such discontinuities are symptomatic of what is being consistently denied. Maghrebi writers are trapped within representations
and identifications that render void concepts such as nation and native

culture. Nowadays, the matrix[16] associated with literary texts has less and less to offer, not because it has become impossible to reclaim anything purely native, but rather because hybridity and/or *métissage* are often turned into mimicking exercises. This is problematic, for example, in the case of the philo-feminism of Algerian writers, which has too often been allied with the dominant, discursive, anti-Islam ideology. Instead of avoiding the pitfalls of Western universalism, the Algerian literary trend of the 1990s proclaimed, loud and clear, the fetishization of the Oriental woman. The novels of that decade consistently buttress the signals of gender and identity hegemony. In Mokeddem's novels, for example *L'Interdite* (1993), the Algerian woman appears as a natural-born victim who transforms herself into a heroine thanks to overrated Western humanistic standards played out at the expense of native Algerian culture. To borrow Said's words, Mokeddem has become, wittingly or not, a "witness for the Western prosecution."[17] Other female writers have been a little more nuanced in their treatment of the plight of women in contemporary Algeria. For example, Latifah Benmansour, while denouncing the Islamic fundamentalist factions of the 1990s civil war in her novels, suggests that solutions to the problem should originate within the Muslim world itself.

It is significant that, in Maghrebi literature in French, the scrutiny of self and society takes place outside the realm of nationalism. Crossing borders, be they national or intellectual, remains the hallmark of the effective decolonization of space and minds. Given that the Western metropolis has long been blind to its own cultural world view as it relates to the Maghreb, finding an appropriate response to latent Orientalism is the great challenge. For Maghrebi writers in French, the postcolonial symbiosis is apparent at the levels of social interaction and semiotics. There is no doubt, for example, that Assia Djebar's election to the *Académie française* was at some level intended to valorize the European intellectual tradition and contain any diasporic voice. It is France, as a Western nation and still an influential power in the Maghreb, that enables or blocks the very existence of the postcolonial symbolic *polis*. The cultural *imprimatur* flows from the old metropolitan centre, and despite the witnessing power of the postnational narrative, there lingers a sense that the much vaunted concept of deterritorialization has been undercut. Much remains to be unlearned, notwithstanding global perceptions of heterogenity and hybridity. As was implicit in the old Orientalist ruses of the past, it is understood as necessary that the Maghreb nations fade away in order for postcolonial literature to take root. Again, in a world of border thinking, the validity of naming is fundamental. Whether it is the migrant figure, the female victim, the disenfranchised father, the tragic leader, or the abused child, disconcerting archetypes are visible in most Maghrebi novels. In this vein, Maghrebi writing continues to paint self-images reminiscent of the outsider figures so emblematic of Orientalist authors. For example, Chateaubriand, Gérard de Nerval, Théophile Gautier, and Gustave Flaubert all tried to step out of the Western modern world, as if the change would open up real transculturation. More recently, three Goncourt Prize winners – Michel Tournier, Didier Van Cauwelaert, and Jean-Christophe Rufin – have tried to tell stories from the perspective of subalternity, only with a Western voice and a subject who remains unable to represent him- or herself.[18] There always seems to be a disconnect between emancipation (displacing narrative authority) and juxtaposition (maintaining a hierarchy of voices). Literature, both national and postcolonial, withstands these attempts and still fails to recognize that the notion of cultural hegemony stretches beyond post-independence reality, whether in the West or in its former colonies.

Latent Orientalism struggles to exist in a world with indeterminate borders where the "career" of ideology is reborn either within academe or in geopolitics.[19] The Islamic Orient, which patently lacks the Western virtues of democracy, modernity, and advanced technology, remains the object of discourse. The canonical politics of interpretation have frozen the Oriental subject in a posture of either need or fear. But the written text and world reality must not be confused with each other; rather, each must accommodate the other. In the case of Maghrebi literature, the quasi-absence of autobiography as a literary genre suggests that there has been a rethinking of the individual voice in favour of a collective account. The idea of a unified self is shattered by the combined experiences of race, gender, and class. The migrant, whether a nineteenth-century French writer or a postcolonial Maghrebi exile, relies on the control of cultural capital over the repression of historical narratives.[20] This is more than a question of literary legacy; the power of latent Orientalism implies an economic structure that articulates and guides historical and ideological determinations. An essentialist position can turn out to be a selling point in cultural settings where identity is no longer a matter of *who?*, but rather *how?* and *where?*[21] Maghrebi writers are aware that they are something more than what theories and ideologies say they are. For example, a key theme in the novels of the Moroccan writer Driss Chraïbi is the constant renewal his protagonists undergo.[22] The seeming narrative cohesion of his works reveals a deep distrust of syncretic or self-righteous linear readings. The author delights in frustratingly objective conclusions, which are often concealed behind the production of knowledge over which Western humanities believes itself the sole proprietor.

A post-independence era fosters the idea that identity is always given, not only because of a logic of migration but also because transgressive discourses hang over narratives. Maghrebi literature manifests divisibility among different states of consciousness, narrative strategies, and imaginaries. No surprise, then, that many authors, in their efforts to establish a unique voice, inject the Arabic language (and, at times Berber dialects) when writing in French. But such intertextuality – which is only the façade, as it were, of the issue at stake – hardly reflects the individual's own geopoetic condition. Although the French language is a natural tool for Maghrebi intellectuals trained in French, there remains a scepticism that calls for a more comparative approach in the writing process itself. So on the one hand, Maghrebi literature in French appears somewhat bland and overrated, while on the other, it trips up scholarly analyses. The mix of historical, psychological, gendered, semi-autobiographical, and ethnic voices referencing the post-colonial condition represents an attempt to distil the Maghreb's own ontology. Mohammed Dib's writings best illustrate this point. For Dib, an Algerian, imagination and origin needed to connect; that is why he worked to expand the power of metaphors instead of relying on collective memory or history. Dib was one of the first Maghrebi writers to forgo the idea of national history and culture atfer independence had been gained. For example, in *Le Sommeil d'Eve* (1989), written when he was close to seventy years old, the adversary to reckon with is neither the colonial past nor any type of post-independence authoritarian regime, but forgetfulness itself. In Dib's writing, the story necessarily remains in dialogue with the reader, with the past, and between cultures. The one who forgets is doomed to lose control of his or her fate. This novel can be read as a model for describing how identity is recomposed both at home and abroad, even while in exile.

It would be far too reductive to suggest that latent Orientalism overcomes nationalist endeavours. In novels by the Moroccan Abdelhak Serhane and the Tunisian Mustapha Tlili, the failures of post-independence states are mentioned as seemingly aesthetic comments levelled at incoherent Arab/Muslim modernity itself rather than at the West's overreaching actions. The question remains: Who benefits, if anyone, from experimental writing? Maghrebi literature in French, although undoubtedly proliferating, seems bereft of any attributes that might actually benefit its sources. There is no obvious rejection of biases when the writers speak for someone else, and their own voices are too often reduced to rehashing familiar discourses of culture and narrative. For example, Tahar Ben Jelloun's best-seller, *L'Enfant de sable* (1985), examines hierarchical oppositions (of traditions, mentality, institutions, etc.) inherent in the postcolonial condition, but it fails to reverse any of them. If, for a writer, the imaginary is not affected, how is reality supposed to be acted upon? The novel's reconstruction of a woman's identity strikes one as distrustful of Moroccan views: there is no speaking subject per se, nor is there any interpreter of Ahmed-the-girl's society. In this literary instance, what is possible is not credible. The global design of gender identity (a daughter raised as if she were a son), as it were, is bypassed in a local impetus to reveal the Oriental Other as inferior and backward, if not dangerous. In this regard, Maghrebi literature distinguishes itself from Caribbean literature in French by relinquishing the epistemological perspective. The vital knowledge of identity matters less than the scope of – or rather the possibility of – different existences in several worlds (Maghrebi, Muslim, female, French). Diverse discourses rise up only to collapse onto one another, and end up streaming into a predictable monotone. Ben Jelloun's emphasis on speaking and storytelling is a narrative strategy, but it is also a means to set aside the world of fiction as if it were incompatible with the competing languages and cultures of the Maghrebi–French encounter. The exotic duplication in Ben Jelloun's novels forces French readers into the same artificial realm as his imagined Morocco. That is the key to their success.

A core tendency in latent Orientalism is most visible in its acts of privileging the past and freezing the present. Maghrebi literature rarely reclaims the old anthropological stance of a pure native voice; however, deeper variations of the idea of cultural oneness must be called into question. The dearth of credible literary institutions in the Maghreb, be they independent or systematized (e.g., academies, book prizes, critical journals), makes the notion of a national or regional literature seem hollow and easily influenced by other cultural and canonical modes, as well as by economic powers. We can surmise that the act of writing in French, while liberating at first, later became a trap of its own. One reason for this could be that, as Said indicated: "The study of Islam [in France] played a far more central role for its own sake than anywhere else in Europe,"[23] and that the notion of the Muslim Other could not be liberated from the system of thought from which it originated. More precisely, a Maghrebi writer is bound to accept the premises of Orientalism at the same time that he or she is denouncing them. The hidden law of Western language,[24] with its insistence on resolving its own bourgeois neuroses, always debunks the subject's authority. Furthermore, chronological and spatial accounts, as well as historical developments, end up being limited by language itself, and French has become the major conduit of Maghrebi literature. And setting aside the cultural gap, the act of writing in French elicits questions of representation, experience, and textuality. To discover the author's actual intentions, we require the regulating power of discourse. Francophone literature by Maghrebi writers becomes the representative link between two entities lacking a point of origin and trying to make their own systems of meaning intelligible. For example, one does not need to believe in Rachid Mimouni's genealogies to make historical reconstruction correspond to a given reality. And when Tunisia does not appear, per se, in Fawzi Mellah's novels, the author's aim is probably to produce a composite place called the Maghreb out of cultural and political fragments. After the initial trauma of colonization, neither the writer nor the reader can rely any more on the integrity of self-identity and history. No wonder, for example, that novels by *pied-noir* writers[25] have presented a completely different picture of Algeria. It is as if the shared fragments of narratives and memory were only available by way of translation. One common language, French, spoken by diverse tongues, generates distinguishing manifestations and fails to organize the hoped-for event that a cultural coming together should be. From his childhood memories, Tunisian writer Abdelwahab Meddeb acknowledges this potentiality: "By learning French it is possible to come to terms with those who hold power. This would also bring about technological advancement, even recognition and material comfort. Thanks to this symbolical structure, the appeal was compelling."[26] What strikes one in this type of statement is its detachment, as if writing, or literature, was the constitutive norm for Maghrebi culture, and as if no effort was required to encompass other modes of cultural transmission or expression. It is clear that along with the linguistic issue comes that of cultural moorings.[27]

Whatever Foucault says about humanism, and whatever Said says about Foucault, one can argue that, given the link between humanism and Orientalism, Maghrebi literature in French must be framed within a dialectic of *engagement/désengagement*. Inherent in the Maghrebi postcolonial condition is an understanding that history is, right now, being made in regions formerly deprived of discourse. But a dissection of Western cultural ideologies by "Oriental" novelists has hardly occurred yet, because these writers have been unable to provide any real alternative to the postnational imaginary other than turning acculturation into syncretism.[28] Indeed, little attention has been paid to the postcolonial regeneration that has taken place in the West itself. Instead of reading from nineteenth-century travellers who set out to escape a "nihilistic" Europe, Maghrebi writers see in the West the last possible refuge from a "decadent" and "undercivilized" Orient. The very conditions of being an exile, a migrant, or an asylum seeker undo the subaltern discourse, as if the density of collective memory requires its own ground, both physical and epistemic. For example, in the case of North Africa, cultural alienation has resulted in antagonism between a minority Berber identity and a hegemonic Arab Maghreb. Kateb Yacine, Mouloud Mammeri, and Nabile Farès have argued in this direction of cultural identity, turning fiction writing into a commitment to their origin.[29] The fundamental question comes down to this: What does the subaltern past allow them to do? It is puzzling that Maghrebi literature remains bogged down in the old colonial paradigm of ethnic divisions, which had once been applied for the sake of foreign domination. Fewer and fewer writers have delved into the denotative and territorial discourse inherent in Maghrebi identity itself. The novelist-poet Tahar Djaout, clearly of Kabyle descent, never raised the necessity of mapping people and cultures within Algerian nationhood. Is escaping indigenism[30] the best strategy for questioning the authority of Orientalism? It seems that this strategy merely bypasses the conservative label of authenticity, a label applied too often by the former colonized themselves. The idea of purity of culture, formalized by post-independence regimes, has yet to be truly established in the works of exiled authors. The main reason may be that genuine archival and cultural rituals were never constitutive of colonial and postcolonial societies. Nearly everything needed to be (re)invented, and francophone writers banked on Western knowledge and science. As a result, they came up with what I would call *Maghrebtopia*.

The invention of the self in contemporary Maghrebi literature strikes one as familiarly detached. This becomes more of an issue when the process is reflective and transcendent, individual and collective, commodified and fantasy-driven, or put simply, a frantic escape from the Western canon. In these terms, *Maghrebtopia* is the art of worrying, of trying to make the absent present in someone else's language. By extrapolation, tools of Orientalism offer the possibility of bettering oneself in the eyes of the former or actual dominant power. If we view this process as a kind of symbolic circumcision, we must wonder whether a full castration is not looming. Fortunately, even if something is missing or obliterated in Maghrebi literature in French, the texts still produce their own signifying structures. One could point to the differences between Maghrebi literature and other world productions in French. There is indeed a double-exposition for and within writers of the Maghreb, one that both corrupts and enriches their output. The laws of Orientalism refer to a fixed point made intelligible only as a representation, whereas Maghrebi literature's own theoretical project is to signify the reference and to uncover ideological or cultural desire by way of the initial circumcision (colonialism, religious dogma, post-independence ideologies, exile, native tongue, etc.). In the surge of post-independence euphoria, aspects of the national culture may go missing, but at least everything is visible. For Algeria, Morocco, and Tunisia, the process behind the idea of nation or culture is highly qualitative, shaped by a dialectic of worlds lifted by doubt, fear, maladaptation, and ambiguity. Independence symbolizes a clear-cut separation, yet it seems that there are several "fathers" (the nation, Islam, Arab or Berber culture, Western political traditions, Orientalism, economic hegemony, etc.) imposing their laws on literature. In his poetry, Abdellatif Laâbi describes the situation for the Maghrebi intellectual and how creation itself verges on chaos and rebirth:

> We are indeed alone empty sick and tired
> at the foot of the Wall of walls of truthful lamentations
> surrounding us from below and above
> with its signature of disaster.[31]

The work of art creates an effect of divisibility that actually overlaps the unidimensional colonial grid. The principle of dichotomy (West vs East, Christian vs Muslim, Caucasian vs Semite, canonicity vs *Maghrebtopia*, etc.) helps formulate a kinship, if not the superiority, of one culture in relation to another. Orientalism does not engage in a potentially varied *topos* of superiority; rather, it holds to a fixed image of superiority as everything that the Other inherently lacks. The discourse of *Maghrebtopia* reflects this particular function of the Other within the realm of narratives. This is one of Said's operative premises when he writes in

Orientalism that "for a number of evident reasons the Orient was always in the position both of outsider and incorporated weak partner
for the West."[32] In this respect, independence as the ultimate destiny is
the continuation of an ideological fiction.

It should come as no surprise that Maghrebi writers' attempts to
cope with Otherness are a reformulation of the postcolonial condition,
limited for the most part by a system of impossible universality. Any
critique of Eurocentrism has proven futile because the discourse stems
from a humanist tradition, which in the postnational age is presumed
to be global and all-embracing. As for broader theoretical projects, they
tend to force writers away from multilingual paradigms, which rarely
relate to core literary considerations. In *Amour bilingue*, Abdelkebir
Khatibi puts it this way: "From then on I am fully free from being bi-
lingual on my own terms. Freedom of happiness that tears me apart,
only to advise me of the thinking of emptiness."[33] Thus *Maghrebtopia*
posits a permanent space of difference even while seeking a logic system that takes its cue from radical rootlessness. If the postcolonial
condition is to rid itself of Orientalism, it must be accepted that the
Maghreb is an *extension* of France, not its Other. Tangible arguments
can be made to connect the history of Algeria to that of France, and
vice versa. Literature invokes an even deeper connection, one that sub-
sumes designs and myths, embarking on an inward journey within the
individual and the Western exilic condition. Novels by Maghrebi writers, predicated on an antihegemonic imaginary, transgress the frame
of any single Maghrebi unit or voice per se. Authority, instead of being
transferred, is diffused. This sets in motion a counter-discourse that
is best exemplified by the state of the postcolonial mind. Camus, for
example, taught himself how to fight his other self, how to disown
the pursuit of independence. By contrast, Algerian writers have turned
their independence into a conquest, not of France, but of that which is
probably most sacred: its culture.

Could it be that latent Orientalism is a double-edged sword? The
ideology behind Orientalism has served to maintain both national and
individual unconsciousness, but it has also led to the recognition and
empowerment of those "Others." The paradigm of transfer that rides
alongside the postcolonial condition does not replicate the debilitating
state of the former colonized. It is a matter of transcendence, although
without the helpful and natural inscription of a national discourse.[34]
It is striking that almost no novel in French by an exiled Maghrebi author offers a resolution based on the fact of nationhood. The conflicts

and resolutions in these works continually re-enact an obsession with a *lack* of place. There can be little doubt that the innovations of Orientalism (naming, designing, attracting/repulsing, inventing, etc.) remain instrumental in tracing one's own empty signifier within the illusion of postcolonial mobility, both intellectual and physical. The advantage for Maghrebi writers is that, having laboured inside the system, they are saved by its shifting ambivalences. The metaphor of the double-edged sword implies that literature has become both a commodity and an intrusion.

Once racial exclusivity and cultural arrogance have been vanquished from the latent Orientalist scene, what is left is the traumatic trinity of language, nation, and assimilation. For an insight into how problematic the situation is for the writer, one must calculate the density of the symbolic field. One key theme, related to nearly all others, is that of the nomad. This theme comes as a reply to the Orientalist representation of nobility and spiritual possession. In works of Maghrebi literature, the reader must gather for him- or herself a feeling for the origin, the extension, even the timelessness of each work, until it is possible to receive the meaning from its recovered traces. In Abdelwahab Meddeb's *Talismano*, for example, the saturated language becomes the vehicle of a weak but nonetheless significant metaphor for the urgency of escaping Western history: "Let's take up to the desert again and the mountains, let's break away from this history the final cataclysm of which could catch us unawares."[35] The experience of freedom evoked lies, not in an invitation to a journey in the Atlas Mountains or the Sahara Desert, but in the thought process itself. Maghrebi literature in French seems to be a terrain of both verbal-intertextual/lingual and symbolic-physical worlds, even while coping with the anxiety of separation from the motherland and the mother tongue. It is on this ground that Orientalism is contested and reshaped and can never add up in a world where totalization spurns from ideological fantasy. Could it be that the "Oriental" has developed this uncanny way of displacing the horizon, where there is no origin yet where it all started – in the West, the new Maghreb?[36]

5 André Gide and Imperial Dystopia

In earlier chapters I discussed an approach to Orientalism partly rooted in historicism; Said's tantalizing and ambivalent argument; how postcolonial studies can negotiate Orientalism's legacy; and how Orientalism has unfolded for Maghrebi intellectuals. To make my ideas clear in relation to literature, I now present a case study of French writing on the Maghreb. Here, I want to emphasize the challenge of *littérature engagée* in the colonial condition. It is difficult to argue with the idea that nineteenth-century French literature delved more deeply than any other century's into the history of – and therefore the attraction to – the Orientalist *topos*. At no other time in European history did cultural praxis utilize so profoundly its own material representations to create a basis where the narrative forms were the experimental mode of a sublime mission.[1] For a sense of the scope and implications of the Orient in the French popular imagination, one need only consider that the original title of *La Comédie humaine* – the longest and most panoramic literary endeavour of the nineteenth century – was *Les 1001 Nuits de l'Occident*. Balzac changed that title, perhaps because he became more preoccupied with the subversive social nature of his work than with its supposedly exotic forebear.

My treatment of Orientalism in French literature will focus on how, in the twentieth century, it accentuated a discourse of self-interpretation whose primary interest was to generate self-dialogue. Rarely has a literary genre engendered evaluation and interpretation so impressively in parallel. Beginning with André Gide at the turn of the century, one can detect on the European moral horizon a presentiment of decline and, at the same time, a metaphysical presence underscoring a powerful historical unity.[2] On the one hand, there is a sense of civilization's decay; on the other, a quest to maintain a coherent identity when confronted with overwhelming power. I will try to show that contemporary literature, taken as a cultural institution, reflects the rise of ideology about knowledge as much as it represents a technique of domination. The broader suggestion that ideology and aesthetic judgments are highly arbitrary affairs whose goal has been to enhance canonical writing draws from a post-structural celebration of discontinuity. Armed with Gide's emblematic example, I will underscore the ambivalent and multifaceted relation of an *engagé* intellectual to colonial ideology and reality.

In a way that scholarly, privileged, and emblematic ideologies have not (Marxism, feminism, Western aesthetics, etc.), Otherness has been able to replicate the strategies of metropolitan domination as a representational system of right and duty on a global scale. While it is highly likely that the notion of Otherness grew as a by-product of colonial ideology, it is literature that underwent a change in orientation and praxis, caught as it was between a colonial periphery (which was a central contributor to two world wars, to colonial exhibitions in Paris, to French expeditions across Africa and Asia, to the cheap import of exotic produce, etc.) and an imperial *métropole* too self-absorbed to acknowledge plurality.

Throughout the nineteenth century, probably starting with Chateaubriand and extending into the late twentieth century as far as Genet, the French literary fascination for the Arab/Muslim world continued unabated, amounting to a kind of loyalty. It is safe to say that among the many lands where French writers journeyed, Algeria epitomized a historical *hors-texte* – that is to say, it never was acknowledged on its own terms because under the guise of radical colonialism, its history required France's narrative. The relationship between a need to bear witness and the temptation to indulge in fantasy was as obsessive as it was self-reflexive. Many writers fit into the *topos* of Orientalist uniformity (guilt-free sex, exotic agency, performative identity to achieve authority, etc.), but André Gide stands out for his anti-epistemic position and for his use of aesthetics and ethics to drive his point home.[3] No author provided a more profound, effective, and disturbing contribution to the subject of French colonial Otherness than Gide. His engagement with issues of Otherness and the Arab/Muslim world is manifold but best illustrated in *L'Immoraliste* (1902), *Amyntas* (1906; composed between 1899 and 1904), and *Si le grain ne meurt* (1919). One could add to that list *Carnet d'Égypte* (1939) or his *Journal 1939–1949*, in which he treated Africa as the reification of experience under brutal colonization, notably in Congo and Chad. Gide's life is well documented, and he worked hard to that end, particularly by maintaining multiple epistolary relationships. While he never set foot in Asia or the Americas, he travelled extensively in North Africa: six journeys between October 1893 and December 1902. Then he settled down in Algiers between May 1942 and April 1945, after disassociating himself from the collaborationist writers in Paris. He also visited Egypt in April 1939, and returned again in April 1946, spending several weeks in Lebanon as well.

Along with his singular and subversive reworking of Western morals, Gide is closely associated with two key principles of the French Revolution – individual freedom and universal responsibility – that turned literature into a performative tool, "committed literature" (so it was termed after the Dreyfus affair).[4] Yet strangely enough, Gide failed to break with the totalizing cultural context of France's Third Republic, most evident in its colonial undertakings. Even the most progressive of intellectuals accepted that France's civilizing mission overseas was both genuine and proper.[5] This was not blind arrogance so much as poor judgment. Insisting on creating a historical community without collective responsibility and denying the existence of legal standards placed the crimes of colonial occupation on the African continent and the war crimes of Europe on the same level in terms of unacceptable behaviour.

Furthermore, French politicians and social theorists deemed true assimilation through universal rights to be impossible because the colonial subjects would always be outsiders whose understanding of those rights could never be more than shallow.[6] No wonder narratives about or from the various colonies bore some degree of mystical undercurrent! Arab women were lascivious, and black men were beastly, and if this reinforced the comfortable bourgeois identity of the time, fed by capital investment and return, then fine. Progressive writers like Gide provided colonized peoples with history in exchange for both markets and fertile ground for fantasy. In Gide's case, that history turned out to be deeply intimate, as we will see.

Most writings on the Orient had been works of fiction.[7] Gide made the experience deeply personal by resorting to autobiography or autobiographical literary playfulness (who, if not Gide himself, is Michel in *L'Immoraliste*?). Boundaries did not exist solely in space; they also existed in language, and Gide was keen to invert them. Unlike scholars of Orientalism interested in philology or religion, Gide considered it self-evident that true knowledge was to be found within the Oriental subject. This may be why some of his key protagonists were Arabs, with proper names and roles within the narratives, not just stock characters such as those in the short stories of Albert Camus, for example. In an age when favourable representations of the Orient tended to polarize communities,[8] Gide in his works fostered interracial desire, not just homoeroticism. Setting aside hypotheses related to moral discourse and cultural logocentrism, important questions lurk in Gide's writings about the Arab/Berber world. Why is the colonial condition deliberately disregarded in these works, even though he discusses it in his essays on sub-Saharan Africa? Did Gide, like Job, his favourite Biblical character, seek to be tested and to reconcile body and soul with a host of clashing horizons (e.g., French Algeria versus France, lapsed Protestant versus observant Catholic)? Were his stories set in the Arab world his attempt to recognize cultural perversion and move beyond a sexual understanding of it? Greater attention to the confusion represented by the poetic thrust of sexuality and ideology is warranted. We will examine to what extent, in André Gide's writings on North Africa, Orientalism fed its own historical conflict and mutated into a dichotomy of imperial mimicry and intellectual dissonance.

One thing that Gide's works of fiction do *not* do is herald the Western world as the absolute political authority. His literary wanderings do not supplement nationalism, be it based on literature, religion, language, or economic hegemony. Gide writes – to use a very appropriate French term – with a *méthode*, a specific literary strategy, in this case based on desire. To put it simply, the libido itself, no matter how rampant, cannot be conceived independently of representations. Pleasing ones at that. To use Barthes's hypothesis, pleasure brings comfort and reinforces the ego by making it compatible with cultural expectations.[9] Gide was also well aware that Beauty, by virtue of its imaginative capacity, was not a valid concept when cultural encounters were being assessed. The Arab and Berber adolescents he met in Tunisia and Algeria intensified his desire for accepted differences (in contrast to the non-identity promoted by the Orientalist ideology). North Africa became the treasure house of a signifier named desire, with one possible trajectory – from subject to ego. Gide refuted the demand that Beauty be cast as a literary deity. Language was to be emptied of its cultural alienations, then invested with the content of aesthetic and ethical possession, something that included subversion and transgression, at least in the bourgeois mode of sex commodification.[10] For too long, European writers and travellers had treated Beauty in Kantian terms, as something whose particulars could be summarized and simplified. Thus, the Kasbah of Algiers was beautiful, but its people (prostitutes, criminals, pedophiles, zealots, Hashishins) were dangerously ugly. Beauty was not just selective; it also shirked ethical standards.

Nothing North African seemed to contain Beauty at its core. Arguably, Westerners were incapable of appreciating the foreignness of the foreigner in his own land. Gide did not see Beauty in abject poverty alone (e.g., in drinking tea in dirty glasses or sleeping in bug-infested beds), or in sexual promiscuity with the young men he sought there. Rather, he traced out a new order that imperialist France was unable to control, by making the Oriental the subject of its own representation, but never of assimilation. In a way, Gide saw something that was non-negotiable from the perspectives of both capital and culture. This realization has had incalculable consequences for the topics at hand and for French readers as well. At the opening of *Amyntas*,[11] Gide states his terms unambiguously: "[…] no compromise just yet between the civilization of the Orient and ours which looks unattractive especially when it claims to mend things."[12]

Amyntas does not fit into any pre-existing literary genre. It is a travelogue, a diary, and an existential essay as well. The text depicts a time and place largely unknown to French readers of the early twentieth century. Gide's self-positioning as a man who professed to ignore Christian and political dogmas has had a powerful impact on how we read the works of the European travellers who pre-dated him. Before him, writers churned out a patronizing, sentimental whitewash of their own value systems. Instead of a self-reflective perspective on his own story or identity, Gide offers his readers a blunt representation of the strangeness of the self. In Algeria, he comes across not as an intruder but as the exemplification of Otherness. In a sense, he has freed himself from the struggle against archival memory and idealist assumptions.[13] His experience opens up to this: "Anguish dwells only in us; this country is, on the contrary, altogether calm; yet, an issue grips us: is it the before-life or the after-life?"[14] To make a colonized land the source of this feeling is a tremendous gesture, since "anguish" and "us" are markedly French. In so doing, Gide turns to a metaphysics that is no longer necessary in order to shape Western aesthetics. That is what makes his writing so modern – indeed, liberating.

Gide's encounter with North Africa cannot be reductively equated with sensual promises and erotic appreciation. His main desire is to expunge materiality from literary expectations. By materiality, we specifically mean interpretation, hierarchies, and canons. For Gide, the Orient provides the explanation for how interpretation leads to allegory or credits Western literature as the paramount institution. For him, it is evident that the fantasy of empire is not the source but rather the substance that thwarts regulating norms. Such an endeavour was not free of challenges.

Gide's writing disrupts Orientalist literature; it also seeks fertile and challenging experiences for their own sake. By incorporating the earth science, the texture of stones, the root systems of garden plants, and even the quality of the air, Gide's writing leans towards a mythocritical reading and its archetype of the treasure. Here, the psychological aspect is reunited with the physical through the sheer force of the quest for individual fulfilment. Gide adds himself to the Oriental landscape without replacing the colonial signifier or evading the colonial epistemological category: "Ah, to know when this thick black door, in front of this Arab, opens, what will be in store for him, behind it ... I wish I was this Arab, that what awaits him would await me."[15]

Gide upends Orientalist logic by raising the colonized subject to his own aspirations as a foreigner; still, the terms he uses are somewhat blurry in the presence of the mystique of Islam. By invoking doors and expectations, the author's quest becomes more intuitive than political, even barring factors such as the fiction of switching identities (a Western "I" changed into an Eastern 'he'). That sense of being reduced to a difference within oneself rather than with the Other comes close to the position developed by the Algerian poet Jean Amrouche later on (after Amrouche became established, thanks to Gide's support in the late 1940s).[16] Of course, a modern critique cannot overlook the post-identarian paradigms of hybridity, nomadology, anti-essentialism, and so on that purport to address broader concepts such as nationhood and globalization. Yet in the case of Gide, identity is inherent in the suspect notion of universal and/or canonical literature. This tendency both to celebrate and to question literature coloured literary critique until after the post-structural age, as we can see in Julia Kristeva's comment on Camus's *L'Étranger*: "The strangeness of the European begins with his inner exile."[17] It is difficult not to think that the same idea fits Gide's situation in North Africa. His existential anguish seems accelerated by a metaphysical geography. In *Amyntas*, Gide travels to many places, which always seem both familiar and new. The dramatization of place correlates with a sense of loss and with boundary transgression, and all the while, the traveller remains a distinctly foreign element.

The special attention paid to detail in Gide's diary undermines the all-encompassing, high-level frame of the colonial endeavour, exactly like an alternative version of the misguided French undertaking in Africa. This happens not just in political terms (although Gide moved closer to the Communist Party in the 1930s), but also and indeed mainly in terms of his aesthetic and idealistic responses. The question now is this: Did Gide simply substitute Orientalism for another pattern of domination?

Whether in the field of theory or by way of individual experience (existential, metaphysical, erotic, etc.), Gide's writing in and from North Africa challenges the representation of the canon, while setting aside any constructive judgment on Arab/Muslim cultures. One should not be fooled by the fragmented, wandering Gidian type of narrative, which supposedly runs counter to the traditional scholarly travelogue of the Orient. Rethinking the writing process is key to contemplating a solution to the problem of unidirectional history written from the perspective of the conqueror. That is why Gide eschewed the saturated realism that is so overwhelmingly present in colonial literature, with its depravity, disorder, corruption, fanaticism, and all sorts of other evils that amounted to nothing less than the complete justification of imperial designs.

There is no pre-existing text that would force itself onto Gide's touristic performance, although he was a committed tourist. Even the homosexual and pedofilic overtones are kept separate from the colonial frame, unlike those of Gustave Flaubert in Egypt[18] and Tunisia, and Henry de Montherlant in Algeria,[19] for example. Yet in the assumed harmony between Gide and North Africa, there is no room for the Other to contribute to his own story. The writer's fascination often extends to glaringly patronizing statements: "Arabs get used to us, we seem less foreign to them, and their practice, clouded at first, changes its ways."[20] In that sense, the value system of desire displaced from France to North Africa only serves to validate a subjective point of view. The organic metropolitan ideology of Orientalism, shaped by stock literary references to *La chanson de Roland*, *Les Lettres persanes*, *Les Orientales*, *Itinéraire de Paris à Jérusalem*, and so on is slowly emptied of its wholesale endorsement of what French culture stands for. Gide argued for a decentring or skewing of both subjectivity and desire, even though he failed to free himself from his paramount erotic script. His shift of identification was from heterosexual to homosexual rather than from imperial to independent. He opposed the literary system for signifying difference and attempted to remodel his world against two other figures: Proust, whom he deemed a hypocrite for having always declined to acknowledge his own homosexuality, and Wilde, because when they met in Algiers, the English writer humiliated him by pointing out that his heterosexuality was a mirage[21] and affirmed its true nature by introducing him to the young Mohamed.[22]

In its strictest sense, canonical literature projected one category of conformity and individuation that would have condemned Gide to endless repetition. But at the same time, desire, in all its warm and fulfilling sameness, was far from peaceful territory. Even so, it was a perfect means to redirect the focus from national republican fascination to enlightened narcissism. Gide's vision of and commitment to the Orient needed to accommodate paradigms of European culture that had already been debunked by other writers before him.[23] One difficulty was to relinquish the full-fledged colonial agitation that was smothering everything else at the turn of the century.[24] His experience, based on many journeys to North Africa, enabled him to quickly figure out that Western culture was dedicated to capital rather than to culture: "Next to us, in front of a wretched hut where three Arab men take refuge, a woman clad in saffron-colored rags washes a skinny five-year-old girl, she is standing naked in a black cauldron [...] If you are not familiar with this country, for starters, imagine just that: nothing."[25]

The class disparity that was so evident in Zola's novels, for example, is no neutral clearinghouse that can be adapted to overseas narratives. Gide seeks to invalidate Europe's sense of conducting rational and beneficial mission in its colonies. The highly principled ideological engineering of the French is erased by any possibility of self-expression (Gide remains the speaker) and self-determination (natives are turned into fetishes). At the same time, Gide unwittingly creates a mythical land that is doomed to be left adrift by history. He seems caught between something he does not know (the Oriental and his story) and something he does not like (the republican betrayal of the revolution's democratic principles). The point is that, if there were no locus of accumulation of power, mostly economic, fed by stealing land and controlling resources, there would be no need for canonical establishment. The wretched, as they appear in Hugo and Zola, cannot compare with colonized victims, despite those writers' progressive messianism, because, as Ricoeur puts it, "the system got rid of what constituted their *raison d'être*."[26]

Yet Gide is neither a historian nor a politician. As the narrative branches off in different directions, he tries to cut across the literary genre itself. It can be argued, by the same token, that Gide's capital is desire. The metaphor of the desert expanse develops as an accumulation of both freedom and repressed emotions. Fredric Jameson identified "the place of the strategy of containment in Conrad"[27] in the sea; it is easy to see that the desert plays the same role for Gide. The desert is limitless yet has been turned into a space of control, with, for example, the establishment of French military bases, the sending out of scientific expeditions whose ambition is to rationalize the imperial terrain, and the closing of traditional trade routes for fear of foreign influence. There is no possible escape from this kingdom.

What is easy to dismiss is Gide's belief that in Algeria he can escape the moral strictures of Christian orthodoxy through a show of individual piety. Religion may be a complex ingredient in the colonial mix, but it is never a political starting point for Gide. His conflicted (mostly Protestant) Christian values tell only half the story. For him, religion amounts to repressed content concealed beneath the formal surface of the colonial condition: he can identify neither with the *missionnaires* nor with the faith of the natives. Thus, religion only contributes to the escapism associated with desire and separation from cultural and canonical expectations. Indeed, Gide credits the "Arabs" for helping him scrutinize the imperialist ethos, a label that also applies to him: "I had to step aside to hide my tears from the others. Within the piety of this vanquished people [...] within their hopeless faith in something else, so the desert's grief was rising."[28] He must conceal his tears from outsiders, just as he does from the outsider within himself. In a strange twist of logic, the brutalized colonized people find themselves living in a negative landscape, one in which space, like individuals regardless of their origin, is itself acculturated. Only Gide seems to position himself on another level, one on which body and spirit intersect. What is perplexing is that Gide uses "Arabs" as an index to measure nature's power over culture. He is substituting colonial logocentrism for another kind; thus, his quest for status and meaning ends up silencing the Other.

Together with the dramatization of space, the acting out of colonized homoeroticism adds to Western ideological momentum. Because of this contradiction, it is safe to say that Gide denies assimilation from within. When, for example, he teaches the young Athman the rudiments of French literature, Michel immediately anticipates an amusing outcome, mostly touching on matters of credibility: "Athman reads like Bouvard and writes like Pécuchet. He studies like one possessed and writes down just about anything."[29] Gide's modernity is characterized by the manner in which he tells another man's story by talking about himself. What we have here conveys the denunciation of a given colonial order, while the experience remains a free-floating narcissistic object.

Gide criticizes the grandiose totalitarian framework of French imperialism even while overlooking his complicity in it. No wonder that, for example, he mentions money never as if it were an idle constraint, but very much as a consideration in the segregated European neighbourhoods and the Arab slums. The author rarely derides the imaginative treatment of his position, but he fully acknowledges having become a self-hating benefactor, especially by way of a touch of materialism. This is one of the rare instances in which the colonized is able to turn money into a Trojan horse: "The hotels are full of travellers; they are swarmed by charlatans and they pay a lot of money for the fake ceremonies staged for them."[30]

Gide's textual complicity in his rendering of North Africa receives a sounder understanding in *L'Immoraliste*. The moral issue evoked in the title points to several possibilities, yet Gide carries on with his unique vision of the Muslim Orient. At first, the issue of immorality leads towards France: the hero, while on a honeymoon trip to Italy and Algeria, ends up being more interested in Arab boys than in his wife of a few weeks. The narrative suggests that sex affects the colonizer, his values, and the social contract with which he is expected to comply. His fallibility clouds the Frenchman's authority, and this movement seems propelled by Gide's sentences, which transform a given reality into a series of impressions that foreshadow the loss of Western narrative confidence. Where the binding ideology is religion together with the bourgeois order, and aesthetics becomes the tool of mediation in the conflict of modern subjectivity.

Gide transforms the novel genre into a tale told by two characters: a narrator, and Michel, who believes he is in charge of his own narrative, which is actually written for a Monsieur D.R. Nothing is stable, or perhaps credible. And therein lies the irony in *L'Immoraliste*. By challenging the meaning of "moral" and its process of consciousness-taking, Gide can open up his story (it is not a novel, according to his own words!) to the practice of sex instead of limiting himself to the external discursive effect of sexuality.[31] Sex cannot be the universal ground, the felicitous object of Western narratives. For Gide, sex is more likely what makes sexuality stumble over itself. The question that comes to mind is this: If rejecting the bourgeois order is conceived within its own cultural frame, isn't it therefore bound up with its own metaphysics? Certainly the extension of the rebellion to the colonial empire must somehow compound the issue at hand. One wonders whether the convergence of sex and place does not help atone for the rarefied vision of an already post-Christian world slowly unfolding towards fascism. Wasn't colonialism the exotic rehearsal of Europe's own nihilistic upheaval?[32]

In *L'Immoraliste*, geographical descriptions serve their own purpose. First, they do justice to a historical crime: Algeria was occupied by France. Second, space re-enacts the ideological dreams of an outside world that would fit within one's own narrative. Because of his desire, first for the Italian coachman and then for the Algerian youngster, Michel seems to be the only character who is able to acknowledge the world's diversity. Even so, his understanding of place is more iconic and intellectual than that of a tourist's chance encounter. To that extent, Michel emulates his social class: travelling entails recognizing place as already identified in a wider scholarly frame (Roman ruins, Moorish mosaics, ancient Carthage, etc.). Third, at the prestigious *Collège de France*, he is a professor of philology whose field of study is the barbarians of northern Europe. The reference to high culture is an exercise in self-criticism, and furthermore, the contrast with popular and forbidden romance strips the virtue from imperialism. Michel belongs to the Goths, whom he seems to know well. Knowledge, value, and possession are intimately linked: "The moral meaning, perhaps, I said, with an unnatural smile. Oh, simply that of ownership."[33] It is obvious that despite the exotic *topos* (the heat, the music, the whiteness of Algiers, the women by the river, etc.), Michel feels at home in Algeria: "I forgot my fatigue and discomfort. With each new step, I approached ecstasy, silent elation, and exaltation of the senses and the flesh."[34]

The much-vaunted bipolar vision advocated in Orientalism takes its cue from within the European world itself. Algeria becomes the other France where Michel can be and act his true self. North Africa (Algeria and Tunisia, in the narrative) comes to life only through images; the land seems to possess no materiality. French monuments and places of power (town halls, schools, banks, gendarmeries, etc.) are noticeably missing. Gide's Orient is a system of identification where the meaning of desire hovers between the historical and the contemporary. There is neither nostalgia for native cultures (Berber, Islamic, Arabian) nor hope in the imperialist present. Support for political causes in Gide's writing would have to wait until the 1920s. As of his writing in the early 1900s, Gide is a qualified observer, free of everything except his own native culture.

Michel's sightseeing verges on voyeurism, the kind that is unwilling to leave much out. Fredric Jameson talked about "cognitive mapping"[35] with regard to how colonial empires surveyed other cultures; Gide addresses a moral problem that touches on the Oriental subject deemed a commodity. The power of consciousness is all the more conspicuous when we observe how Michel cherry-picks boys as companions: for their visibly feminine features and prepubescence. The sensual/sexual demands made on the Arab boys by the narrator are not just exclusive and selfish; they are also demystifying, so long as the evanescent satisfaction Michel receives comes as a rebuke of the European's myth of re-creating one's family in the extended self of the empire.[36]

The narrative in *L'Immoraliste* unfolds in a dystopian mode: just as with the Europeans' powers in Africa, or in the New World a few centuries before, Michel wants to rule over and debase the boys he discovers: "Bachir followed me, talking the whole way; loyal and agile like a dog."[37]

Gide's character always seeks what seems authentic in the Algerian landscape, be it an urban neighbourhood or a village on the edge of the desert. The author conflates his scholarly knowledge, always historical in nature, with his intimate expectations, which are mostly promiscuous and therefore immoral in content because they are based on a power relationship. No principled classification emerges from the journey apart from a desire to stand out from the European crowd in Tunis or Algiers. One may argue that this narcissistic desire is akin to the very ideology Gide craves to debunk: the cultural difference (based on the moral paradigm) defaults to the empty French bourgeois model. Gide's reality construction – that is, that Arab boys are readily available – fails to question the fiction process in terms of ideology. Does the Algeria he is writing about exist, or is it yet more colonial misrepresentation?

To return to voyeurism, it is evident that scenes and objects, supposedly produced by the narrator's memory, must be delivered to the metropolitan readers as if they were paintings or photographs (especially postcards). And what they are invited to see is not so much one particular colonial condition (Gide was not attracted to black men or to Indochinese boys) as an acting out of some cultural anticonformity. His erotic competition, his pleasure in being surrounded by many Arab boys, goes to the heart of the liberal view by declaring him to be the one who is able to understand these people. The cultural integrity of the natives is shredded by this patronizing exploitation; over and over, the Arabs are reified and passive, just as in Delacroix's paintings of Morocco, in postcards of Algeria by the Geiser brothers, and later in Camus's short stories. Unable to step out of this role, Oriental natives are condemned to stage their own exclusion, as illustrated in that scene of the perpetual return: "I do not recognize the children, but the children recognize me. Informed of my arrival, they all rush in. Is it possible at all that they are the same ones!"[38]

By fact alone, as well as by its literary challenge, L'Immoraliste cannot be compared to any other work of the time. Gide elaborates on a personal journey while striving to bridge the gap between culture and colonialism. Yet the cliché only camouflages the fractures within French society itself. One cannot blame Gide for not condemning colonialism altogether. After all, even Karl Marx disapproved of the colonized's revolts against European powers (e.g., India against England).[39] Stepping on historical materialism's preserves, one ascertains that, according to Marx, it was in the interest of both parties to establish a new social order, regardless of the sacrifices this entailed. For Gide, the colonial world was a vector of individuation as well as an opportunity to negotiate identity in opposition to difference. After all, Algeria was the other France, a place where Algerians dwelled in another matrix in the zone of capital accumulation and the cultural *tabula rasa*.

Michel is haunted by images and impressions; however, no clear understanding of the Orientalist situation underpins the narrative. It almost boils down to a matter of sheer consumption: "I sat down on the first bench I came upon. I was hoping a kid would appear [...] The one who showed up a little while later was a fourteen-year-old boy, tall, not shy at all, who immediately gave himself."[40]

With the Arab boys, desire bears on an expression of the quantitative (their number, the frequency, the bargain rates, etc.), and this aesthetic of repetition aims at neutralizing the moral fault of a pedophiliac married man and his ambiguity. It is common, therefore it cannot be a sin or a crime. Michel attempts to naturalize both landscape and people; furthermore, he knows their feelings and thoughts, which are supposedly guided by greed and desire. In a sense, because Michel finds himself presented with generous possibilities for experimenting in homoerotic play, Algeria is turned into nothing more than the ground for an Orientalist praxis. And in the end, it is all about quality rather than quantity. Moreover, the children's identity is always introduced under the umbrella of the empirical, as if to provide some degree of homogeneity. This is a return to the rhetoric of the Oriental's oneness. Gide proves unable to represent in depth or at length the subject he claims he knows so intimately. He is mixing his journey with the natives' status quo, partly for strategic reasons – for example, his alleged obsession with the desert has mostly to do with being cut off from European society and exploring at will the terrain of pedophilia. The desert scene evolves into a voyeuristic *topos*; at the same time, Michel needs the screen of distance. Contrary to what was previously postulated because of Gide's humanistic and liberal posturing, he is actually expanding the boundaries of Orientalism under the guise of taking the side of the colonized.

L'Immoraliste takes the reader back to a paramount question: What does desire have to do with colonialism? In many respects, the narrative can be characterized as a tirade against the writer's feeling of exclusion. A section of the story involves Michel, front and centre: he does not care much for his wife after she miscarries – basically, he allows her to die of tuberculosis. This part of *L'Immoraliste* keeps telling us what it is – a moral tale that will never be erased because the hero repeatedly fails to reinvent himself: "And I would compare myself to palimpsests […] What was that hidden text? In order to read, didn't I need to first erase the recent texts?"[41] As the narrative unfolds along different moral pitfalls, it becomes clear that Gide's project is fundamentally logocentric. Most significant for the argument of Orientalism is that the discourse of idealization (married life, the colonized's safe condition, the availability of sex, etc.) offers itself to critical strategies. For example, Michel's economic and political privileges become negative expressions of sexual fulfilment. The myth of assimilation[42] boils down to a lubricant of selfishness, arrogance, and most of all, a trick to strip the colonized of their subjectivity. The distinction is at least as important as the segregation the colonizer firmly maintained, be it based on housing, employment, education, or language.

Even though Gide goes to great lengths to secularize his view of love and sexual relations – by, for example, emphasizing his interest in boys over his recent marriage – he draws on a horizon of continuity that is at least one part theology: the glorification of sacred desire. The Arab boys are always desirable by nature, and once in the hands of the European man, they become the servants of his affections. In theory, this may well provide a model of inversion; still, the collective voice and point of view fail to add up to a coherent whole. The real perversion here lies in the switch from the legal, sacred couple (Michel and Marceline) to a cleaving of the subject himself (due to a different original sin), who becomes unable to recognize himself in his desire and ends up a castaway in the literal and metaphorical desert in search of redemption. The logic of *L'Immoraliste* traces two cases of alienation that are trying to exploit each other. Michel is never loved by any of the boys; Gide's writing amounts to an attempt to relive or resurrect his dreams of the Orient. Back home at his Normandy estate, Michel tries to seduce a farmboy, without success. The hero on his quest quickly becomes saddled with melancholia. While the Arab boys lose their innocence, Michel finds himself in a state of mourning, yet with no guilt attached. A very mature Derrida, in his reading of colonial monolinguism, has problematized this particular state of loss with regard to a cultural authority reduced to what he calls "the hegemony of the homogeneous."[43]

Gide's original pursuit of the Oriental treasure is transformed into a bourgeois narrative saturated with dystopian universalism. There are no dates in *L'Immoraliste*, as if to halt the historical hemorrhage brought about by the colonial endeavour. Seasons, sometimes months, are provided, but only to shape the importance of Michel's flight towards the Orient. This strategy also helps blend history into fiction, and vice versa. Just before the episode of his "friendship" with Moktir, an Arab boy he has invited to his rented accommodation, Michel quotes the Bible. Michel's capacity to balance moral issues depends on how he has experienced them at a given time. Of course the situation is not immune from interpretation. One may wonder whether Michel's evolution is not the exact opposite of that of a Christ-like character: from the sacred to the morally unsound, with little room left for redemption. Gide piggybacks both on morals, by juggling values and individual desire, and on politics, by denouncing the deceptive simplicity of the colonial condition.

In *L'Immoraliste*, place – or perhaps location – engages in an exchange of meaning, with little symbiotic relationship possible. For example, the narrative presents no interaction between the French travellers and the French colonizers. Here, Marceline, Michel's wife, is the perfect foil for the old-fashioned patronizing posture, with her well-intended deeds that amount to a static national model of authority. Gide demonstrates, perhaps unwittingly, that cultural grounds for mutual understanding were few and far between within the French colonial frame. In the end, Marceline is never truly at home anywhere. So it is she who must be sacrificed: "Marceline is trying to sit down in her bed [...] the bedsheets, her hands, her gown, are covered with blood [...] I am trying to spot a place where I plant a horrid kiss on her face, drenched as it is in sweat."[44] Setting aside the Judas–Jesus reference, the imaginary models are too familiar with rather clueless characters and their tentative grasp of social forms, of creeds, or simply of space.[45] In the end, Marceline's life has become non–place-specific, for her love hinges on a man whose experience transcends borders; his expansive cosmopolitanism never addresses local issues. In the end, Michel cannot be fully separated from either France or Algeria. Reflecting the homogeneous nature of colonial literature, he is the prosecution witness for the failure of imperialism. Marceline is buried in a village on the edge of the desert. Here again, place is another means to grasp the full significance of identity. By becoming an extension of France, the Orient ceases to be a powerful paradigm of nomadic possibilities. Gide's Algeria smacks of romanticism of the worse kind because it is turned into a righteous instrument of the anthropomorphic norm, whereby narrative resources dry up and merge into a narcissistic call devoid of tragic purpose: "Take me away from here now, and give me reasons to be. I, for one, cannot see any."[46]

In the process of knitting together pedophilic desire and an obsession with the Arab Orient, Gide converts a political situation into an existential one by way of a narrative capable of providing some metaphysical challenge. As with *Si le grain ne meurt* and *Amyntas*, the main argument of *L'Immoraliste* consists in sketching the horizon of being, along with what is predictable or disturbing. Subversion is rarely on the agenda; rather, Gide seeks to realign himself with a new order. In the end, Michel stays in Algeria for a time after Marceline's death; he shares his home with a prostitute and, at times, with her younger brother. While movement and relationships were valorized at the outset, the new concern that overrides everything else is that Michel has become a prisoner of his own life. He has failed to free himself by overthrowing the social prohibitions related to sex and colonial identity. The problem for Michel – and, by the same token, for Gide – is that he could not see that identity is a product, not an origin. Orientalism was so bent on positing essentialism that intellectuals, most of whom demonstrated progressive colours and petulant affection for the wretched, did not see that the struggle needed to take place on another plane.

Ultimately, one wonders how a writer with a social conscience such as Gide[47] could come to terms with the colonial condition and with how colonized peoples were framed as fetishes. In a famous Sartrean scheme, we know that the sway of colonialism wanders in circles;[48] but another side of the argument may be that literature is only a reminder of repressed Western violence. Gide's narrative calls for scepticism with regard not just to the stereotyping of the Oriental subject but also to the silencing of a subject who tells no tale. But again, the author's premises could not be misinterpreted or rejected because European power had already crystallized in its own alienation. Michel symbolizes the alienated French figure. He is confused, but he is never bewildered by contradictions. Michel is indeed a non-transcendental character. The beauty of *L'Immoraliste* is that it operates through two antagonistic proper nouns: Algeria and France. Yet Gide could have taken the issue a step further and argued that political culture begins at home, that violence is both the starting point and the endgame of colonialism, and that Orientalism has lived off established formulas of sexual inhibitions repressed in the home country.

6 Fables of Maghreb Nationhood

One might expect postcolonial theories to conduct a less one-sided historical and cultural analysis – and interpretation – through a better handling of mediation, or what we have called "representation," as Said would view it. In this chapter, I find that the most promising approach is to examine the evolution of the Maghreb's nationhood, for the sake of clarity as well as to avoid embracing the imperial vista that postcolonial studies so vigorously opposes. Independence entails more than the end of colonization; it also means introducing modernity in such a way that the new citizen becomes the measure *and* the centre of the postcolonial condition. In the Maghreb this has been a long process. The question of nationalism is implicit in its political origins (Enlightenment and Marxism) but also in its discontinuity with the Western tradition. Following up on issues of French representation of the Maghrebi subject, I will discuss to what extent it is not enough simply to suggest that Orientalism represented a turn towards naturalizing the Maghebi Other. I will focus on political activism and literature, a pairing that went a long way towards contesting the colonial unconscious in the first half of the twentieth century. While often going to great lengths to avoid politics per se, Orientalism, in its association with colonialism, in effect established a political orthodoxy opposed to nationhood in the Orient. From this particular perspective, and without referring to aesthetics and sciences, Orientalism created a realists' utopia, largely by theorizing the infeasibility of nationhood outside the French sphere. This time around the situation did not emerge from deep within the cultural constructs of the eighteenth-century Enlightenment or the anti-infidel narratives of the Christian Middle Ages. The dynamic in all its absurdity derived, instead, from the fact that Orientalism's bulwark against nationhood was the modern concept of the nation itself. Throughout the nineteenth century, the French model of national identification carried on with the concept of "nationhood" as its theoretical blind spot. For example, the Third Republic's obsession with national commemorative events heightened the tension between the revolution's universal premises and local loyalties within France itself.[1] What can be said, then, about Orientalism's symbolic menace beyond the national borders? Perhaps that the fantasy of excluding any other national "us" became the hallmark of a free-floating virtue that ignored the resistance it generated among the colonized. More specifically, the fantasy of Orientalism grew out of the perception among its pseudoscientific practitioners that society was homogeneous and needed to maintain an inherent purity.[2] Faced with the "narcissism of self-generation,"[3] this continuous narrative (in both space and time) of the French nation could not meet the conceptual indeterminacy and the instability of knowledge outside its borders. In theory, just as in practice, France with its colonial empire could not reinvent democracy by starting from a distorted image. Perhaps it is less salient to work out how to couch the colonial situation within French universalism than to grasp that nationhood resists political theory even though it is the handiest tool for generating collective power. The situation of France and Algeria, or rather one against the other, is probably the best example of this.

The significance of colonialism is that it did not present itself simply as an ideological performance that extended the artificiality of French nationhood beyond its natural borders. Colonialism also loosened the bounds of belonging in space and time for colonized peoples. While borders in Europe were being drawn many times over, in war after war, colonial possessions slowly turned outward the forces of nationalism and the Industrial Revolution; in this way they themselves became loci of power. So in a sense, colonialism bowed to the worst possible threat by depoliticizing its own ideology. The colonial ideology switched from a modality of analysis, as expounded during the Third Republic, to a modality of practice, permeated by geographies and by the nomenclature of multiple identities. Domination was thereby naturalized and even fetishized, because it never confronted a different source of knowledge. So one may wonder: What were the pre-existing identities that had been suppressed throughout North Africa, especially in Algeria? How relevant were they when faced with the colonial cultural onslaught? How did imperial identity stake out a part of the world and operate within it before it actually produced a framework for the

Algerian nation in 1962? And lastly, how does the concept of nation impact our reading of Orientalism today?

From the mid-nineteenth century on, the French nation was characterized by its values, interests, and common ethnic background, on its actual territory and indeed anywhere in the world where French people settled down. For peoples of the Maghreb, the semantic scales pulled in the exact opposite direction by subtly shrinking the discursive space where a sustained political unity could be developed. The importance of French ideals was slowly matched by that of Maghrebi myths that had taken root over centuries, based on both religion and local ethnic identities. Still, what shape could nationhood take without sovereignty? The colonial condition was such that nationhood was more than a challenging concept; it was something that had been "stolen" by the performative power of colonial Frenchness. Colonies were in effect a new country that comfortably slipped into old hegemonic modes, fed by Orientalist representations and a nationalist yoking of identity to political institutions. In nineteenth-century North Africa, the Arabic language and the Islamic faith, although highly relevant, failed to counter French Otherness because they never emerged as a force at the macro level. Algeria was a patchwork of ethnic groups (Berbers, Arabs, Jews, Turks) that were often too busy fighting one another to shore up their legitimacy or to derive benefits from the new colonial power. This suggests why the Emir Abdelkader, in his armed resistance against the French invaders (1832–47), was unable to unite the Algerian factions or to convince the Moroccan king to provide crucial military support when it was most needed.[4]

It is fair to say that nationalism throughout North Africa was shaped by nineteenth-century European ideologies, as well as by the need to somehow develop political coherence and ultimately resist colonial rule by force of arms. All the while, the asymmetrical historical situation generated mirages insofar as the occupation confounded any coherent national narrative. A historical fact about Algeria that is often overlooked is that while France was striving for absolute control, it brought considerable military force to bear on establishing new aristocratic native families, with the goal of suppressing any national sentiment.[5] These extended families, called *khalifas*, *naïbs*, or *bachagas*, re-established feudalism within the colonial institutional frame. Behind the veil of colonial rule, the imaginary Maghreb created its own blank state. The central trope of political discourse mobilized a new point of view: that discourse was to retreat before the supranational, commanding colonial arrangement. To take root, this dysfunctional system (dysfunctional because illegitimate) needed to eliminate dissenting voices and forces.[6] It is no coincidence that early Algerian nationalist leaders were exiled to distant lands of no return, as far away as the South Pacific (e.g., to New Caledonia).[7] Nor is it a coincidence that Maghrebi inmates were lumped together with Republican forces during the 1871 Paris Commune. The idea behind these harsh policies was that native national unity had to be made too costly to ever be realistic.

A paradox of colonial rule was that instead of holding colonized peoples stranded in a regressive state in which history was deemed illegible, it actually generated political power. This was a dramatic departure from Orientalist binary constructions that rendered cultural difference barely intelligible because Maghrebis were supposedly caught in some teleologically warped essence. By means of this French ideological take, democracy was happening "now" while the value system of the Arab/Muslim Other was supposedly lost in time. Islam, the foundation of Maghrebi cultures, was no longer consonant with the rule of law and became strapped down by misleading labels. The symbolic system of colonial rule, articulated with its own language and logic, unintentionally spawned a movement based on Islamic reforms and cultural dynamism. Exclusive identities thoughout North Africa were as powerful and goal-oriented as the colonial nationalism of the early period. In the twentieth century, the native elites, trained in the French schools and colleges in France,[8] helped brush the dust from the fossilized body of native customs and traditions that had once prepared the ground for colonization. For one thing, until the twentieth century, critical attention among Muslim scholars had hardly been directed at challenging Western political philosophy and historical materialism. Colonialism had caught the Islamic intellectual sphere off guard.[9] Then, wielding Western intellectual tools, Maghrebi nationalists, most of them secularized, began questioning France's dominance in terms of both laws and cultural presuppositions. Colonialism had propelled the natives towards following French forms of intellectual inquiry. Some may argue that this encounter was overdue, but the subaltern did not accept unreflectively what was "presented" to him. The process took time, access to education was limited, and education itself was closely tied to colonial ideology.[10] The Maghrebi elites were mainly low-ranking civil servants, non-commissioned soldiers, pharmacists and physicians, or teachers. By 1962, there were fewer than 10,000 French citizens of Algerian descent in a country of 7 million Algerian natives.[11] As a consequence, among the Muslim population, the notion of an elite took a different route in terms of internalizing the value of citizenship and rethinking the nationhood reference. For one thing, the elite did not speak for the nation, and they were viewed by Algerians at large as living proof of colonial contamination. The French education system was expected to emancipate its pupils by validating the glorious colonial undertaking. In many ways, it failed to do so – too few Algerian natives attended French schools for cultural assimilation to take root. By the 1920s, the widespread representations of French culture were being shaped into new ones throughout North Africa, in ways that turned the distant territory into a contentious centre of power. Had it not been for the Second World War, the independence struggles would have started much earlier. Indeed, there was more in the air than unrest and demands. In 1920, the Destour Party was founded in Tunis, with the unambiguous goal of drafting a constitution for an independent Tunisia.[12] As if to drive the point home regarding France's political worries vis-à-vis its colonies in North Africa, a decree of March 1949 stipulated that bills issued by the Ministry of Education concerning Algeria would have to be approved by the interior minister. This only strengthened the links between nationalism and the politics of culture. Imperial France had long ago convinced itself that it had stabilized North Africa by bringing technological progress and a market economy. But it was quickly becoming clear that antagonism toward colonial status was permeating every aspect of North Africa's civil society and that the future was going to be a bloody one.[13]

The people of the Maghreb never recognized the dominant culture as legitimate.[14] At the same time, the colonial power viewed the natives as incapable of critical resistance (and of self-government) – as meriting, at best, patronizing empathy. Under its universalizing mode, whatever colonial rule claimed to offer, it always left something out. But eventually, cumulative subjective change brought about class and national consciousness.[15] Once collective anxiety was displaced from culture to politics, a national awakening began. By the interwar period, it was clear that French colonialism amounted to a clash of two nationalisms: one that oppressed the colonized, and another that was to liberate them. In the national struggle throughout North Africa in the twentieth century, the French institutional powers hijacked the concept of a native elite in order to transform it into a harmless, neutral ideological means to control the rest of the colonized populations. National historiography became an ideological tool in the hands of the *Front de*

Libération Nationale (the National Liberation Front; FLN), which developed its own comprehensive, universal pretensions. The native elites had to ensure that they did not impede intercultural communication, but also that they did not curb the emancipation dreams of their fellow Maghrebis. This vacillating in-between-ness well illustrates the "third space" of the colonial condition.[16] A gradual shift took place from the elite to the general population, from the lofty ideals of French republicanism to a rather nationalist individuation of the colonial subject. Was it that notions such as "nation" and "freedom" were so overdetermined by France's history as to be left alone by the colonized? In an ironic twist, Mohamed Larbi Madi, a founder of the FLN, wrote from a French prison: "Soon you are going to celebrate in Paris the anniversary of Bastille Day. We stand with you in thoughts for we certainly recall its meaning. And such a recollection keeps our faith strong, and gives meaning to our hopes."[17]

The Algerian freedom fighter set out to hinder French political projects in the colony, portraying them as already obsolete. It turned out that Orientalism, as a result of its fixed representations, had itself become fossilized. The habit of metaphorically casting the Arab as a historical subject succeeded only in articulating resistance, often beyond the colonial borders, as became the case with liberation pan-Arabism from the 1940s through the 1960s. In the late 1950s, France began to consider extending citizenship to the natives and granting broader access to public education, but by then it was too late to salvage the empire. The tropes of domination could only be transposed onto the deconstructive enunciation of self-determination and independence. Once history began to "accelerate," especially after the First World War, the nationalism arising from the colonial condition began breaking moulds, shaping new representations, and encouraging the colonized to struggle for historicizing political power. All of this was transpiring worldwide by mid-century, and it inscribed the present of the colonized, whether on the Indian Subcontinent or in the Arab world, onto the timelessly imagined Orientalist paradigm. Furthermore, the counter-power of liberation was being elaborated not from beyond the unknown or unimaginable fringes of the metropolis, from Paris or London, but right from the heart of it. Intellectuals and anticolonial activists, such as Césaire, Senghor, Bourguiba, Messali Hadj, and Ho Chi Minh, all located imperialism in the heart of the modern state, whose very strength was to promulgate world-systems against those it intended to dominate if not eliminate. So, although this was not originally an expected political outcome with regard to France, the patterns of authority dismantled their own cognitive landscapes.

Given that colonized peoples had little if any say in what was enacted in their own lands, it comes as no surprise that elaborate programs for reform, and later for national liberation, took root outside North Africa, mainly in France. By 1919, an estimated 100,000 Algerians had settled in France. This accidental community was dazzled not so much by the *métropole*'s technological or economic achievements as by its political organization. What the *émigrés* had seen and known back home was quite different: abject poverty, colonial oppression, religious superstition, the tyranny of local leaders appointed by the French authorities, and a close-mindedness that had become as corrosive as any imperial ideology. The sharp decline in living standards in Algeria had caused a steady flow of immigrants, overwhelmingly male, to the *métropole* from the countryside.[18] These former peasants and day labourers were well aware of what it meant to lose one's own land. They were also the keepers of the resistance spirit that had been fostered nearly a century earlier by the Emir Abdelkader, who had drawn his fighters largely from the countryside. It is safe to say that before they became nationalist militants, the *émigrés* were patriots; and their world view was not the *leitmotiv* of some social project, but rather was deeply rooted in the reality of nationhood that had been so far denied them. Their views on nationhood could not be changed by theoretical enunciations on such issues as intercultural assimilation, or later on, a shared community of interests, as advocated by Albert Camus and other left-wing thinkers, for example. But the polymorphousness of the struggle confounded the identity epistemology, which had been associated for too long with religion and ethnic syncretisms. In other words, the grand overarching sense of national belonging developed slowly and in multiple layers, regardless of social background. Human dignity, shared citizenship, and nationalist aspirations evolved over many years, often painfully. In Morocco, for example, the war in the Rif (1921–6) epitomized the inner turmoil within a kingdom torn between the demands of the French and Spanish protectorates and the identity and rights claims of the Berbers. In the course of the twentieth century, the much-vaunted Orient turned into a schizophrenic space, split into two directions: from France to the Maghreb, and from the Maghreb to France. Assertions of Algerian-ness and Moroccan-ness were a response not only to political oppression and appalling economic conditions but also to the fact that France was no longer identified with talismanic pronouncements on democracy and the *mission civilisatrice*. So the main question in the colonies, as well as in France with its immigrant workers, could have been this: Who were the real people, and for what nation?

In the narrative of Orientalism in North Africa, there was no room for peoples and nations. But at the same time, France itself reiterated the failure of the imperialist ethos to pursue any sublime mission – one predicated on the overblown imaginary figures of the colonized and the colonizer. Against this alienated condition, the insular critiques of the liberation struggles expanded into dramatized political relationships. Under the leadership of Messali Hadj, the *Étoile Nord Africaine* (*North African Star*; ENA) was founded in 1925 in Paris, as a labour organization close to the Communist Party; soon after, it evolved into a nationalist movement. In 1929 the French government tried to dissolve the ENA, and soon after, its leaders were sentenced to prison for re-establishing it as an underground organization. Liberation movements became far more attractive to North African intellectuals and immigrant workers than the pipe dreams of colonial assimilation and watered-down reforms. Nationhood brought with it an ontological possibility as well as a novel self-conscious reflexivity rooted in faith, language, and land. The independence discourse evoked history in contrasting Western ideologies with national constructionist accounts. The same discourse pointed to the crucial need to start imagining a model of actual territorial rootedness and, against the odds, a globalized culture able to endure the impact of colonial hybridity. The challenge for the new nations would be to reorient the epistemic premises of the West towards new identity territories.

At the same time, France slowly began disavowing its own brand of overseas nationalism.[19] Even conservative critics, such as the well-known journalist Raymond Cartier, advocated unilateral withdrawal from the empire as a precondition for salvaging the original spirit of the French nation-state.[20] The outmoded dialectics of progressive–regressive nationhood regarding the "Arabs" reappeared as a discursive ploy that applied empty nationalistic claims and offered a strategic escape from a war in Algeria that was locked into the same self-defeating paradigm of what had happened in Indochina between 1945 and 1954. The Orientalist pull derived from the notion that under France's patronage, the colonies had been subsumed into national identities. Within this frame, national independence throughout Africa – and the Maghreb in particular – was linked to a modernization program that mobilized the West's icons and ideologies. In a pamphlet published in 1957, Raymond

Aron declared that the time had come for Algerians to make their own history because economics and demographics were no longer on the side of the colonial undertaking.[21] In light of the hegemony exercised by global Orientalism, national sovereignty was to gain the upper hand because it was truly political, or rather, it was a stark reminder of the significance of a "from now on" identification of history with the people. Ironically, this consisted in filling up the emptiness – created by the colonial anti-*logos* – in the classic manner of humanism by turning the colonized into a subject in his or her own right and by restoring some original presence (historical, cultural, and economic). There is no need to underscore how this exercise in national relabelling was resoundly ahistorical, and the fiasco of the FLN, which meddled with myths and national memory, only helped put the case to rest. Before independence, the self-projecting French ego and its strategic use of essentialism had proved incapable of accounting for views of other political contexts as well as historical modes of consciousness. This was one reason why the French could never have won the Algerian war. Military might only replicated an outdated geopolitics. In an attempt to skirt this strategic impasse, which was unsustainable both economically and on the diplomatic front, Raymond Aron developed an argument that embraced some sort of a transnational flow of capital instead of pointing to the historical fault lines of colonialism.[22] Another part of his historical analysis fed on the old paradigm of a clash of civilizations: he believed that the European minority could not live in and adapt to an Algerian republic. In essence, the former rulers could not morph into non-French citizens. This puzzling position would lead us to believe that the European population of Algeria did not "own" their history, that it was given to them by circumstances that compelled them to obsessively invoke their origins.

Of more consequence for a discussion of Maghrebi nationhood is that throughout the liberation struggle, the natives had to turn the political gaze on themselves rather than against the French. The North African liberation movements that originated in France in the 1930s were seemingly governed by the demands by workers and unions, by political configurations reacting to the rise of fascism, and by metropolitan audiences with a weak interest in the colonies; nevertheless, those same movements informed the essential character and desire of the colonized peoples in terms of what had previously been sketched out in the Orientalist discourse. Members of different cultural and ethnic backgrounds converged on Paris and organized against the colonial establishment, and this helped strengthen the boundaries of nationalism and revitalize France's self-image as the crossroads of intercultural dialogue. An example was *Le Paria*, a magazine founded in 1922 in Paris by Louis Hunkanrin of Dahomey, Max Clainville-Bloncourt of Guadeloupe, and Ho Chi Minh of Indochina that was published from 1922 to 1926. The journal claimed to be giving a voice to all people subjected to colonial rule, thereby establishing the first "inter-colonial union." Despite *Le Paria*'s communist slant, Algerians and Moroccans were eager contributors to it. They ensured that their Islamic faith did not fence out ideological communication and collective struggle, especially from the socialist atheistic side. Pragmatic subalterns were perfectly capable of organizing and speaking for themselves. France's military setbacks in the world wars against Germany did not help end · colonial occupation and institutional dependency; they did, though, ensure that triumphalist imperialism and its supporters were from now on open to attack.

The argument that a purely imperialistic solution could quash expectations of nationhood among a colonized people rooted in their own religion, culture, historiography, and native soil found itself strongly challenged. The independence struggles were founded on the premises of cultural authenticity underlying the epistemological pendulum between what was truly foreign and what stood for home. By the early twentieth century, the project of a global French nation found itself relying more and more on exhorbitant and anomalous narratives as well as political sleight of hand in order to maintain its ideological usefulness. The nationalist concept and imaginary that France derived from its colonial experience was broad in its geographic and cultural reach, but it was applied only in a narrow and technical sense, and this became more troublesome when the market system of exploitation was "put on stage," quite literally. In 1930–1, France organized in quick succession both the centenary celebrations of Algerian colonization and the Colonial Exhibition, with the avowed purpose of impressing the French people with the *grandeur* of overseas France. These political displays came attached to an anachronistic and chimerical mandate to proclaim and reinforce France's cultural world mission, and not just as a rival to the British empire. These exhibitions were extremely popular, with about 8 million visitors between May and November 1931 for the Colonial Exhibition alone. In his inaugural speech, Paul Reynaud, the colonial minister, flatly declared that "colonization is the greatest feat of History. Does it ring true at all that on this day we are celebrating a crowning moment that is close to falling into decline? Never have a soaring spirit and its outpouring been so powerful as they are today."[23] The discourse on differentiated hierarchies and perspectives went so far as to claim that the colonies could become the birthplace of a new European man, a true pioneer for the French race in every sense.[24] However, political opposition to these archaic valorizations of the nation lacked a centre and a privileged point of view. The Communist Party, with the vocal support of Surrealist artists like Aragon, Éluard, and Tanguy, organized a counter-exhibition from September to November that denounced the excesses of imperial France and promoted the native arts of Africa, Asia, and the Pacific Islands, although this project met with little success. With no genuine working class existing in the colonies, left-wing intellectuals and activists stood between two centres of attraction: national assimilation, and cultural association. Both meant the continuation of the colonial paradigm: from a fixed symbolic order (represented by the civilizing mission) to patronizing overtones that denied the true realization and rewards of independence. Whatever the French political spectrum had to offer, the notion of full-fledged independence had not yet gained traction in the national political consciousness. Even left-wing intellectuals were busy papering over the natives' identities, out of sheer ignorance or perhaps because acknowledgment of them might flare up into an engine of social change that would slip out of their control. So it is no mystery why Maghrebis set out to redefine their own culture. After all, even Sartre's account of "situational engagement," in his preface to Senghor's *Anthology of African Poetry*,[25] while it addressed the complexity of the epistemological roots of the colonized, was only able to frame the liberation movements within the Marxist doxa and its limits on emancipatory humanism. The word "anticolonialism" had been coined in the name of French republican values and designated what only the colonized peoples longed for. In Hegelian fashion, anticolonialism in the 1930s turned out to be a form of alienation, from which a brighter future could not be distinguished. In that sense, the rightful aspirations to self-determination had run up against a profound sense of betrayal over what France had failed to achieve beyond its own borders. The nationalist militants from the colonies wanted to wrench their political reality loose from centuries of oppression.[26] One obvious conundrum was that they applied Western concepts and methods without endorsing them. Furthermore, they had become a diasporic people, which forced them to think and act in more syncretic terms than their fellow militants who had remained at home. France continued to rely on a morally uncertain principle of "vital space" to maintain its empire; meanwhile, resistance from the colonized sprang from an egalitarian ideology slowly turned upside down until it became fully validated by a total break-up.[27] It can be argued that the native soil as the foundation for nationhood was all the more relevant since it set the stage for postcolonial modernity in an ethically crucial way: the temporal dislocation resulting from colonial occupation could, at long last, be spatialized. Recall that Orientalism engaged in deep scientific conversations concerning cities and dynasties of the Maghreb, for example, while eschewing discussion of the nations of this same area.[28] For too long, Muslim natives had been caught in a metaphysical construction. The contours of Orientalist discourse were congruent with an always inadequately explained self-determination. Logically, nationhood and independence were to reclaim a historical point of origin. Because of this deflation of ideological authority, it was not so much a question of catching up with one's own history as defeating the terms of cooperation inherent in the new Occident–Orient paradigm.

The 1930 exhibition celebrating the 100th anniversary of the French colonization of Algeria demonstrated the extent to which France had squandered its moral prestige. The exhibition had been meant to foster a sense of cultural proximity between France and Algeria, yet the event was choreographed to generate a sense of ethnic superiority and to offer a facile justification for the "self-ordained" colonial project. Algeria was important not just to vindicate France's republican nation-state; indeed, the exhibition promoted itself as offering a programmatic view of the "global nation." Foreign cultures and peoples were documented within an ideology of knowledge with design, something that did not seem to obviate the need for racially inflected Orientalist theories. For example, the use of the French language helped underscore how far France was willing to go to escape the consequences of its imperialistic ambitions. All the same, the absolute denial of Algerian nationhood was based on the political meaning of France – a meaning detached from its own principles. As soon as the task of colonial domination and exploitation began to operate with full force, the *leitmotif* of democracy and Western superiority collapsed into a device aimed at its own image. The colonial exhibitions, and the attention paid to them in the media, offered evidence of France's racist unconscious. The purpose of the colonial ideology was to turn an allegory of power into a political tool that could shape the consciousness and minds of French citizens. Given the French government's significant investment in these

colonial exhibitions, it was clear that the paradigms of French historiography had settled into an unstable orthodoxy. The method and the
dynamic were prescriptive and doctrinal. Instead of being entertained,
French visitors were "educated." The sea of performative visibility on
offer was premised on the distinct characteristics of the colonized peoples within the nation's culture. Quite a feat. One goal was to show
the global *indigènes* within a broader pseudoscientific framework, and
here, the effect of shaping the natives with an objective discourse consisted precisely in "protecting" all sense of their identity from interpretation. The allusions to empire legitimated the reference system of
an unstable republic even while hiding other peoples behind the veil
of a monarchic-type order. Under the colonial fallacy, the boundaries
between a French "us" and a native Algerian "we" did not run along
territorial lines, but rather through a desired national entity that naturalized segregation and disenfranchisement. The colonial exhibitions,
the metropolitan media, and even the film industry contributed to the
new arrangements of history to the extent that the essence of the colonies no longer lay within some exotic frame or economic advantage.[29]
Rather, that essence was set out as some vital quality important to the
state and its organization. With a nod to social Darwinism, the colonies, especially Algeria, symbolized the healthy, forward-looking part
of France and – by extension – of Europe as well. In the 1920s, Albert
Sarraut, probably the most influential French colonial minister during
the Third Republic, could state in a seemingly rational fashion: "We are
living through times where the very future of life dictates that we must
expand our vision beyond horizons we are familiar with."[30]

The political traditions that had altered identities throughout Europe
were predicated on the drawing and subsequent erasing of difference
in the colonies. More specifically, the universalist foundations of French
politics allowed for a myth of objectivity and a rational policy process,
admittedly in a nationalistic mode. For example, under colonial rule it
was not uncommon to see more land appropriated by the government
after the First World War, based largely on the ludicrous argument that
there had been no such a thing as a system of private property before
the advent of colonialism. Every cultural misunderstanding vindicated
France's right to pursue its unilateral economic interests and to realize its geopolitical aspirations. The 1930 exhibition of the centenary of
Algeria's colonization brought the naming and knowing of the empire
into the modern archive of history. To make good on its intention of creating a history of its own, France recoded the categories of Orientalism

from representation according to inception. How so? Through displacement, disguise, and numerous disjunctive processes that underpinned and eventually mapped out a single prescribed version of history. Within the highly ritualized framework of the French republican celebration, Algeria stood out as sacred ground. The budget for the exhibition was astronomical – more than 130 million French francs for an event that lasted from January till July 1930.[31] In Algeria, most of the celebratory events were military in nature; in Algiers, for example, there was erected a statue of General Lamoricière, who was lauded for his victories against the natives' resistance, which involved slaughtering hundreds of thousands of civilians in the exercise of absolute power. There were also travelling exhibitions of photographs, bearing on military exploits and the lives of European pioneers who had settled on the "unforgiving" Algerian soil. This self-serving collaboration between the centralized French state and local branches of colonial power insisted on the historicity of the imperialist system; this amounted to a political argument based on the idea that the ties between France and Algeria were unbreakable. Was the colonial situation an instance of positivistic reduction of political theory?[32] In Algeria the anniversary exhibition helped embody unified communities, yet coherent identities were missing and an Orientalist mindset was folded into the mix. In the sciences, for example, a neuropsychiatric school was founded in Algiers, where Professor Antoine Porot conducted a famous study that supposedly indicated that the Maghrebi brain cortex was dwarfed, which allegedly proved that the natives were mentally inferior.[33]

The masquerade of the centenary exhibition ushered in a new, more vigilant stage of the nationalist struggle by contributing to Maghrebis' understanding of how politics worked and by validating their collective conversation, at least among *émigrés*. Very early, the Communist Party's influence on Maghrebi nationalist militants wore off. Even as they struggled against capitalism, the independence activists opposed the unidirectional importation of conceptual apparatuses largely shaped by European and Soviet perspectives and experiences. The concept of class struggle was meaningless within the colonial situation and was perhaps even dangerous for nations that needed to remain united against a single enemy. Also, most of the North African leaders belonged to the bourgeois class back home and had by then been compromised by their strong ties to the colonial establishment. The political challenge was to reconcile Marxist temptations with nostalgia for a mythical homeland and the demands of Islam, of which intellectuals had little knowledge.

Even so, the unsettled situation in the 1930s demanded that Maghrebi activists not only reject the magical narratives of the colonial culture but also appropriate status quo methods for their own purposes. It is fair to say that the nationalist struggle did not arise from a linear set of correspondences between oppression and self-determination but rather from opposition to both traditional native cultures and the unstable (if not misleading) French republican discourse. The various North African political movements did not see eye to eye, being divided at times over matters of socialist theory, at other times over matters of religion. Sometimes they were mesmerized by the conspiracy-addled French colonizers; other times, when they came back home, by the politics of the Near East as discussed by Syrian intellectuals, in particular, who lived in exile in Paris.[34] Independence leaders found it hard to apply their ideas in a world where the models they had experienced in France either did not exist or, worse still, were controlled by Europeans.[35]

Trade unions, political parties, and even athletic associations were rolled into one Western sphere of influence. Only religion seemed to offer a pure political path. So, at least until the Second World War, Maghrebi leaders and militants conceived of themselves as Muslims before they claimed any political label. Islam was what unambiguously separated the true natives from the colonizers. And religion brought with it a social model that did not rely on myths of Western modernity and that gave meaning to the origins and cultural practices of the peoples of the Maghreb. This religious element within the nationalist movement meant there was less room for compromise with the colonial world. By 1945, hostility to the colonial state had swept away any expectations for meaningful dialogue, even among those intellectuals for whom French cultural and political life had held some appeal. For practical political purposes, the ideal of assimilation had lost any traction it might have enjoyed in the past. As a cultural alternative, Islam was more powerful, and the colonial power had few means to oppose it in the political arena. Relatively few militants were religious, yet religion turned out to be vital to their understanding of their state of dependency. Realizing they had no control over transnational capitalism, the militants turned to religion as an original essence that would enable nationalistic truth to take hold. Is it possible to talk about a metaphysics of nationhood? Nationalist militants felt justified in reaching the paradoxical conclusion that it could; for them, there was room for both a deep-rooted faith and a brand-new idea of the nation. While French humanists entangled themselves in the Industrial Revolution and historical materialism, the Maghrebis' identity grew stronger because their debates arose from the very roots of their nations. Orientalist essentialism – its cultural and psychic servitude – was methodically turned upside down. This pre-modern historical certainty would surely bypass the colonial experience. There was, however, a major difference between the Algerian independence movement on the one hand, and on the other, the Moroccan and Tunisian independence movements, which kept the door open to negotiation and compromise with the French, simply because their politics of national identity seldom traversed the canonical divide of religion and historical obliteration that characterized the Algerian colonial experience. For example, the first Moroccan national organization, the *Comité National d'Action*, was founded in 1933. The party brought together the secularized urban bourgeois (mostly from Rabat and Fez) and leaders from Islamic schools. Their goal was to bring about comprehensive reforms within the French protectorate. Independence was never on the agenda, and membership was limited to a few thousand men. Yet the organization was dissolved by the French authorities in March 1937. Only in 1943 was a true liberation political party founded in Morocco when the Istiqlal Party succeeded in merging all the political forces of opposition to the French protectorate.[36] Their charter demanded immediate independence and the founding of a constitutional monarchy.[37] By 1952, with the support of the United States and the Arab League, the nationalist movement was growing in both numbers and influence. By March 1956 the Istiqlal Party was a key participant in the political negotiations over Moroccan independence. The Moroccan nationalist movement enjoyed unity and cultural coherence. Mediation regarding the consequences of French imperial rule was diverted by a search for democratic consensus revolving around the king. History would prove Moroccan nationalists wrong as far as civil rights, gender equality, and economic emancipation were concerned.

Early in the independence struggle, Algerians wanted to oppose an Arab/Islamic core to the French Jacobine tradition. One advantage of resorting to religion was that the movement would benefit from a collective dynamic.[38] The cultural fetish located in colonial rule was from then on conceived of as a necessity, a vehicle for social transformation. The colonized had to unlearn Otherness, and that process could not be embedded across all the North African nations in the same manner. The peoples of the Maghreb had all embarked on a struggle for nationhood and identity; however, Moroccans and Tunisians chose to explore political constructs whose discourses conformed to the narratives of Western liberal democracy. Also, Morocco and Tunisia had relatively small European populations and thus were more attuned to the *topos* of authentic native identity. Algerians, by contrast, tended to enforce an essentialist subversion in order to counterbalance the *tabula rasa* applied to their own recent history. Algerians needed to locate the concerns of identity in a more remote historical structure, given that the colonial undertaking had pushed deeper the organizing cultural assumptions. All the while, the Orientalist posture allowed simplifications based on binary modes of opposition. For example, instead of articulating true humanist cognition from the bottom up, the colonial exhibitions exemplified and implemented both racial taxonomy and the first stage of hybrid modernity. The struggle for nationhood urged one to ask: How does one assess the advent of emancipation and independence in a world in which normativity consists in enforcing ideological fantasies? Just like a traumatized body, a colonized nation has to invent survival strategies. The harsher the colonial impact, the more potent the insurrectionary agency. The Algerian historian Mostefa Lacheraf had this take on the situation: "In Algeria, society had been more deeply wounded than the nation, and yet it was the latter, not society itself, that became the ultimate goal, and held all the stakes. This truly meant attempting the impossible when everything was determined in an indirect fashion by the attitude of the enemy who denied the Algerian nation because they had no hold on its spiritual wholeness, its hidden reserves of recovery."[39]

Orientalism had opened the door for patriotism, but by the 1950s its ideology had been soldered to modal approaches and theoretical dead ends. By definition, there was no such thing as a destiny process, nor was it possible to attain a *telos* for the colonized. To rationalize the uncanny nature of the colonial *imago*, liberation movements sought what would best promote universal freedom and national aspirations. One dimension of the deconstruction of nationalist Orientalism appeared in what was later called "francophone literature." Maghrebi writers had been contributing to newspapers and literary reviews as early as the late nineteenth century. The first recorded short story in French by a native North African author was *La Vengeance du Cheikh*, by Si M'Hamed Ben Rahal, in Algiers in 1891. The first novel was *Ahmed Ben Mustapha, Goumier* by Si Ahmed Bencherîf, in 1920. These works were derivative of the European canon and vaguely autobiographical. Their importance lay elsewhere: they had been written for objective purposes, notably that of restoring the presence of the subaltern to literature and history. Existential anguish in the face of cultural and national desintegration had precipitated a search for a signifying project that would sustain a sovereign self-identity. How better than by resorting the language of the enemy? Writing in French did not mean turning towards the future and erasing the past – a highly literary and glorious Arabic past at that. The truth was that most of the Maghrebi elite trained in French schools had been poorly educated in formal Arabic. So despite their admirable intentions, too often French was their default language. After the First World War, a wave of Maghrebi francophone writers drew on non-linear as well as more complex critical relationships between aesthetic value and political purpose. While French editors and readers judged Maghrebi authors for their ability to create plausible characters and plots associated with the native exotic, it became obvious that there was more to their efforts than that. What had been rejected and deformed by the colonizers was now being reintroduced behind the veil of non-contentious cultural politics, mostly because there were hardly any native readers. Fiction writing, especially after the Second World War, cultivated an anticipatory consciousness, resorting to either saturated realism or autobiographical scenarios that dramatized subjectivity. This barely challenged the prevailing orthodoxies, be they French or native, but eventually literature would compete with politics for the spotlight in the emancipation movement, which became the defining feature of postcolonial literature until the early 1980s.

What matters most is that francophone literature slowly aligned itself with the dominant historical narrative. Something more was needed to shoulder the political struggle, even if the writing itself could hardly be deemed nationalistic. Perhaps the emphasis on the literary process added more rootedness to an identity issue that had been buried under decades of self-hatred and the subjugation of a national consciousness. The central point to draw from this form of reorientation is that, as it sought a unified vision of subject and nation, it conceived of new possibilities where before there had been no prototype, no true account. It should not be surprising that it was in Algeria, where colonialism had been most enduring and most brutal, that francophone literature first appeared. Fiction writing by Maghrebi authors was a tool for a reductive ideology and a place where decolonization of the self could begin. Still, were these native intellectuals liberated from an alienation from their own history, and from the symbolic structure of language? The French language made Arabic look older. Furthermore, fiction writing brought out social issues related to origin and mimesis. Orientalism had posited Arab culture in terms of confrontation, to the point of negating its scientific legacy (from the ninth century onwards); now, francophone literature from the Maghreb was setting the challenge of nationhood on a steeper course by keeping to an "I" that spoke both for the individual and for collective resistance. Mouloud Feraoun, the last novelist of the colonial period, who was assassinated in March 1962 during the final truce, wrote in his diary: "Is it possible that while labels abound, I don't have my own? What is mine? Somebody tell me what I am!"[40]

7 A View from *Diversité*: Writing and Nation

It is in the postcolonial condition and literature of contemporary France that I find my strongest illustration of the impact of latent Orientalism. Indeed, this is certainly a better option than becoming the negotiated term in my own cultural impermanence in a country where unease with postcolonial politics has been considerable – probably as considerable as the unease with moral relativism and with the many incarnations of the *mission civilisatrice*. *Beur* literature will highlight the particular notion of a social text and its many challenges. But my purpose is not to market postcolonial Frenchness, which has been created, as we will see, out of a process of unlearning and an estrangement of identity. Rather, I will draw on the domain of subjectivity and what has been alluded to as the fabrication of the cultural subject while old national parameters continue to erode …

In chapter 22 of *Le tiers-livre de Pantagruel*, Rabelais merged fantasy with cultural realism in his depiction of the *marrabais*, the Christianized Arabs and Jews of sixteenth-century Spain. Rabelais's creation of degenerate monsters reflected political realities in Western Europe, where nationhood was gathering momentum and purity was on the agenda. The word *marrabais*, a compound of *mécréant–Arabes–Rabelais*, underscored the dangers of miscegenation in France at a time when purity of national language and culture was an emerging concept.[1] Half a century later, in Shakespeare's *The Tempest* (Act I, scene ii), Caliban, whose mother is from Algiers, threatens to corrupt Prospero's lineage by populating the island with his (Caliban's) descendants. These challenges of physical presence, displacement, and destiny are not simply critical tools that have sprung up in postcolonial theories. The semantics and subject matter of identity, both national and individual, did not materialize in opposition to the tenets of imperial control until the late nineteenth and early twentieth centuries. But the story is much older and runs deeper. In Europe alone, national identity has been acted upon for centuries, albeit with a single shared purpose – to read oneself as advanced, superior, and self-aware. This fantasy of domination culminated in the colonized's voluntary submission. More precisely, this ideological illusion rested on a sense that domination worked because the colonized Other desired to become like the European. The great trick of Orientalism was to transpose fear onto recognition; the French, to become fully French, had to build a dependency on the Other. For this reason the colonial designation itself took different names over the course of more than a century.[2] So, what can we read in this condition? Does it apply to twentieth-century North African immigrant communities in France? To what extent can the descendants of the former colonized become qualified French citizens? These questions draw us towards the vast field of cultural studies and its irksome relative categories and treasure trove of rhetorical activism. Certainly the postcolonial condition in France seems mired in "being," "representation," "minority," "the real," and "subjectivity," yet the discourse itself is overwhelmingly subsumed by amorphous, transcontinental nomenclatures. Latent Orientalism is all the more potent because national character and sovereignty, both in France and in Europe, have been withering away; it all comes down to entropy. To be clear, the ideas I have chosen face their own challenges; what matters most is that we pursue them in such a way that their value is vested in the autonomous subject, both postcolonial and academic.

The identity framework initially seems to have been determined by the dominant culture, within the boundaries of a nation that still yearned to prove itself at the expense of the Other. The immigration of Arabs and blacks was at first a continuation of their colonial status. A strategy to abjure tendencies towards independence helped control North African immigrants. This political and economic platform operated rather smoothly, largely because the immigrants bowed down on their basic rights and even felt grateful for improvements in their economic condition; this helped buttress both French power and the immigrants' own humanity. In France, the purity of colonial hierarchies was maintained by political and class structures, as well as by varying degrees of material comfort – or at least the promise of it. This dynamic changed for the children of postcolonial immigrants, who valued and claimed the principle of universality and French citizens's rights. The

abstract universalism of the Enlightenment (established as the foundation of the civilizing mission) yielded when faced with the reality of col-
liding worlds. The children of immigrants co-opted the right to vote that
had been denied to their parents (most of whom kept their citizenships
from their newly independent native lands); they also self-consciously
resisted dealing with language and citizenship issues. A monolinguism
with few guarantees of dialogue took root. Where Arabic was the language of the parents, French was always the children's mother tongue.
Language was a conduit for the pain that official history dismissed or
failed to convey. Between a Maghrebi background and French citizenship, the identity feature has hardly been understood for what it is: a
defensive strategy for coping with historical silence and social invisibility. Little wonder that the first wave of expression from immigrants'
children arose in the heart of French cultural fetishism: in literature,
and at the exact time when the Ministry of Culture heightened its visibility while the Ministry of the Colonies faded away. The symmetry is
striking and raises this question: How do we theorize France's national
character from the vantage point of postcolonial culture?

Between 1977 and 2007,[3] *Beur* writers in France published more
than 170 novels, plays, autobiographies, and diaries.[4] A mere number,
though, does not capture the breadth of the revolution that has occurred
in French letters. Were all of these works merely fledgling expressions
of life in the *banlieue*, or are they symptoms of a multicultural transition
in France? The abundance of articles and essays about *Beur* literature,
on both sides of the Atlantic, strongly suggests that literary criticism
is substituting socio-scientific terminology for the terminology of the
old anthropological paradigm. Michel Laronde, Alec Hargreaves, and
Mireille Rosello have offered forceful accounts and critiques of how,
since the mid-1980s, a new literary semantics has fused with the age-old
concept of a national language. How is France's identity being tested
by its postcolonial citizens? One need not be reminded that assimilation was shaped by steady and violent contact between the dominant
nation-state and the peoples of its empire. Rosello suggests that *Beur*
authors balk at playing identity politics, that they have been "reluctant
witnesses."[5] Of course, the spectral power of France has ceased to be
operative because French truly is the mother tongue: colonial suppres-
sion simply does not function any longer. It has been replaced by the
rhetoric of identity, something that drags *Beur* literature onto the lop-
sided terrain of the postcolonial condition and its rationalizations and
historical legacies. For example, the deconstructive turn of *Beur* literary

writing (its use of slang, hip hop, American English, Arabic, and French) is conveniently construed as an urge to preserve one's own foreignness, or what the French mainstream media call resistance to *intégration*. So even if within the confines of the French republic, identity is somehow untangled (they are French, aren't they?), it still needs to be deciphered. One matter in particular calls for attention: literary critics have left the *Beur* literary phenomenon largely unexplored while they sketch cultural confrontations between the Christian and Islamic cultural spheres and parse out the differences between the Maghrebi migrations to France and those of Poles, Italians, or Spaniards. Furthermore, those who argue from a postcolonial critique (especially a Marxist one) that *Beur* literature is the product of a linear view of history fail to note or to explain that in similar circumstances, a similar mass movement had sprung up even earlier in Britain, among the children of immigrants from the Indian Subcontinent. Latent Orientalism is marked by a defensive depiction of the pain and despair of the now-French Other, which gathers new meaning for the colonial trace it represents within the postcolonial condition. It is no longer a matter of imposing representations from the outside, but of letting the subjects themselves reprise the ancient figures of irrationality, violence, laziness, and social inadequacy that were once applied to them. No wonder the *banlieue* becomes saturated with the stigma of lawlessness and linguistic breakdown, along with the menace of a "foreign" core, something that especially sullies the purity of a public education system that is meant to turn students into citizens. As a consequence of the challenge to linguistic high culture, cultural chauvinism has become embedded in all French institutions. Alain Finkielkraut, a declared foe of postmodernism and postcolonial studies, has been one vocal advocate of national culture against what he calls "tribal cultures," lamenting that third-generation French citizens, descended from families from the former colonies, hate France.[6] The fantasy of civic and cultural uniformity is not the only culprit here. One wonders whether the publishing industry itself does not validate a patronizing, beneficent intervention in the name of a recognition that is failing everywhere else in French society.[7] The year after the November 2005 riots that broke out in the suburbs, there was a near doubling in the number of novels published by *Beur* authors. Did this surge relate less to literary aesthetics than to a historicist orientation in the face of Orientalist anxiety over the foreign-yet-French body?[8]

Scholars engaged in francophone studies too often find themselves in a state of what could be called anticolonial indenture, whereby they use

Beur literature as a surrogate for all crises of authority in contemporary French culture. Perhaps this new literature from within France reflects an effort to break away from both French and francophone canons. Hargreaves, a prominent scholar on *Beur* literature, contends that this may always have been "a culture without a name."[9] That is probably an accurate assessment, but it raises a question: Are we postulating a theory of cultural default, as if *Beur* literature amounted to a counterpart of national allegories (the performativity of French national language and culture post-empire)?

Actually, the literary disruption involves more than mere cultural classification or authoritative labelling. *Beur* works reach into the heart of a neocolonial ethos that is alive and well. Political and media discourses, for example, engage in an endless performative act of signifying French citizens of immigrant backgrounds as a threat to French identity and to institutions such as French public schools and the French tradition of secularism. When we fail to recognize this, we turn *Beur* into a postcolonial, academic pursuit that is itself a matter of representation and narcissism. This discourse on representation fails to acknowledge its own hegemonic momentum. The impression that results is that *Beur* literature has been placed on a continuum of liberation discourse, when in fact it never truly transcended colonial castration. *Beur* authors write because they feel threatened with non-signification, not because they are motivated by some uninhibited aesthetic endeavour, as we will discuss later. It should not be surprising that it is in Britain and North America, where postcolonial theories have flourished, the *Beur* literary subject is now attuned to what critics and scholars generate in their resolutely culturalist approach. This perspective is not a problem except insofar as ontological certainty is not guaranteed just because someone else claims to identify *Beur*'s difference.[10] One must determine how critical methods – language analyses, for example – can effectively disclose the merits and the spectrum of differences within a national literature. Immigration literatures in Germany, Britain, and France may share some basic assumptions (e.g., mother tongue issues, social-class consciousness, religious practices); by contrast, *Beur* literature has claimed a core of aesthetic *and* ideological intentions. The latter show, for example, the extent to which the issue of integration remains predominantly a political one. Inasmuch as assimilation policies failed during colonial times, the integration "buzzword" raises to awareness forms of cultural denial that are already familiar.[11] Identity itself, as seen in *Beur* literature, becomes a quality conveying contingent meanings, time- and place-specific, all of which are nonetheless entrenched in an ineradicable brand of French universalism. For non-postcolonial French citizens, the effective result is domestic imperialism: the *Beur* generation is relegated to second-class citizenship, a situation identical to the predicament of their parents or grandparents during colonial times. For example, the omnipresent symbolization of the dialectics between margin and centre (*banlieue/centre-ville*) continues to signify the denial of commonality, which in turn authorizes institutions and economic powers to stigmatize the people of the suburbs. In this sense, that *Beur* writers are being commodified by the publishing industry is a small but painful marker of identity, a means for them to protect themselves against the loss of everything else.

Beur literature's own awareness of its altered state of identity defines it in the first place. The texts are characterized by a mutating verbal activity that promotes the emergence of a new Hexagonal literature. Baring their nomadic cultures (from Maghreb to France, from *banlieue* to downtown), *Beur* writers display qualities that have little to do with the ethnic chic that has grown out of post-structuralism. *Beur* borrows from Maghrebi oral traditions (e.g., Berber tales, prayers, Arabo-Islamic narratives), Parisian slang, and an iconoclastic tradition that can be traced back to Villon's poetry. However new this fusion of genres and cultures may be, its roots are not. A withdrawal into a so far non-identified self (Arab, Berber, French, or all three?) and an outward impulse towards a referential language (French) seem to reveal the distinctively transitory nature of *Beur* literature. The mixing of codes has been prompted by an essential quality of literature: verbal creation and identity validation. This may be one reason why *Beur* authors tend to ignore the classic French literary style of writing and the intrinsic imagery of an established culture. The frenzy for social intelligibility, especially as it relates to the documentary dimension, should not mask the striving for literary form. In an early novel, Fouad Laroui[12] did away with the stock character of the mother overwhelmed with work (at home and moonlighting) who gets no respect for all she does: "Enough of all that! I do not want to abuse her. She's got to get off here (out of time, out of plot) with some consideration. I will not talk about Mina any longer."[13] Most of these novels tell the journeys of their protagonists through diverse social spheres; they also assign a new kind of power to words, when, for example, their authors realize there is no reliability in *either* linguistic source, Maghrebi or French. Rhetorical devices such as faulty grammar, the mutilation of standard French, and the juxtaposition of verbs, tenses, and varied lexical fields all strip the language of its established literary value. Stylistic expectations are indeed affected by this postcolonial *poiesis*. Over time, the once crystalline social frame of the author – what Mallarmé called "le Monsieur" and Barthes the *persona* – and his or her work becomes impenetrable to readers who know the *banlieue* and Islamic culture only through television news and Islamic culture via a latent Orientalist proxy.

Beur works resemble post-1970s African American novels[14] not because the French writers try to give an account of their racially charged daily lives, but because they strive to find their own voices within a dominant culture, while being wary of essentialist traps. French culture oppressed their parents under colonial rule and then again under the economic exploitation that attended postcolonial immigration to France. Over the same time frame, from the early 1950s to the mid-1970s, the parents'generation were never really considered potential constituents by any political party, including the Communist Party, because they could not vote and thus were less "valuable" than the traditional French working class. Politically and socially excluded from mainstream France, immigrant parents most often felt they had no choice but to force upon their French-born children an integration that had eluded them for so long. In this acquiescent attitude, we find an early sign that in the middle course of assimilation there would be no homecoming. From then on, home rested on the former enemy's territory. Place and time were challenged at all levels, individual and institutional, and this made *Beur* writers anxious to catch up with social reality. This is suggested by their works, which are saturated with discourses of integration, or by what Barthes, in a different identity context, called *la demande d'amour*.[15] But *Beur* feelings always wash about in a highly politicized space. Passive Orientalism has changed into active representation. There is nothing accidental in the social anguish of *Beur* narratives; discourse and creation work towards a unified view of literary production in order to heal a fractured image of the French Maghrebi self. The literary weaknesses of early *Beur* writings in the 1980s – weaknesses often construed as proof of authenticity (in stories revolving almost exclusively around life in the suburban ghettos) – actually bore the seeds of uniqueness. By echoing one another in contemporary France, *Beur* writers were talking to and about their own country with a distinctive language that was bound to become institutionalized by the publishing industry and through self-recognition. Characters and plots pointed towards a reality outside the merely socio-political sphere.

The paradox is that the stability of aesthetics and ideologies is achieved through the fluid relationships the writer sets into motion. In *Georgette!*, for example, Farida Belghoul explores the intricate relationship and mutual expectations between a daughter and her father.[16] In that sense, *Beur* literature is embedded in a discourse of production, although not necessarily along Marxist lines, because it relates to individuals rather than to history as the controlled, distant narrative of class subjugation. Yet the fact remains that whatever the eventual fate of their books may be, *Beur* authors are not committed to a literary movement, nor have they been fully accepted within their own ethnocultural community. The immediate effect of such an existential dilemma is to establish new standards for both writing and reading. *Beur* writers are blamed for not making serious efforts to integrate themselves into French universalism; at the same time, immigrant families view them as foresaking their original culture. This double-bind transcends cultural relativism within the frame of French literature through a unique style. The linguistic combinations (e.g., French and Arabic dialects, various slangs, cultural pastiches) form a discourse that has blazed a new path for literature without rejecting the language of the *Académie* per se. The most striking aspect of these works is their autobiographical content: they are more than sociological accounts – they are quests for order of the self. The notoriously taxing determination of the self in colonial times is from then on read as a device to valorize the identity momentum of the postcolonial condition. Omnipresent humour and raw realism has so far managed to accommodate the conflicts of the narrative voice, set in a larger frame of identity overflow. Just as African American writers tried to "lynch" or to jazz up the English language, *Beur* authors have sought to shape the French language into a verbal game, one that rejects any assumed objectivity validated by centuries of literature. More often than not, this involves a close scrutiny of the national ethos – of anything but a discourse of selfhood translated into words.

Beur writing is based on one fundamental premise: sacrifice. Authors who create by writing in tongues cut themselves off from their community even while remaining at the margins of a strongly Jacobinic literary world. This haunting position closely aligns that of their readers. Indeed, *Beur* novels are not bought and read by the *banlieue* people, the kith and kin of the authors. This literary "immolation" becomes conspicuous in family representations in the novels, which, regardless of their sometimes humorous or ironic content, tend to depict relatives and friends as victims. Behind the hidden (or not so hidden) issues of race and class, pain serves as the object for the stories, refuting through its very expression the fallacy that a lack of cultural maturity is attributable to linguistic dislocation. This linguistic disparity is underscored by the differences between an educated centre and an underdeveloped periphery in contemporary France.[17] *Beur* literature counterbalances the cultural see-saw by returning the world of the margins to the centre. It also turns the physical visibility of *Beur* youngsters, as a stigmatized and dangerous population group, into an intellectual one, as if the *foreign* body were replaced by a home-grown language and, it follows, a validated narrative.

Yet the postcolonial, theoretical language of a centre–periphery paradigm reveals itself as a code for colonial capitalism. The overarching trope of *Beur* fiction is one of the many incarnations of the profits yielded by cultural exploitation (e.g., by publishing houses, the media, and academe). The broad idea of French integration consists of literary productions that resurrect the whole concept of foreignness, except that the situation is no longer a matter of cross-cultural negotiations between East and West; rather, those negotiations are conducted *within* France as a postcolonial nation. Once the postcolonial culture (in literature as well as music) has replenished the national ethos in the guise of some benevolent multiculturalism – although the French cringe at that word – the pitfalls of a masquerading identity are not far off for *Beur* artists.

Although the issue of style remains open to subjective responses, for *Beur* writers, accommodating several cultural backgrounds produces greater richness of meanings. Their translinguistic exercises are reminiscent of invocations that eventually call attention to a changing culture. The stories allude heavily to the social realities of the *banlieue*: police harassment, drug trafficking, high unemployment, gender issues, discrimination, the place of Islam, and failing schools. But they also bear an irrational side-characteristic of spiritual experience. *Beur* writers are re-creating a world they know all too well, but they are also separating themselves from it by the very act of writing. This process of separation appears both systematic and inspired: systematic because the same structures (narratives, lexical fields, themes) are used time and time again; inspired because it is a new phenomenon in French literature that is helping redefine the cultural order and a sense of identity within society itself. Writers like Artaud, Desnos, and Michaux have experimented with a language-beyond-a-language and cultural transfers (notably with Asia), but their experiments remained sporadic, highly individualized, and limited to the field of poetry. The language of classical French literature and that of the media are rendered unusable in *Beur* fiction because of changes to both the function and the spirit of writing. *Beur* authors no longer conceive of immigrants and their children as victims unable or unwilling to talk back when confronted with the neocolonial reality of France. Their spirit and function have changed also because they do not underplay institutional violence, according to which, for example, the paradigm of universal humanism is defined in terms of French culture, as represented by the official language, public schools, the justice system, militant secularism,[18] and centralization. While the new literature highlights the extent of the damage done to non-Gallic French citizens, it cannot be taken as some kind of social project speaking for the oppressed. Indeed, *Beur* writers tend to separate themselves from any process of subjugation, be they postcolonial victims or members of the dominant culture. In their works there is a sense that writing is first and foremost talking to oneself. The *Beur*'s literary affinity consists of dramatizing selfhood under the fetishistic demands of French *diversité*. In this light, the autobiographical and schizoid dimensions of *Beur* literature acquire the status of outer-directed assertions as well as inner-directed testimonies. *Beur* practitioners denounce the unfairness of the job market, an unmistakable hallmark of discrimination: "We are unemployment fodder as they were cannon fodder ... And what about the hundreds of mailed résumés – for nothing! What about job interviews – for nothing! What about open applications – for nothing! Even worse, internships: lies, legal tricks, a mockery of jobs, damn it all – Oualououououou!"[19]

The awareness of a dual position, French and foreign (i.e., non-postcolonial, non-Christian) at the same time, shows the line of separation between francophone and *Beur* literatures. It is within itself that literature becomes a awareness of one's Otherness in the sphere of identification that French literature has always been. For example, Dumas *père*, Zola, Proust, Beckett, Sarraute, Kundera, Makine, and Dai Sijie are all considered French writers *par excellence*, even though none of them qualifies as truly Gallic.[20] However, the principal difference between those writers and *Beur* novelists lies within the former colonial frame and its unavoidable cultural inheritance. The novels enunciate the invocations of cultural commitment and the legitimizing strategies for national identity. In *Beur* writing, Otherness still needs to be domesticated against homegrown exoticism.

In a sense, *Beur* literature bears the promise of redemption, but whose redemption? The geographical literalization of intermingled Maghreb and France induces in *Beur* writers a conviction that literature has become both a blessing and a challenge. It is from the particular point of view of mixed cultural identities that the meeting of tongues can become a tool for denouncing historical conditioning and cultural deprivation. Language itself is a series of subjective vibrations that are close to Barthes's famous concept of adding up in order to erase: "While talking, I can never rub out, erase, cancel; all I can do is to say 'I cancel, I erase, I correct', that is I still talk."[21]

The language of *Beur* writers seems almost French because, while the syntax and the lexical fields are predetermined, the writer's own identity remains unknown – or rather, appears unstable, because of his or her awareness that there are no models on which to base one's own cultural assumptions. It is not surprising that *Beur* writers are acutely aware of language, be it used for caricature or for pseudorealistic purposes. Laroui, for example, plays with words and with the reader at the same time: "I was chased after by the tors. The what? The tors. The collec-tors! What's the matter? Can't you understand French?"[22] The verbal scheme expresses the sense of continuous transition of the self that flies in the face of the ethos of a classic French aesthetic as best represented in its literature. It is not surprising, then, that a self-declared far-right writer and Islam-basher like Renaud Camus, for example, is also an advocate for pure, classical French writing.[23] He turns culture into an accessory for letting racism off the hook. In this sort of confrontation, *Beur* literature does not obsess over singularity or foster "anti-French" taxonomies; rather, it "extends" itself, just like the multiple branches of the transit system that runs between the *banlieues* and Paris – a connection of sorts.

Under the veil of postcolonial status, something remains hidden or undiscovered. Perhaps that something is a response to the republican obsession with *intégration*, or perhaps it relates more to an unsettling Maghrebi heritage. The exterior materiality (mostly identity politics) gives way to textual indeterminacy – something that tends to explain the emphasis on realism in *Beur* novels. For example, the deterministic grasp of space – one in which the *banlieue* itself becomes a character – establishes a sense of separateness, a sort of metaphor for individuality. The newer generation (Rachid Djaïdani and Mohamed Razane, for example) expect to be read against the elder generations (like Mehdi Charef or Azouz Begag), but then they break away from ethnic constraints. This dialectics of "us" versus "them" (all of whom are French) is propelled by a struggle for objectivity and recognition. In a sense, latent

Orientalism sits right there, unconscious, even amorphous, yet something that creates new levels of resistance against alienation, or rather an overidentification with a cultural learning curve that would overtake generic distinctions. In this context, *Beur* literature distinguishes itself utterly from so-called francophone literature, which requires not only a clear historical, institutional, sociocultural, and ethnic identification but also subcategories such as Maghrebi, sub-Saharan, Caribbean, Asian, Acadian, Québécois, and European. Furthermore, *Beur* literature is not rooted in historical, confrontational modes of "us" (i.e., former colonized people) *versus* France, where the language assumes political ramifications as well as ideological slippage. On the contrary, *Beur* novels read like a convulsion from the inside; they express a strong desire to belong even while asserting one's own cultural features. So literature is less a matter of exorcising some colonial sin than of trying to use culture in every possible way because it is theirs, and the language is only a property of the writing. The struggle to assert oneself becomes a function of the writing itself, a way to play with language so as to take the edge off words and refract them into a consciousness of *Beur*-ness in society at large. The writing helps project a postcolonial symbolic order that supersedes worn-out claims of Otherness in favour of a much vaunted legitimacy.

This literary dialogue is all the more disquieting in women's writings (Farida Belghoul, Djura, Leila Houari, Tassadit Imache, or Soraya Nini), as if these writers were calling into question *all* dominant discourses. They compete to be heard both at home and in their books. Generally, the point of view of the writer provides a sense of unity, although early *Beur* literature seemed to be mostly in the same thematic vein: exploring a socially closed and determined world with social stereotypes and stock characters within a pre-established system (confrontations in the classrooms, *banlieue*/downtown oppositions, dysfunctional families, racism and self-hatred, representations of the police as the arch-enemy, conflicts with employers, and various forms of denied love). Then in the 1990s came more political disillusionment, when the artifice became all too visible or predictable, so *Beur* authors shifted to a more reactive type of writing, as if its first incarnation had been necessary to denounce all forms of authority. Violence was a historical *and* aesthetic extension of the deconstructive drifts so natural to their identity crises. A dynamic begins to take shape in this literature as it becomes the component of a new expression that is neither sociological theory nor part of a multiculturalist manifesto. Instead of simply tackling issues regarding the soul or consciousness in a work of art, *Beur* literature has evolved into a matter of writing in a new language that refuses to be a commodity, fetishized through the dialectics of French latent Orientalism. More recent *Beur* writing seems to bring into being the conventions of anticonformist individualism with dissonant, schizophrenic characters. In one of her most recent novels, *Des nouvelles de Kora* (2009), Tassadit Imache alludes to identity as an unstable mental condition that predetermines the subject's desire for her roots. France and Algeria fail to embody the imaginary safe and atoning power. Eventually, the mother projects more ambiguity, more splitting of the signified of identity and being: "To live, you'll find out dear daughter, is to manufacture forgetfulness and lies."[24]

French literary institutions (the publishing establishment, the literary prizes, the Paris-based media, the academic institutions) inevitably position themselves as ahead of or behind *Beur* literature. With *Beur* writing, one can talk about a critical movement in all possible meanings of that term. This is a cultural as well as a temporal process, whose purpose is to clarify itself in order to elude the complexities of social realism. *Beur-ness* as a cultural archetype is to be replaced by *Beur-ness* as an artistic identity. In that sense, *Beur* literature should be subordinated to political conjecture because its authors want to unplug themselves from representations of the oppressed, downtrodden minority as mediated by French cultural and economic actors. The mixing of languages parallels the confusion of cultural issues with questions of race. Not surprisingly, the stories themselves bear a performative charge rather than a simple identification with words, as if the writers were churning the waters between cultures. By strongly personalizing themselves and motives, the authors establish a specific cultural space for themselves while maintaining French as an imprimatur of significance. This dual existence explains why *Beur* literature rarely touches on the Maghrebi culture of the parents, who are not French citizens and are often still strongly attached to their native lands. The children of immigrants are unlikely to turn to Algeria, Morocco, or Tunisia for their cultural antecedents. This cultural distance draws on an identity argument that claims to negate the immigrant parents' own identity. In this sense, *Beur* writers are trying to construct a more powerful platform for themselves by being first writers, then *Beur*. This emphasis on creation constitutes a final break from colonial castration. That is why the Maghreb is rarely a destination; there is no bonding ritual with some lost paradise. Not surprisingly, what that seems to interest the most recent *Beur* writers more than anything else is American hip hop, not the Maghreb's musical or literary traditions. This is obvious in Rachid Djaïdani's *Mon nerf*, in which the main character appears to be both mentally unstable and dead as well as carried away by his own semantic music and aliteration rythms: "I'll head for the train station and melt into the guts of my train, my choo-choo, my suburban railroad car. To run away to my shrink and spill the beans."[25]

Once the paradigmatic movement has been identified, a key condition for literary creation has been met, albeit with a certain amount of selection. The *Beur* writer chooses from images or situations that pre-existed him but that the subject under the French assimilationist steamroller either denied or knew nothing about.

In this sense, *Beur* writing is informed by identity conflicts that tend to preclude any conception of a hegemonic culture because more often than not, the writer's experience is based on the model of a colonized people. French literature is thus reshaped and made accountable for what needs to be formulated with regard to the sustained negation of equal participation in the dominant culture. This offers no pretext for bourgeois bewilderments about artistic traditions or for the intellectual essentialism embedded in elite *Grandes Écoles*. *Beur* writers leave aside that which does not interest them about French literature, an entity that is embedded in a system that would exorcise their foreignness. Writing becomes a flight from the fixation on or repetition of an Orientalist present that wishes to shape the *Beur* writer into a referential token of literature – a demarcation between history (colonization and immigration) and the archival sphere of (French) universal textuality. Here, publishers' attitudes ought to alert us to the patronizing project (and fantasy) of mapping French *diversité* in terms of the postcolonial condition. If such a project were to succeed, *Beur* literature would find itself mediated not through writing, rhetoric, and style, but through a twisted referent based on essentialism and globalized construction. France would then be able to boast its own multiculturalist fetish with these "French-Arabs," just as the British have with their Anglo-Indian or Anglo-Pakistani writers and the Germans with their Turkish-German writers.

Beur writers pick and choose elements of French culture and language in order to construct a new literary system capable of addressing their own identities. By denying the French language its pre-existing values, they make it new. They expand the borders of cultural politics – something that has always made the intellectual establishment uneasy. But this exercise in "undoing" the possibilities of a national literature does not amount to theorizing some homegrown deconstruction. For one thing, does *Beur* literature exist in itself or is it a historical by-product that has taken the shape of a cultural commodity? Put another way, are *Beur* writers fashioning a new literary subjectivity into something French, thereby creating more instability?[26] Alienation, like possession, is more about the subject than the culture: *Beur* novels do not represent French culture; they are French culture with the imaginary wholeness of identification. This distinction is something that latent Orientalism, with its narcissism about nationhood, has never allowed, because *différence* means division.

Perhaps these writers became influential because they generated forms of power by countering their parents' situations as well as that of the suburban community at large. One wonders where the multicultural paradigm then stands. Against the dialectics of cultural and multicultural realities, *Beur* literature opposes a typological difference within the whole of French culture. By betting on, or playing down, the opposition inherent in a dialectic of "us *versus* them," *Beur* writing tends to reinforce the essence of French culture, in terms of both duration and change. Ambivalence helps avoid any reliance on racial and cultural stereotypes. This literature adds a qualitative dimension to a multicultural concept that is not yet fully understood within French institutional life, both political and cultural. Contrary to the Anglo-Saxon model, in France it is not the society that is multicultural but the individual. The far from perfect "separate but equal" British model becomes in France a disavowing moment for the postcolonial subject: citizenship is reiterated not just in terms of conformity but also within the time lag of the former colonial situation. So it is not surprising that *Beur* writers are never conferred the authority of intellectuals; their works are unequivocally framed within the postcolonial experience, that is to say, they are perceived as a matter of flowing identity rather than representative ideas.

The allegorical place of such a reality is the city, which in *Beur* literature happens to be divisible (into ethnic neighbourhoods, foreign languages spoken, and the emergence of value systems). This split suggests mediation, just like graffiti in the suburban housing project or tags on subway cars that claim "I am here" yet remain anonymous. The city also represents the sum total of its various aspects. Such a literary representation often shows a subject at home among those separate modes but also torn between different worlds. These novels help redefine the concerns within the French postmodern cultural consciousness.

For example, Paul Smaïl depicts the urban native space of his protagonist hero as follows: "Apart from the far away University of Paris-X, that is to say Nanterre, to where I used to commute by train, I have spent all my life within a territory marked out by La Fourche, La Chapelle, La République, La Trinité [all located in working-class districts in the northeast of Paris]."[27] Here the actual locations point in the direction of one interpretation, always assumed and rarely acknowledged: the city becomes the confirmation of the subject with a clear identity, that is, a born-and-bred Parisian. The supposed foreignness of *Beur*, both physically and linguistically speaking, transcends the boundaries of the "here *versus* there" of latent Orientalism. These relics of the industrial age, with their working-class neighbourhoods, coexist with a postcolonial repossession of space, which in this particular novel contains an extra layer of cultural simulacra. But of course, what is missing is the Orientalist, moralist view of cultural enlightenment and technological improvement even while ghettos underscore France's record of "multicultural" achievements.

A prevailing development in *Beur* literature is that it explores the complex relationship between convergence and division within French society over the past thirty years. Guiding the act of writing is the opposition to Jacobinic visions of French culture and its language on the one hand and the protean identity of the Franco-Maghrebi subject on the other. This highly significant *topos* helps locate the direction of daily life in the *banlieue* and in working-class Parisian neighbourhoods. It took a long time for French institutions (the media, political parties, academe) to recognize this cultural mediation: *Beur* novels first appeared in the early 1980s, at a time when a *Beur* generation existed, although more as a political oddity than as a cultural symbol. The tongues they wrote in attracted curiosity, if not scepticism, from the French literary establishment. Nowadays, at a time when the literary imagination in Franco-French literature has fallen prey to self-indulgence, narcissism, nationalism, and autobiographical exhibitionism, *Beur* novelists show a love for linguistic exploration and are refashioning public discourse after their own experience. This gift for cultural translation has kept the texts alive but also left them quickly outdated. No wonder that after thirty-plus years, not a single *Beur* writer has been awarded a major literary prize in France. This exclusion speaks to more than a national literary system that long ago lost its *panache*.

Beur literature proves that literary solipsism ("I am what I write") is a variant of sociological solipsism ("I am what I live"); it also transcends the mere communicative function of writing in favour of a quest for experimentation. This decentring of *the* French culture from within has sharply demystified European as well as Maghrebi narratives. *Beur* novels are less indebted to intellectual trends than to an exceptional boldness of expression, without mistaking politics for history. In that sense, these new French writers work out everything that corresponds to a determined historical period in terms of temporality (the emergence of a new generation), difference (the emergence of a new literature), and heterogeneity (the underscoring of ethnic identities over Franco-French assumptions). Their language is performative in character and aesthetic in content; however, the transfer of *Beur* literature into films or rap music testifies to the limited range of the generation's voice. A concern for Arab and Berber origins and explorations of French reality and language can heighten emotions but rarely achieves aesthetic fulfilment. Personal history and sociological self-consciousness are not enough to make literature. All of the linguistic, cultural, and ideological codes that *Beur* novelists have inherited have helped fix the moment of truth when the *reality* of being French meets the *sensation* of it. It is all about being within a fiction, but is it explicit enough? In *Les ANI du Tassili*, Akli Tadjer illustrates that cruel moment when the hero takes a symbolic reverse passage across the Mediterranean and realizes that he cannot understand Algerian culture, much less fit into it, and that he is a Frenchman in spite of himself.[28] Thus *Beur* identity appears to be informed by both cultural criticism and emancipatory pronouncements.

Of course, the *topos* of transnationality conflates globalization with French universalism without addressing the latent Orientalism that feeds on cultural difference or a sense of superiority. Early works were too often autobiographical; *Beur* writing offers new literary forms that stake out an individual space along the French ideological spectrum. Unlike the novelists of the *Nouveau Roman*, whose break from traditional structures and the bourgeois content of high realism coincided with the purest use of the French language and a strictly Gallic perspective, *Beur* novelists occupy the dissonant space between identity and culture in contemporary France. The conflation of form with language is facilitated by committing attention both to a reality kept silent for too long and to a need to map out a new imaginary landscape. *Beur* writers, preoccupied with the modes in which their fellow *Beur* are constituted into French subjects, turn their literary scrutiny towards everyday language, family breakdowns, racial and sexual violence, and the workplace, as well as to the political impact of the school system and the media. As if to make amends for the failures of the colonial undertaking, the French institutional system has pretended to integrate at any cost French citizens of foreign origins, yet evading material history does not make *Beur* literature any more legitimate within France's cultural institutions. In this respect, the convergence of what fiction or autobiographical characters feel, think, and say has become a constant feature of *Beur* literature: that is the new script of national character where cultural transfer happens. The novelist turns out to be both a transmitter and an advocate of this important dimension of contemporary French culture. One can say that *Beur* literariness calls attention to itself by bringing out affective meaning (personal experience) and a referential function (an inescapable postcolonial condition). Rosello observes about this particular subversive state: "'French' culture can conceive of itself as an autonomous entity only because its foundational discourses foster a sort of amnesia about its origins."[29] In the particular case of *Beur* literature, the novelist's position within the culture reflects as much a linguistic venture as a dramatization of recent French history. The unique use of codes generates a transmutation from social experience (life in the *banlieue*) to aesthetic pursuit, one that belongs neither to what francophone Maghrebi literature stands for nor to the literature produced by middle-class French authors. *Beur* literature's attitude towards writing contradicts past tradition. For *Beur* novelists a book is rarely a projection of a single point of view or a single aspect of society. It is rather a process of relativizing the writer's status and an insight into the genealogy of French discourses. *Beur* writers translate the position of the postcolonial subject in society and history. There is a story that needs to be told, regardless of the genre used or the socio-historical contexts, in which the radical act of writing makes it even more difficult to answer subject-centred questions such as, "Who is the I that says I for us *Beur* people?" As Michael Riffaterre put it regarding reception theories: "History is pertinent only to the circumstances of literary production, that is, to the genesis of the work of art and to its reception."[30] There is a sense that there is no historical origin, no natural affirmation of linguistic codes (Arabic is not recognized outside the home/*banlieue*, and at home French is mutilated, consciously or not), and a decline of the idea that the unique French culture legitimates the claims of *Beur* writers to poetic necessity. The world of the *banlieue* cannot be left without formulations about a new territory, filled at first with graffiti, then with novels. Yet these original formulations tend to fade away as *Beur* novelists try to create their autonomous literary selves.

In *Beur* literature, French culture is not threatened by plurality but rather enriched by it; this is the much-worked concept of remapping postcolonial France, *sans* the magic name of Benedict Anderson and his "imagined communities," which may share few interests in contemporary France. The age-old duality of "us versus them," reinforced by the ideologies of the French Republic and latent Orientalism, is shattered because that Other, who is also French, albeit not Gallic (in the national-identitarian meaning) and even less Christian, claims an identity of citizenship, rights, and language. The challenge for France is that there exists sameness yet no affiliation. So while *Beur* literature is self-inscriptive, it is also divested of its signifiers. The French publishing establishment is well aware that the *Beur* phenomenon is what we call today a culture, inseparable from the idea of France, both for historical reasons (colonialism) and sociological ones (the emergence of post-immigration generations). *Beur* literarary artistry is not limited to trendy multicultural codes whereby France, like the United States, produces a crop of multicultural writers. It is, rather, a matter of possessing the language. The truths of French literature pale beside the *Beur* world's version of reality. The displacement factor from the margins to the centre disappears along with the cultural complexities ("Who are those French writers who don't even have Christian names?"). Farida Belghoul explains the delicate balancing act between value and fact in fiction writing: "If I were writing in Arabic, there would be a sort of continuity; by choosing French I have the feeling that I am trampling on my heritage."[31]

The affective and intellectual charge generated by the imposition of language sets aside other cultures in terms of both production and meanings. At the same time, as it has slowly transformed itself (as of 2013, there have been at least four *Beur* generations), French society has learned to address some of its accepted ideas such as anti-Islamic prejudice and stereotypes of the *banlieue* world, even though those peripherals of the postcolonial condition are patently French.[32]

The argument for cultural exchanges through *Beur* literature becomes the marker of self-cognitive status as well as public knowledge. In Charef's first seminal novel, one of the characters replies to a police officer: "I am a Frenchman. I live in my own country. What do you take me for? An Arab, or what?"[33] The language itself points to a controversial notion, a way not only of communicating but also of being. In France, French equals non-Arab, but what about Arabs who are French? Clearly, there is no cultural determinism here but rather a series of principles that are either validated or rejected. The subaltern, proletarian figure is cast as a radical foreigner because of language and religion. This is perhaps how French can turn into a tool for resentment, not simply the premise for national identity. Such a reality calls to mind a literature at a crossroads between languages, histories, gender, and religion, where it is no longer the object that bears the brunt of criticism but the subject. That is why *Beur* writers seem to assume their new positions as speakers and creators within a national culture in crisis, those crises being the inevitable integration of France within the European Union, the loss of power on the international scene, an obsession with preserving its language, issues of immigration, and the place of Islam within a secular framework, not to mention the tide against political correctness that is opposing postcolonial theory. If it is language that has established *Beur* literature as such, then writers have managed to examine French culture from their own vantage point, be it in the *banlieue* or even the Maghreb.

In that cultural transition, from what is seen to what is chosen to be told, literary works turn out to be less sociologically oriented and more situated within the framework of complex novelty, with literature serving as a point of departure from the constraints of high culture, as if writing itself had become the metaphor for migration. *Beur* linguistic relativism is a paradoxical branch of multiculturalism, since it is rooted in a belief in, or an attachment to, a specific culture – namely, French. This literature, though, keeps open cultural windows that authenticate the French language as a medium for communication, whatever its claims to exclusivity. Yet those linguistic formulations do not mean that the *Beur* world speaks French. It is simply programmed with a language that causes writers to hold beliefs about the connection between language and identity. In a way, *Beur* literature is a corrective to French ethnocentrism, having situated itself as far as it can from neocolonial mimesis. This writing turns the glances inward with a new language of identity struggle, thereby forcing other Frenchmen to speak on their own.

French readers are often required to decode Maghrebi references, be they linguistic or cultural. This interplay of translation reflects a conscious resistance to voyeuristic exoticism. Latent Orientalism, which operates with identificatory mechanisms, is activated and set back to an aggressive mode of external images and Otherness. The writing visualizes power inasmuch as it represents an expropriation of the dominant culture. Yet the disavowal is incomplete, because *Beur* literature fulfils only partly the promise of citizenship by turning the suburban subject into an authoritative symbol. The *Beur* desire for recognition is ambivalent and may reveal a neocolonial continuum in the guise of intercultural interpretation. This sort of literary pragmatism may be inspired by Maghrebi francophone literature, which attempts to write out any neocolonial takeover, although the vast majority of works continue to be published in Paris, largely for French readers.

Because of their early literary contradictions or limitations (their works comprise mostly autobiographical accounts, repetitive *topoi*, and stylistically coarse and stereotypical representations), *Beur* novels tend to demonstrate that French society has been derailed from its ethnocentric dynamic. In such a system, the unidimensional national subject manages to speak in the name of the new citizen involved in cultural exchanges. *Beur* literature chronicles the slow erosion of the French literary canon by playing those two subjects – national and *Beur* – against each other. It is not surprising that most *Beur* novelists are suspicious of morally upstanding protagonists (indeed, all are afflicted with many flaws) and are unwilling to incorporate genealogical inquiries into their stories. At the core of this type of writing is the validity of the subject. What identity? What language? What function? Unsurprisingly, French academe tends to treat *Beur* literature as part of francophone studies. There is still a temptation to think of the French world as possessing a static essence, particularly in how it privileges language and a universal narrative. Insurmountable cultural barriers are less significant for French-Arab writers, who tend to identify their works with Hexagonal literature, not that of the Maghreb. One writer goes so far as to state: "They [*Beur* writers] are motivated by references that belong to French culture and are activated by their will to become French."[34] Without being too categorical or parochial, *Beur* literature succeeds in isolating the forces that govern the postcolonial condition in France, namely Orientalist attraction and post-9/11 political revulsion towards the Arab world. What seems true about these forces is that the original culture and language of the parents, who were born and raised in the Maghreb, hold little relevance for the children born in France. Too often the Arabic language (or rather the Berber and Arabic dialects spoken throughout North Africa) presents the *Beur* generation with a disjunctive reality. They never fully mastered Arabic in the first place, so it comes to symbolize the patterns of exclusion and humiliation endured by their parents in their daily lives. No wonder this particular literature seems shaped by an alliance of antagonisms describing the process of a spirit gradually becoming self-conscious and thereby enriching itself.

With an abundance of possible meanings, *Beur* novels have produced a language in themselves, but one that is different from that of the *banlieue* because they are reclaiming imagination for their authors even while exorcising postcolonial hierarchies. A balancing act between self-hatred and self-esteem remains inscribed in a discourse that sets the pace for an emancipatory literature, or at least a discourse in search of its significant centre. These forms of language stake out the never-ending quest for self-development in a culture that conceives of identity from the perspective of repression (in all senses). For example, in her *Journal*, Sakinna Boukhedenna underscores the challenge she had to face:

> It's in France that I learned how to be an Arab.
> It's in Algeria that I learned how to be an immigrant.[35]

Both the parents' culture and canonical French literature are faithless mirrors. Literature helps act out the fantasy of origin, not that the origin is unknown; rather, it is repressed. This structure of desire – masochistic in French culture, sadistic in Maghreb cultures – strikes one as a unique characteristic of the postcolonial condition. Whereas the parents reproduce an identified language, *Beur* writing creates a sense of awareness that in some ways resembles a theory of liberation within the looming cultural battles of the Hexagon. This literature can be violent, comical, highly poetic, or realistic, but it always seems to point to the limits of a dialogue within a country where culture matters more than anything else precisely because it is political. *Beur* literature is impregnated with meanings – both meanings related to identifying issues, and more traditional meanings – that address the creative process itself. The novelty in the particular case of *Beur* writers is that meanings do not cancel one another out; on the contrary, they create correspondences. Codes and cultures are conceived as a series of levels that progressively dissociate themselves from the referents of a strictly political reality. For example, the attitude towards language (slang in particular) become more critical than trusting in order to negotiate the passage to the writers' own identities. In the Orientalist paradigm, the *banlieue* languages are true exotic tokens. The old sexual and religious divisions are less pertinent than the analytical conditions – and therefore the domination – of knowledge and its indictment within the institutional powers. When critics and journalists interview *Beur* writers, the authors joke that their interest lies in producing creative works, not in writing about petty crime.[36] As long as they write, they are still searching for something legitimate.

The purpose of such a literary system is to break from the social levels of identification of what *Beur* people are supposed to be like, particularly at a time of overwhelming media scrutiny. The novels resolve into a dynamic animated by identity as well as linguistic experimentation. In recent works, plots avoid traditional depictions of the *banlieue*, opting instead for a more introspective exploration.[37] The body becomes the location of speculation and discourse. The question of materiality, historical *and* economic, is slowly substituted for the fabula of subjectivity. In the work of Nina Bouraoui (though she is not technically a *Beur* because she spent her childhood in Algeria and her mother is of French stock), the body is symptomatic of literary *jouissance* (satisfaction), something far more threatening to bourgeois *vanitas* than trying to settle old scores with colonial history.

The shift may be one reason why *Beur* novels cannot be characterized as minority literature. In discourse about the nature of Frenchness in recent novels, little has been said about the claim regarding relative correspondences of meanings. For this reason, everything is recognizable in *Beur* literature because its patterns are constantly changing, mirroring French urban society itself. Yet on close examination, *Beur* writers temper the revolt of suppressed collective realities with a sense of resistance and reconstruction of the individual. The motifs of the early novels of the 1980s have faded away, as if their authors wanted to emphasize a new attitude towards actual creative conditions. The central elements in the narrative structures and various lexical fields have become inconsistent in their own terms because their authors hold that the experience of victimization itself is neither inevitable nor necessary during the writing process. In Ramdane Issaad's *L'Enchaînement*, the story takes place in every possible country or city but never in the world of the *banlieue*.[38] As for the characters, they are international gangsters, soldiers of fortune, or French call girls, not the usual suspects found in other immigrant literature. The exclusion of the expected codes of *immigrant writing* makes the question of what a *Beur* novel *should* be inconclusive and moot for those still in search of a sociological basis for this literature. Instead of demonstrating and advocating *Beurness*, these novels generate a criticism of cultural meaning within the language itself, from the perspective of the protagonist foreigner. The *banlieue* becomes a metaphor for that which escapes French cultural centrality, both Jacobinic and nationalistic. The historical privileging of the theme of nation is no longer predicated on a process of assimilation. The fragmented cultural experience stands for the whole. In this way,

Beur literature elaborates a very important connection between French nationhood and a postcolonial exchange. The *banlieue* produces a combination of meanings that is translated into writing in tongues and self-enunciation as communication capital.

Beur novelists feel and create from the tongue of the mother (Arabic, Berber) into the mother tongue (French), and vice versa. Translation itself becomes a narrative form, something that could be called, under the sweep of postcolonial "hurray" discourse, a sort of "domestic transnational" endeavour. The law of fiction is both in and on the tongue, and it keeps *Beur* subjects going from one cultural sphere to the next,. despite denials from the outside world, but above all from themselves. So the question remains: When is migration over? *Beur* literature appears as a singular quest to communicate a collective loss. However, writers find themselves confronted with a crucial choice: they must either root themselves in a given language (risking an unwanted come-down, or alienation), or set themselves adrift (and be doomed to perpetual exile). This search for a unique locus between cultures and languages points to the impossibility of dwelling fully inside both canonical French literature and the Maghrebi francophone world. The double-paradox is that although the French language is the mother tongue for *Beur* people, it is simultaneously a language of exclusion that has been revised through different degrees of slang from the *banlieue* and its syntax (backward slang or *verlan*). As for Arabic, if it is indeed the tongue of the mother, it remains essentially foreign to the children born in France. In the particular case of *Beur* writers, being "in migration" implies being unable to distance oneself from the original tongue, as well as the illusion of integration, which is eventually symbolized by the publication of their books.

If literature does modify the identity of the one who writes, it hardly affects the postcolonial community in France. What could be perceived as "home exoticism" for Franco-French people becomes expected and predictable, when not overrated, for potential *Beur* readers. They know the context and the values, even though the latter may appear fragmented. On the one hand, Maghrebi cultures are almost inaccessible; on the other, integration has been so successful that for those left out of this "success" their Frenchness is openly disputed or denied, most flagrantly in race-based discrimination in the housing and job markets. Hence the function of languages involves more a quest than a reshuffling of relations. More often than not, *Beur* writers know just enough dialectical Arabic to cease idealizing it as cultural treasure. Moreover, the cultural link continues to exist in the mother's voice. Their original identity, then, has not been completely erased through the ordeal of immigration to France. What matters most is that by keeping in touch – willingly or not – with the mother tongue(s), *Beur* writers elevate the principle of emancipation in symbolic rather than historical terms. They ask to be taken seriously within the framework of their cultural and linguistic ambiguities. This interplay between several spheres makes *Beur* literature seem schizophrenic, when in fact what it is doing is denying French literature its utopian ideal – that is, one culture embodied in one language. Beyond its palpable presence, *Beur* literature brings readers back simultaneously to the starting point of the primacy of their culture and face to face with a new perspective in which language exists on its own, like a spirit poised to pass on stories.

8 The Challenge of Identities and the French Republic

What identifies feminism within postcolonial studies is not the establishment of a distinct field of research but the correlative movement between the two spheres. In France the matter turns more complex because of its barely addressed colonial memory and the recently stronger ideological take on Islam – a take in which secularism looms large in the debate. Even postcoloniality has become a code language for avoiding recognizing the multicultural state of affairs in France. Intellectuals, politicians, and the media seem to be missing the salience of the postcolonial condition to the contemporary situation. A recent illustration of what amounts to cultural autism came up in what the French called the *querelle du postcolonial*, with Jean-François Bayart, an Africanist and political science scholar. Bayart's argument epitomizes France's defensiveness: "In the present circumstances, one could not be accused of being too polemical or spiteful in seeing the sudden success of postcolonial studies, and the excoriation of French backwardness as something like a niche strategy carried out by academics eager to corner a part of the market, a form of coquettishness halfway between American snobbishness and French masochism."[1]

This has been painfully clear in analysing the reaction to suburban riots, especially those of 2005, and the ongoing witch-hunt against Muslim women. It has become commonplace to poke fun at the French for developing their own resistance to "Otherness" theory, yet I want to pay special attention to the current identity challenge from the point of view of the postcolonial observer. I will not be bemoaning neocolonial hegemony for its own sake, and I will not be claiming that postcolonial *intégration* is only a matter of time. This is a cultural distortion that has gained currency with the greater visibility of the far-right candidate during the presidential election in the spring of 2012. In view of the deeply entrenched culture war now raging in French society, we should assume from now on that the postcolonial is real.

Cast as a disruptive discourse in France, postcolonial theory may turn out to be the best tool to reset French identity by demarcating new intersubjective frontiers: a sobering corrective when *différence* takes over from the mantra of assimilation. The rise of postcolonial identities throughout Europe, especially in France, has significantly problematized the ongoing political and cultural debates over identity politics.[2] The implications for national inquiries often seek to challenge the West's epistemic assumptions about itself. In truth, Western academics often need to question their own personal stakes in parsing postcolonial issues; such an exercise can be either redemptive or patronizing.[3] In much of Europe, conceptions of collective identity are marked by imprecision as well as by a tendency to conflate geography with faith or to gaze at faith-based identity through the stereotypic prism of national identity. In France, a Muslim is considered primarily to be someone who traces his native ancestry to the Maghreb; in Britain, a Muslim is inextricably wedded to a Pakistani national identity; and, in Germany, Muslim means Turkish. But if the issues at the core of Muslim identity were actually faith-related, they would ultimately and objectively be equal all over Europe –which is, of course, far from the reality. In fact, issues and conflicts stem from antagonistic historical narratives and cultural misunderstandings. By stigmatizing one particular group of citizens – that is, Muslims – European societies cast down their own value system and turn faith into a common denominator for all of those who already feel discriminated against and socially ostracized. The dynamics of what one means by the postcolonial condition are thus structured differently according to national identities, historical nexus (issues regarding France and Algeria, the Cold War, France and the European Union, etc.) as well as by the capacity of citizenship to serve as a new basis for political power.

This chapter examines how Islam in France has forced a conversation across cultural and ideological locations, bringing home the impact of both the postcolonial condition and globalization. In this postcolonial context, one example that runs across the issues of individual freedoms and republican principles is the headscarf, something that will be discussed in detail. Yet the main issue in contemporary France does not boil down to how to accommodate peoples of radically different ethnic, cultural, and religious backgrounds. This is less a matter of immigration from the South to the North than it is of emerging citizens in the West. The complexity that globalization imposes on the nation's home politics works to alter its political arrangements in terms, for example, of a shift from difference to minority status, and from minority status to citizenship.[4] It is noteworthy that in France, the appeal for forms of national loyalty – based on universalism – have turned out to be both contingent and unique, as if nationhood functioned as a substitute for the nation-state. The French postmodern political formula simultaneously operates within civil law and enjoys common acceptance. So it is not surprising that, as we will see, the debate over the Islamic headscarf has transcended the traditional French left–right opposition.[5] As early as the 1990s the polarized structure of identity between a certain idea of Frenchness and the visibility of French Muslims had slowly shut down the alternative of mutual recognition within a truly multicultural France. It is no surprise that victims of racism and discrimination often talk of a two-tiered citizenship that hems them in and curbs their rights. The nexus of conflict stands between identity (law) and sameness (culture), especially regarding questions related to history and values. Is it possible at all to be French and Muslim in the twenty-first century? Is the scapegoating of French Muslims establishing a new national covenant at a time when the republic has been questioning its own constitution?[6] Too often, matters of social reciprocity and common interest (social class, public education, housing, etc.) suffer from the divisiveness of other identities that have been thrust forward in the public sphere and in political counter-discourses in the hope of restoring a place for kinship – critical secularism being put forward as one of these. Naturally, this brand of neonationalism, not clearly in the open, feeds on the gifts of land, memory, and customs that supposedly come with French citizenship – on all, that is, that is unavailable to immigrants and their children.

Although recognized by law as French, the children of immigrants find themselves relegated to the country's socio-economic backwaters. It is as though the instrumental principles of law – the *jus soli*, for example – had been subverted by aspects of social recognition that continue, sometimes after several generations, to construe some French citizens as *immigrés*. For them only, citizenship is not a quality but a process. We touch here on the problematic encounter between liberal humanism – conceived in terms of individual rights – and the contemporary form of universalism. As Naomi Schor has observed, "we might speak here of a 'spectral universalism,' the shadow of a formerly vigourous and dynamic ideology [...] now reduced to an empty rhetoric in whose cozy and familiar terms present-day ideological battles are fought."[7] These ideological obstacles nonetheless enable a challenging view of identity, both national and individual. Meanwhile, the slow yet irreversible integration of European nations has been deflating both the concept of national sovereignty and the reality of the postcolonial condition, which defies strict national categorical labels such as French or British. Nations like Denmark and Italy, for example, have become receptive, unwittingly or not, to the push and pull of Eurocentrism and globalization, which has been brought to a head in the often tortuous relations these countries have with their own newly arriving Muslim populations. With this new encounter, the home societies of immigrants become their true and only home, but at the same time, ushered in are new models of national cultures previously predicated on historical legacies and ethnically homogeneous populations. It is in this particular context that France has been reinventing – and reinvesting – its values with regard both to legitimacy (of institutions, republican laws, etc.) and to what could be called, for a lack of a better term, national personhood.

Venturing beyond the universal and liberal views that constitute France's cherished self-image, it is easy to argue that cultural politics have reshaped the ethos of the nation and of identity in the twenty-first century. Domination is no longer a function of colonial power, but a commodity inherent in sociocultural structures – for example, the idea that Judeo-Christian culture is self-evident and universal; that neutral, rational, and objective secular principles are markers of Frenchness; and that it is acceptable to interfere in the affairs of other nations while treating one's own national sovereignty as sacred.[8] Regardless of the increasing social integration and the collective sense of shared values among all French citizens, difference, discrimination, and even policies of mass deportation for illegals reveal the cloning of cultural fetishism in modern French nationhood, with the defensive posturing this entails.[9] Citizenship, as France seeks to conceive of it today, defines a process of depersonalization for new immigrants,[10] along with the abstract goal of a shared and conformist cultural life, which embodies authority as a system rather than as a tool for a safe environment.[11] The former Sarkozy government's decision to embark on a national and highly public conversation on what French national identity means and entails demonstrated to what extent the legacy of republican citizenship was open to different interpretations – and, one might add, conflicts.[12] In October 2009, the Minister of Immigration and National Identity launched an electronic forum and held public debates throughout the country to seek out views on identity contingent on membership in an entity where history and politics coalesce.[13] Side by side during the debate over national identity, there were constructive reactions against a new brand of nationalism as well as intensely xenophobic assaults on (mostly) the place of Islam in France. Once again the Oriental Other (a fellow citizen, too) was being talked about and theorized in terms of national loyalty and cultural threat. During this debate, historians, economists, labour market experts, educators, and religious leaders were left out of the government undertaking; moreover, the immigration issue was pushed to centre stage in such a way as to oversimplify the debate and incite nationalist sectarianism. The message was quite unambiguous: some people may claim to be French, but they are not if they do not share the same cultural experiences and national memory as the majority. Sarkozy and his government were caught trying to substitute republican ideals for nationalistic values, even while claiming that the undertaking's purpose was to clarify old debates. Instead of rethinking history within new parameters, French politicians decided that citizenship needed to embody identity.[14] The equation is flawed because the logic of the state swamps this proposition and leads to the stigmatization of a particular group within the French population: Muslims.

Far-right leaders and their conservative representatives in the *Assemblée nationale* had once dwelt on the threat allegedly posed by foreigners, with their allegedly "skyrocketing birthrate and natural propensity for crime."[15] Latent Orientalism never positioned itself far from partisan politics, with leaders suggesting that immigrants had settled in France in order to benefit from France's generous welfare system. Oblique allusions were all it took to keep the old colonial prejudices and stereotypes alive. In a sense, the shanty towns of the 1950s and 1960s,[16] then the suburban ghettos from the 1970s onward, represented one truth of the Orient, close to home. For Maghrebi immigrants, a taste of French economic wealth often led to a feeling of absolute nothingness.[17] Latent Orientalism became the point of entry for neocolonial mimetism. Once the Maghrebi nations had gained independence, the domestic "Arabs" were looked on with scepticism and hostility. The ideas of "independence" and "home" did not square: France was not ready to become a surrogate nation for something it had created in the first place, even with social interactions that remained based largely on the same colonial patterns of submission and exploitation. For example, workplace segregation was all the more striking among the powerful trade unions, which did not sign up immigrant workers, because they were not French and because their demographic did not confer any leverage when it came to negotiating new contracts and reforms. Meanwhile, in French society

at large, immigration was indeed a political topic, and the situation acknowledged the vaunted value of projecting democracy onto peoples
who, in the French psyche, had never been prepared for it.[18] There
were very few competing views of nationhood between the French and
Maghrebi immigrants. All of this led to a tense confrontation between
an alien territory (France) and alien citizens (postcolonial foreigners and
their French-born children). And it came as no surprise that after the terrible killings of 13 November 2015 in Paris, one "strategy" of the execu-
tive power to fight terrorism was to revoke citizenship of French-born
Muslim citizens. This move has been condemned as an assault against
the principles of the constitution and equality among citizens.

It is true that the expansion of rights (relating to job legislation, health
care, and education) in France was part of a more sweeping postwar
democratization process. Laws and welfare benefits were applied
equally, but this mostly served the values of the ethnic majority; immigrants were expected to enjoy this economic emancipation (and to
pay their taxes) while remaining socially and politically invisible. This
social stage was itself a form of alienation – the subject was captured all
over again, his or her specular image deprived of selfhood. Such a representation was so powerful that the children of these people, two or
three generations later, still find themselves entangled in the paradigm
of the *immigré*. Without reading too much national psychology into it,
note that the past participle of *immigré* has been operating as a concept
for something: colonial history. This type of denominative and social
formalism enshrined inequalities and discrimination; it also completely bypassed one striking reality – that immigrants had helped rebuild
France after the Second World War, and that while doing so they were
underpaid and worked and lived in appalling conditions. The former
violence inherent in the relationship between colonizer and colonized
reproduced itself in the form of silent class warfare. In postwar France,
West African and Maghrebi immigrants spurred the economic recovery with both their labour and their consumption. For them, the opportunity to leave poverty and minimal economic prospects behind in
the Maghreb or West Africa amounted almost to an answered prayer.
Having come to France, they forgot their resentment and frustration
over colonial rule, or rather they set aside those things for the sake of the
few material comforts they could now enjoy and for the economic op-
portunities the new country might provide their children. Not surprisingly, the cultural mosaic of the former empire found itself reassembled
in France. Between 1962 and 1999, the number of people of Algerian
descent in France grew to 3.4 million, those of Moroccan descent to

1.9 million, and those of Tunisian descent to 800,000.[19] Yet the process of redefining French discourse on national identity would begin in earnest only when the children of immigrants stirred up cultural unease, not simply because they wanted fair recognition of their rights in the workplace and in housing, but also because, by speaking up, they were confronting their parents' alienation head-on. The first massive show of visibility was *La marche pour l'égalité et contre le racisme*, held in October 1983, which the mainstream media quickly renamed *La marche des Beur*. It started from Marseille in October 1983 with thirty-two people; by the time it reached Paris, that December, more than 60,000 had joined it. In the capital, its leaders were hosted by then President François Mitterrand, who granted immediate documentation and work permits to illegal workers for a period of ten years. This only demonstrated the extent to which *intégration* was tragically mixed up with immigration. The problem would only get worse.

For the children of the postcolonial condition, *intégration* assumed a language of its own. For them, the acquiring of citizenship was part of their personal story *and* their ethnic history. This was not something tied to colonial history; rather, it was an object associated with an unstoppable process – indeed, a cleansing process meant to restore the self-respect that was tragically lacking for the immigrant generation. This identity shift was set in motion by the parents' anticipation of their children being French *à part entière*. Note that among all immigrants, Algerians would be last to apply for French citizenship, out of respect for their own young homeland and the sacrifices that had been made during the war of national liberation. Even so, they felt somehow relieved that their French-born children were automatically and legally French – something that cancelled out the discomfitting option of having to seek French citizenship on their own behalf.[20] Thus for the children, speaking up was not a matter of choice. Slowly, as discrimination against them grew more intense, the immigrants' children learned to avoid universalist determinism. Minority discourse was liminal so long as it retained its cultural heterogeneity. It seems that the parents had made other choices – for example, giving their children Muslim first names and participating in Islamic practices such as the Ramadan fast, when all the while their children were wrestling with the narrative of French citizenship. That narrative, as opposed to the colonial one (founded on images, exotic affects, fables, reification, nostalgia), is based on complex discourses (concerning economics, feminism, legal critique, aesthetic expression, civic rights, etc.) that are too often hampered by a transnational emphasis that generates xenophobia. The public sphere is unapologetically Judeo-Christian, while private homes tend to re-create distinct albeit idealized models of the native land the immigrants left behind. Of course, it may not be possible to study post-colonial identities in contemporary France without addressing French analytical categories where – as Halbwachs noted nearly a century ago – social and individual memory (narrative and trauma for the postcolonial subject) are tied together and make it all the more difficult to assess an organizing concept.[21] So, what is the connection between postcolonial collective memory and historical consciousness when everything else, including citizenship, is challenged?

For the sake of argument, let us postulate that identity must pass through a relationship to another being. Actually, this very relationship accounts for social existence, even in its deepest forms of despair. And by despair we clearly mean that of the children of immigrants, who are confronted with the empirical phenomenon of citizenship, along with the questioning of their Frenchness because, in the eyes of citizens of French stock, people of the postcolonial condition are never going to be French *enough*. It should not be surprising, then, that after the 2005 urban riots, the people of the suburbs were depicted as culturally and racially different from the mainstream French, as if politicians on both the right and the left as well as voices in the media (e.g., Alain Finkielkraut, Caroline Fourest, Éric Zemmour, and Michel Onfray) were trying to create an urban apartheid.[22] The imperative of social uplift (through jobs and better housing) was answered with police containment. Oddly enough, it seems that one "privilege" of universalism for postcolonial individuals has consisted in renouncing one's own identity, the withering away of the experience of Otherness. This kind of discontinuity is fundamentally different from the alienation experienced by their parents, who never doubted their roots no matter how harsh the colonial condition. A West African or Maghrebi background is no longer a historical extension of French identity (the old propaganda of France's empire); rather, it has become a liability, as if the connection between personal identity and the national horizon of French continuity has ceased to function. One permanent manifestation of this cultural entropy is police harassment, including identity checks carried out on French people who are minding their own business, simply because they are "Arab" or "Black." The national fear of social disorder at the hands of a French-yet-foreign body is a remnant of latent Orientalism. It is also a blatant example of one group of people having to bow to the symbolic order of another, as if nothing had been learned from the painful history of relations between France and the Maghreb. French remains the name of the father figure; the labels "Arab" or "African" fail to apply any identitarian discourse that would free the postcolonial subjects from the France's national imaginary. The subaltern is very much alive in France, but instead of having to kowtow to the degrading colonial institutions of old, he is now disciplined by a racialized view of citizenship. It is only a matter of time before the postcolonial subject experiences a loss of his other rights. A national non-governmental agency, HALDE (*Haute Autorité de Lutte contre les Discriminations et pour l'Égalité*), established in 2004 and terminated in 2011, found itself overwhelmed from the beginning by complaints, 50 per cent of which were associated with workplace issues or complaints about job applications. In 2008 to 2009 alone, the agency had to double its workforce and personnel so that it could carry on with its mission.[23]

A significant aspect of the postcolonial condition appears to be its antisystemic legitimacy. The general frustration and anger among the children of immigrants eschews the old left–right opposition. Indeed, their inability to set forth the range of their concerns (workplace discrimination, political invisibility, cultural alienation, etc.) tends to demonstrate that nothing fundamentalist sits at the conjecture of citizenship. Yet, like the people who think they "remember the 1960s" although they were not there, French citizens of the postcolonial condition refer to the globalized, Orientalist evolutionary ideology of the backward, inadequate "Arabs," those who take their cue from an *intégration* that is always on the line. So when French intellectuals openly question Islam's compatibility with Western democracy, they are in a roundabout way targeting their fellow French citizens of Maghrebi or black African background.[24] They are an easy target because of the facile celebration of the primacy of nationhood over citizenship. Unlike in the United States, in France there is no such concept as "we the people." Difference is frowned upon. For the French, the equivalent of "we the people" is an agonizing transition from modernity to globalization, one that involves an imbalance of representation. Within this warped frame, public discourse on Islam contends that the native root of identity signifies civilizational differences. By outsourcing their ideology to the global "there," French ideologues on the left *and* the right can pretend that ethnic diversity and nationhood are crossing paths, each with its own historical baggage. The old colonial discourse, which was informed by a "mission," has slipped into a reverse nationalism that is no longer a path to victory but rather a defensive posture. By the same token, to speak of internal Orientalism is more relevant than referring to latent Orientalism; following in Edward Said's footsteps, the latent Orientalism argument bears mostly on culturalist debates – debates centred on renewed American influence in the Middle East, the rise of the Arab bourgeoisie, Muslim women and education, the "Arab Spring" and Islam, and so on. Internal Orientalism epitomizes matters of national survival contemporaneous with the shift from the former colonial periphery. From that perspective, the *banlieue*, for example, would be a series of gradations of "domestic Orients." Couscous has become a French dish; halal food is available nearly everywhere; Arabic words have been integrated into the French language;[25] transatlantic hip hop has trumped trans-Mediterranean music (raï, andalus, chaâbi) but with a *banlieue* twist; and even suburban ghettos have outpaced the claims to Frenchness of the Eurocentric community. The spectacle of political domination is no longer required, or rather it cannot be sustained, because of the fragmentation of vectors (liberal universalism, belated cosmopolitanism, hardcore secular principles, etc.) that were once kept together by an active but simpler form of nationalism. This is why the disputed concept of citizenship has loosened its grip on the discourse on Otherness. Because the universalist matrix has become so obsolete, French nationhood manufactures difference within itself instead of beyond its national borders, as it did, for example, from 1870 to 1945, in three wars against the same country, Germany. Yet, there is no disputing that Germany is now France's most important economic partner and strongest political ally within the EU; France's "enemy" is now construed as internal, and he holds a French identity card.

Did the postcolonial condition bring about the divorce between republican principles and identity, or did the dialectic of colonial memory and national essence never validate anything acceptable? Whether in political philosophy or in postcolonial critique, alterity and otherness still bear the marks of a colonial imaginary because the last territory to be colonized by the French empire was France itself. Colonial contamination affected not just the national economy but also the collective psyche, as we can see today with ethnocentric reactions in representations of both the State and national history. A scandal that deeply shocked the French arose when supporters, apparently of Maghreb descent, shouted down "La Marseillaise" during a soccer game in Paris between France and Algeria in October 2001, and then again during another game between France and Morocco in November 2007. These incidents suggested there was a lasting colonial fracture in contemporary France.[26] The unruly supporters were trying less to insult France to its core than to display a manifold allegiance, which was another way of debunking the idea of political community. Through this disrespect of national symbols (the national anthem, the flag), there surfaced the fantasy of recovering a lapsed identity among citizens caught in the postcolonial condition. This pairing of the ideas of breaking away and of quest may hold relevance for contemporary postcolonial culture. Still, in the case of *Beur* citizens, it is irrelevant to underscore that anger at France bespeaks confused loyalties to two or more cultures. Nations of the Maghreb remain essentially foreign to the children of immigrants. That is why those lands are so strongly idealized: they are defence mechanisms for times when identity is threatened at home. Indeed, the vast majority of *Beur* have a limited or poor command of Arabic and a knowledge of Islam that too often does not reach beyond cultural rituals. Arabic education in the public school system has been a notable failure. And the Islamic faith has been turned into a cultural fetish, or more recently into a political one.

The colonial ghost may never be far from an understanding of the patterns of rebellion, but there is still no obvious genealogy between the colonial state of silence of the natives and the postcolonial condition marked by hybridity and its identity as a bridge to power. The metaphor of political knowledge (denying visibility behind a screen of objectivity) has changed with the reality of immigration, especially now that new French citizens have proved themselves able to move forward and create a discourse outside the binary, protracted parameters of the worn-out "West versus the rest" dialectic.[27] France is no longer the hegemonic power it was before the Second World War, and the political horizon is not that of self-determination or independence. Everyone lives on the same soil, under the same republican constitution and civil laws. But however useful political praxis may be, such a reality is a tangle of contradictions. For example, whereas citizenship is given, identity is constituted, meaning that something must be available and self-understanding must be projected so that eventually, identity can serve as a tool for emancipation. The children of immigrants refuse to mend the historical cracks; in this vein, the religious revival among the youngest generations has provided a screen for unconscious material associated more with the parents who hid their faith than with the institutions that attempted to suppress Islam's visibility on grounds of secularism. This mute subjectivity, the passive labours of the parents, and the awkward nationality of an independent yet missing native land reveal the true self-projection of French citizenship against an identity not fully intelligible.[28] The greater the dependence on selfhood, the bigger the investment in artificial ploys, be they self-destructive behaviour (e.g., dropping out of school, juvenile delinquency), political hip hop songs, or radical Islam. Anger helps keep identity afloat against the lexical seasickness of ideological stigma. In the particular case of France, the minority's anger fosters internal Orientalism, which feeds a readily available consensus across the political board. More specifically, the continued demonization of Islam demonstrates that there is supposedly a non-Western alternative to successful citizenship and nationhood. A dramatic instance in France has been the "affair" of the Islamic headscarf.

A haunting question underlying the ban on religious signs in French public schools was this: Can French people born to Maghrebi parents play any role in contemporary French society, or must they be the poster children for France's crisis of universalism?[29] In the past, Christian students were never required to choose between visible signs of their faith and the right to a free public education. In addition, the 2004 law has undercut the notion that citizens' rights are upheld by placing more restrictions on individual freedoms, and this has caused a dangerous social fracture between "good citizens" and those of Muslim faith. The law purported to solve social ills by stigmatizing one particular faith. According to Joan W. Scott, "the headscarf controversy opened a searing debate about the meaning of French secularism, the limits of religious toleration, and the founding principles of the republic."[30]

This blurring of the boundaries between private and public, secular and religious, citizens and immigrants, set the stage for an Islam "problem" and changed the terms of the national conversation: more than *integration*, it was France's civilizing mission that had failed. Communalism (*communautarisme*) was blamed on Islam, although it is obvious to everyone (except those afflicted by cognitive blindness) that the *banlieues* are places of economic despair. Sadly enough, most criticism directed at the 2004 law came from outside France,[31] even while the country basked in a kind of self-congratulatory mood reminiscent of the chest-thumping that attended colonial conquests. A prominent feature of the naturalization of Islamophobia in France has been the ongoing cultural and scholarly conversation that seems geared towards consensus against the right to wear any religious sign; all the while, everywhere else – especially in North America – rebuke of the French

2004 law has been persistent and informed.[32] This baffling infringement on freedom of religion and freedom of conscience based on liberal humanism had its roots in the old colonial notion that Islam was a threat to French secular principles and republican order. In 1959, during the Algerian War of Independence, Frantz Fanon rightly pointed to the ideology behind the so-called liberation of the Muslim woman who was asked or forced to remove her veil: "The dream of an absolute subjugation of the Algerian society through its women who leave their veils behind and are made accomplice of the colonizer has never ceased to obsess the political leaders of the colonial undertaking."[33]

The unveiling of women – by force in colonial Algeria, by law today – is playing a significant part in efforts to break down a culture deemed unassimilable. The law became symptomatic of a restorative attempt at a nostalgia back when identity and gender lines where blurred by the imperial nation and its narrative, only this time the *banlieues* are construed as the new territories that needed to be civilized. While the unveiling strategy behind the 2004 law was called a "campaign for the dignity of women,"[34] the true goal was to substitute a sacred national alliance for the slow socio-economic disintegration of the *banlieues*. In a context of reductive colonial history, this posturing strikes one as illiberal; it suggests a gendered strategy for pacifying the suburbs. Not surprisingly, this sort of internal Orientalism turns the Muslim woman into a victim – something that harks back to the fantasy of erotic domination in which the female subject (along with her partner) is always under control because of patriarchy or male predatory patterns of behaviour. The Dominique Strauss-Kahn affair in the spring of 2011 revealed the extent to which France had a "problem" with gender equality – indeed, at the highest level – and it was definitely not because of the actions of its Muslim citizens. This Islamic explanation bespeaks a crowded history of incidents between France and Algeria, thick with cultural complexes, collective amnesia, still unaddressed issues, and an underlying ideological violence. The ethnicization of French politics through a scapegoating of the "Arab" male (construed as an abuser of women) served to increase the standing of the dominant group. French sociologist Nacira Guénif-Souilamas has framed the situation in terms of a biased French feminism that has managed to elude the ambiguities of the assimilationist model of the republic as well as the class issues associated with discrimination.[35] This type of "republican feminism" has come to exist thanks to two foils: the veiled Muslim woman, and the "violent" young man from the *banlieue*. The core argument against this type of French feminism is that it "naturalizes" women through their femininity. The violence of liberal feminism is based on the ongoing subordination of those it claims to be helping or even rescuing. For liberal feminists like Elisabeth Badinter, Geneviève Fraisse, Gisèle Halimi, Elisabeth Roudinesco, and Linda Weil-Curiel, emancipation seems to go hand in hand with the subordination of the "native" woman. And this fantasy of the endangered "native" woman has become the springboard for a new brand of universalized civilization. This idea is eerily similar to the old Orientalist fantasy of the female native who resists the code of Western visibility and desire. No wonder the promise of *intégration* is held out to those who choose to spell out their Islamic faith within a public secular frame. The assimilation discourse seems forever attached to caricatures of the "Arab" in need of being brought into the fold of civilization. In this scenario the French feminists and the media machine (which has been siding with them since the late 1980s) are not oppressors – who take young girls out of public schools – but civilizers. In their struggle for cultural and identity references in a world of irreversible globalization, one in which secularism appears to be the sole source of cultural capital, French disciples of entrenched republican principles have found an organizing theme – a home enemy who supposedly is also an economic burden.[36] This form of legal discrimination (based on a law voted in contravention of the European Convention on Human Rights)[37] has also helped solidify the ground for claims to moral superiority. If the French had a compelling case for Muslim women's "liberation," they could venture into a post-9/11 world by invoking the democratic benefits of the West while avoiding the 2003–11 American militaristic adventure in Iraq, as well as deflecting attention from its own history of domestic discrimination.

Between the first headscarf affair, which came to court in 1989,[38] and the 2004 law banning religious symbols, there had been no fewer than 150 cases nationwide where Muslim female students were barred by school principals from attending public school because they chose to exercise their right to dress in garments that expressed their religion or beliefs. However, as early as 27 November 1989, and then again on 10 July 1995, the *Conseil d'État*[39] ruled that the headscarf was not an ostentatious symbol and could not be banned from schools unless it was being used as a propaganda tool for proselytizing, or unless it compromised health and safety. After institutions stalled on this issue,[40] many media campaigns went into high gear and succeeded in selling French public opinion on the idea that teenage Muslim girls were actually being forced to wear the veil and that it was a symbol of female oppression. Thomas Deltombe's *L'Islam imaginaire* offers a groundbreaking analysis of how the propaganda machine conspired to construe French Muslims as a threat, all the way from postulating an "immigration problem" to preaching a radical approach to *laïcité* (the French brand of secularism), which was portrayed as a last-ditch defence against an alleged homegrown invasion.[41] Many unsaid things now came to the surface, as if the dam of colonial denial had burst. From then on, Islamophobia was more readily permitted in the national conversation. Political and media discourses were carefully organized to normalize and legitimate invidious slanders against Muslims and *immigrés*.[42] Muslim French citizens found themselves caught between a patronizing left and a stigmatizing right. From the 1990s onward, Islamophobia went from being a sideshow of the *Front National*, the far-right party that challenged the political status quo of the mainstream parties, to being a public relations pitch representing Muslims as a clear and present danger to national institutions and to the very soul of the nation. The fact that no Muslim feminist in France or elsewhere had asked the French to free Muslim schoolgirls allowed women to call for a one-sided differentiation between "good Muslims" and "fanatics." Just as in colonial times, "good Muslims" willingly collaborate with the dominant power, usually in a show of self-hatred. An unmistakable feature of "good Muslims" is that they have sold out their received identity, especially with regard to faith. Not surprisingly, feminist "thinkers" in Muslim culture have been co-opted to stand at the forefront of postcolonial *intégration* as well as of battles over faith in France's cultural politics. They do the dirty job of attacking Islam by claiming to do so with an insider's credibility. Their commitment can usually be reduced to political ambition, to a desire to appear in the media and sign book contracts, and sometimes to a mere willingness to engage in staged exercises in Islam-bashing after a woman has been victimized in the suburbs. On close examination, these Muslim "feminists" quickly display a paucity of analytical skills, as well as very little knowledge of Islamic theology and law and of the social sciences in the Arab/Muslim world. As if fulfilling a need to vindicate itself, the Islamphobic ideological framework expanded to other European nations. In the Netherlands there was the case of Ayaan Hirsi Ali, who made up her own story of victimhood at the hands of Muslim "fanatics" back in her native Somalia. But when documented facts surfaced, they contradicted all her made-up claims. In a matter of weeks, she was forced to resign from all her elected positions. As a consequence of the enormity of her deception, her Dutch citizenship was revoked. It is easy to take issue with Hirsi Ali's writings, not just because they are biased and counterfactual, but also because they are grossly under-theorized, packed with overgeneralizations about the Islamic faith and its theology, and substandard in terms of elementary geopolitics in the contemporary Muslim world – not to mention the binary argument that the West is a utopian land while the rest of the world is enveloped in barbaric despair. She has since been hired by a Washington-based conservative think tank. Self-proclaimed Westernized feminists like these have invited Europeans and North Americans to identify vicariously with the condition of Muslim woman from the comfort of their own homes, although the same people continue to turn a blind eye to the unbearable suffering of Palestinian women under illegal foreign occupation, and of Iraqi women who have lost their loved ones in the course of a fabricated war. What is most troubling is not that the former mechanisms of domination are being perpetuated, but that they underwrite so much of the social stigma of postcolonial difference, something that is sure to summon forth an exile from inside.

It is not surprising that France has many examples of these "house Muslim" feminists, as well.[43] A cross-cultural case is that of Djemila Benhabib, who was raised in Algeria and who relocated to Canada from France. She set herself the task of confronting the largest women's organization in Quebec[44] because of its decision to oppose any ban on religious signs in public places such as schools, hospitals, and town halls. In a book with a catchy title, Benhabib has embarked on an exercise in recycled anti-Islam fear-mongering.[45] She recounts the horrors of the Algerian civil war in the 1990s, although she left the country in 1994 with the bulk of the upper-middle-class elite who were able to afford a way out. Her grasp of the history and concept of Islamic theology and of the socio-economic status of women in the Maghreb consists of ill-digested appropriations of the works of more nuanced and thoughtful Muslim feminists from the Maghreb, such as Fatima Mernissi, Ghita al-Khayat, and Marnia Lazreg. Like most self-hating Muslim "intellectuals," Benhabib gives the impression that women live under the rule of three or four verses from the Koran. Her argument is governed by the worn-out Orientalist paradigm of an unchanging historical context in the Muslim sphere and by an essentialist rendering of Islam both as backward and as a permanent threat. Lastly, she repeats the sensationalist argument of economic oppression, arranged marriages, genital mutilations, forced prostitution, and honour killings.

Her function, although she may not be aware of this, is to commodify prevailing clichés while completely missing the truth of a changing and diverse Islamic world of one-and-a-half billion people. Her book, and her promotional tours to publicize it, have been quite successful in France among journalists, academics, and militants of *laïcité*.

In short, the female French citizen of Muslim faith has become a Trojan horse whose purpose has been to discipline the male Muslim subject and to rehabilitate, in a seamless manner, both old and new global stereotypes of Islam. With the spread of Islamophobia in France and the fundamentalist turn in discourse on *laïcité* since the mid-1990s, discrimination has found a target; it has become, in a sense, a voluntary ideology based on faith distinction. A gap has been exposed among French citizens, and as a consequence, latent Orientalism has been internalized and the crudeness of identity politics has been unravelled. For example, on the left the French brand of Islam would ideally be secular and liberal.[46] But to practise Islam as a faith is a dangerous choice because this may lead to a conflation of the public and private spheres – something that is underscored by the positions of those who declare that the end of French universalism is near.[47] Furthermore, too often the Muslim postcolonial subject is expected to reform the Islamic faith from within an analytical framework that is the legacy of the Enlightenment. This equating of religion and secular philosophy naturalizes the metaphor of unveiling the nakedness of postcolonial *intégration*. With such expectations of creating docile Muslims, one can picture the perennial master who continues to lend credibility to a national project; and for France this would mean Islam without Muslims, just as there was a French Algeria without Algerians (only *indigènes*). It turns out that, in the case of female Muslim high school students, French sociologists have demonstrated time and time again that the headscarf actually represents a strong symbol for *intégration* because the young women have a native command of the cultural codes and want to stand out and assert their individual identities, whereas traditional Muslim students, because of their fear of not fitting in, usually take off their scarves on their own in order to blend in with non-Muslim peers.[48] Against all ideological expectations, wearing the Islamic headscarf has been evidence of a switch from tradition to modernity: visibility in a public place is a token of liberation. Could it be that the much vaunted French social contract has become moot, perhaps irrelevant? Sociologist Françoise Gaspard asks this question: "By expelling girls from public schools aren't we applying sexist standards because we shatter the balance between boys and girls when it comes to our educational responsibilities?"[49]

Said once reminded us that true humanism is sustained by collective and critical understanding. What has been missing altogether from the debate is the question of feminism, or more precisely Islamic feminism.[50] The latter postulates that faith and individual rights are mutually inclusive. This brand of feminism also operates on a rejection of dichotomies: the colonial ideology on the one hand, and a radical take on Islam on the other.[51] In essence, Islamic feminists like Al Akhbar Zila Mir Hosseini (an Iranian) and Asma Lamrabet (a Moroccan) want to reclaim a normative reconciliation between Islam and women's rights that has been hijacked both by Islamic medieval jurisprudence and by the colonial narratives of patriarchy and class domination. They advocate a reversal of perspective and a search for the marginal discourse that would underscore what the hegemonic principles are. The transnational story behind the postcolonial condition has affected both the Islamic periphery and the secular centre. Under the guise of the *laïcité* discourse, we are witnessing a shift from one controlling power (religious patriarchy) to another (the State), with the blessing of already secularized women. Mainstream (i.e., Western) feminists have failed to question their own premises, or what could be called traditional knowledge of women's rights, as well as their privileged explanatory power, which shuts down contradictory discussion. For example, the famous French psychoanalyst Elisabeth Roudinesco stated that a law banning the Islamic headscarf was as necessary as the law banning incest.[52] So long as Islam is construed as a backward belief system, impervious to change, as well as a cultural ruse about to morph into a contingent presence in the French republican space, there can be no genuine, constructive dialogue. French feminists remain captive to their narrative of upward cultural mobility, that is to say of controlling the flow of bourgeois ideologies. Is it possible that the headscarf issue is all about social class, with one group (of women) patronizing another one? Removing the headscarf in the name of (republican) equality has little to do with equality between men and women. Rather, it is about women only, as if Muslim schoolgirls were expected to fall from one gender system to a new one with the blessing of a law and its colonial implication – that French Muslims are being saved by their French secular sisters!

If this kind of discrimination and cultural blindness continues to provide grounds for exclusivist political discourse and intellectual posturing, it is equally clear that it has become impossible to separate personal identity from nationhood in France today. True emancipation can occur only if the children of immigrants realize that the "French Muslim" is a construct that serves as an ideology for consensus. But what kind of consensus? That affirmation of cultural subjectivity relies on a national essentialist narrative, because citizens, Muslims, and others can only be what they are. What needs to be derived from the postcolonial experience can be inserted into French politics as true features of universalism. In the specific case of the headscarf, the argument points to the spirit of *laïcité* that was originally built on respect and neutrality.[53] For Aristide Briand, one of the fathers of the 1905 law, *laïcité* contained three key principles: freedom of conscience, separation of Church and State, and equal respect for all faiths.[54] Yet the word *laïcité*, deemed a neologism, never appeared in the text of the 1905 law and its articles – an irony that makes current interpretations all the more debatable. In the early twentieth century in France, 98.5 per cent of people who claimed a religion were Catholic, 1 per cent were Protestants, and less than 0.5 per cent were Jewish. The clear target of the 1905 law was the Catholic Church, which was perceived as obedient to Rome. Not surprisingly, Pope Pius X became one of the harshest critics of the French law. This historical context highlights the French republican struggle for legitimacy against political countercurrents, which included the power of the Catholic Church in public life (especially in education, civil law, foreign affairs, and matters affecting freedom of the press). By the same token, the law was supposed to apply equally in France *and* in its colonies. Yet a series a decrees in 1907, 1917, 1922, and 1947 confirmed that Muslims in Algeria were to be excluded from the reach of secular law because Islam was supposedly incompatible with the republic. To this day, on the French island of Mayotte, which is Muslim, the 1905 law does not apply.

The concept of *laïcité*, to say the least, remains open to interpretation. Briand wanted it that way in order to appease the tensions within French society and seek common ground. The Dreyfus affair had brought civil life in France to the brink of explosion. The time had come for a national healing. A favourite word that stuck in the spirit of the law was *neutralité*. For example, when the basilica of the Sacré-Coeur was under construction in Paris (it was completed in 1922), authorized by a vote in the National Assembly in 1873, Briand, in his capacity as prime minister, decided that Muslims needed their own place of worship in Paris. Although the idea of a mosque in Paris had been suggested a long time before,[55] it took the deaths of more than 100,000 North African soldiers during the First World War to make the decision a reality. The site, the old Pitié Hospital, was chosen by Briand himself. Work began in 1922, and the mosque was completed in

1926. From then on, because the state did not recognize one particular religion, it could not ignore any. *Neutralité* was where public order and freedom of religion met.

If the state has no right to interpret religious symbols and people's beliefs, why does the 2004 law do precisely that? Proponents of a ban on Islamic headscarves in public schools claim that preventing violence against young women was the motivation behind its enactment, ostensibly in order to validate *neutralité* (i.e., rather than coercion).[56] So the republic, and its principles, are constructed as a lived entity that guarantees constancy, predictability, and legitimate expectations as far as the dominant culture is concerned. Contrary to the official mantra of *laïcité*, there is no such thing as ethnic or religious loyalty; what truly sustains identity is the name-bearing process of citizenship. This is one reason why Islamophobic discourses and acts are hurtful. It is not because they promote a degrading view of faith, but because they reshape citizenship into something that is not meaningful. They break the symbolic relationship that acknowledges Muslims as French. One wonders whether the national conversation that began with *laïcité* is not encroaching perilously on the territory of *égalité*.

The old rhetorical strategies aimed at generating a discourse of difference, immune to axiomatic resistance, are slowly re-entering mainstream debates over French identity. For example, by making any association with Islam objectionable, law and ethics have unwittingly helped rehabilitate essentialist positions. Orientalism is thereby internalized when it accounts for precisely this kind of construction of the "Other" French citizen. In a true show of France's cultural exceptionalism, the political theory of secularism and universalism owes a historical debt to the postcolonial condition. Whether it be the Islamic headscarf, social segregation in the *banlieue*, or job discrimination, citizens of the postcolonial state provide a mirror image to their fellow Frenchmen of the traumatic insufficiencies of national history. What politics and culture repress is that citizenship is the lived extension of identity. The ease with which *laïcité* and *égalité* feed into historical issues is a consequence of the failure to reimagine nationhood. Whether or not the fetishized intellectualization of the Muslim Other is complicit in resurrecting the old Orientalist demons, it seems that France remains unable to relocate itself on the global multicultural map. It is a sad sign when the republic aligns itself against identity and freedom because the work of representation is no longer that of an inadequate Orient but that of a self-defeating West.

Epilogue: Elusive Convergence?

Historians advise against deconstructing historiography, just as literature scholars eschew the binarity of history and fiction. Their point is well taken. But sometimes one needs to keep telling oneself that a cogent, valid examination of key concepts and disciplines such as latent Orientalism and postcolonial studies deserves better than a rehashing of, for example, the challenges of neo-Marxism, the presumptions of neoliberalism, the emphases on anything "post-" and on any new "-ism," or the resilience of Othering in a globalized world. Ever since scholars speculated on the nature of the West/East encounter, more work has continued to question human behaviour that provides the framework for very complex issues ranging from, say, cultural empathy to geopolitics. Even if language continues to be invested with the content of ideological alienation (one recalls the coinage of "enemy combatant" after 9/11, for example), it remains to square the postcolonial reality with the now long-lasting signifier of Islam on the world scene.

One case in point that offers a lead to a deeper understanding of how latent Orientalism operates rests in the terrorism representation. Interestingly enough, terrorism is always constructed in narratives of self-recognition. First, terrorism happens when the victims hail from Europe, North America, or Israel. The terrible violence, with mind-boggling death tolls, in other parts of the world (Chechnya, Iraq, Afghanistan, Palestine, Somalia, Syria, etc.) is normalized to the point of irrationality. Within the Islamic sphere, terrorism boils down to the documentary nature of figures (2,000 killed in Pakistan in 2012, 500 killed in Iraq on a monthly basis, a death toll of nearly 300,000 in Syria as of December 2015), while in the West it stands as a matter of moral urgency ("Why these abominable acts?"). Second, and in relation to the first point, terrorists are always non-Westerners; there are defined by their Oriental ethnic background and faith, or by association when a "loner" converts to Islam. At the same time, state terrorism (Russia in Chechnya, the United States in Iraq, Israel in South Lebanon and Gaza, etc.) is never recognized as such, in the name of self-defence or geopolitical interests. Finally, it is necessary to pretend that terrorism came about through spontaneous generation – an ideological posturing that betrays a constant revisionist take on history. Yet it is an open secret that Saddam Hussein and Osama Ben Laden were on the CIA payroll and that until 1987, Israel provided financial support to Hamas (including schools and mosques) in order to undermine Palestinian unity under Yasser Arafat's PLO. The absolute alterity that terrorism represents is also an airtight strategy whose purpose is to bring Western nations together around the idea of civilizational superiority, something that amounts to a grand exercise in sidetracking both elementary reasoning and accountability.[1] So, what does "terrorism" teach us about the seriousness of contemporary Orientalism, or rather the preposterous reiterations that are everywhere present, from Hollywood blockbusters to NATO military interventions in Afghanistan and Libya? Perhaps that establishing dialogue between facts and politics is not easy. Circumstances change, and the Arab/Muslim world shares the blame for dragging its feet on democracy, yet Orientalism's ascendance expresses itself not in its power to represent – linking humanistic knowledge to fantasy – but rather in an individual who from now on exists in real time and life. A particular event that epitomizes the tragic spiralling down within the postcolonial condition, and that is relevant to the general argument of this book, is the crime committed by Mohamed Merah, a Frenchman born to Algerian parents (as was I), in Toulouse (my hometown, too), in March 2012. This twenty-three-year-old man shot dead seven people, including children inside a Jewish school, in an act that reappropriates the Islam simulacrum of what *jihad* is not and cannot be. Reclaiming the racism and the symbolic violence of latent Orientalism by redirecting it back onto symbolic victims (Jews, the military), Merah was able to recast the postcolonial identity in its most radical signifying system, that is, as "us absolutely versus them." Through this horrible crime, France was forced to confront its own transformation within what could be dubbed transnational hatred. And the contingent materiality of the postcolonial condition has only taken a more dramatic turn: hundreds of French youth, largely of Maghrebi descent, have been joining the ranks of the various jihadist movements in Syria. It is clear now, with blood being shed in all places, that the French, in particular, can no longer uncritically buy into the essentializing discourse of identity and nationhood vis-à-vis the kind of "Arabs" they have been trying to make since the colonial era. The hero or martyr posturing by some of these postcolonial youth is more than a speech-act *à la* Frantz Fanon in *Black Skin, White Masks* (self-hating French Muslims passing for warriors like in the time of the Prophet Muhammad). Violence plays along like some achievement that engages in a counter-intuitive understanding of world citizenry. In that sense, those "terrorists" have created their parallel globalized world, or what Althusser called in his definition of ideology "the imaginary relationship of individuals to their real conditions of existence."[2] It is possible to contend that the postcolonial condition has broken down the realms of the symbolic (society and its kinship system) and the real (history itself), where individuals no longer recognize or experience life itself.

My ambition in this book has been to unearth and articulate a negative aesthetics and an ideology that have been navigating from violence to reconciliation and back, both in the academic world and between national cultures, that of France and the Maghreb, for example. A convergence? Not just yet. We first need to recapture a moment of innocence in the face of centuries of civilizational errancy.

Notes

1 States of Postcolonial Reading

1 "Let us never forget that we have taken over Algeria not by the law of the *jungle*, but by the law of *civilization*." Vialar, *Première letter*, 233. My translation.

2 Bernard Lewis, David Kopf, John MacKenzie, Daniel Varisco, and Robert Irwin have unapologetically questioned Edward Said's works at times for his supposedly polemical pro-Arab stance, his ahistorical approach to culture, and his crude approach to a rich and diverse field of study, as well as for claiming that Orientalism boils down to a single systemic discipline.

3 Iqbal Abbas and Ibrahim Pour, eds., *The Complete Collection of Twenty Essays by Qazvini* (Teheran: Donya-ye Ketab, 1984), 25. Special thanks to Hamid Dabashi for the reference in his *Post-Orientalism: Knowledge and Power in Time of Terror* (2008), 75.

4 Too often, new methods of studying the Arab/Muslim world are construed as essentially anti-Western and anti-Zionist. We will see in the last chapter to what extent anti-Muslim policies in France (and throughout Europe) directed at women who wear the headscarf play into this latent Orientalist ideology of simple binary thinking, reductive opposition, and archetypes of representation.

5 Said, *Orientalism*, 259.

6 Bernard Lewis, "The Question of Orientalism," *New York Review of Books*, 24 June 1982.

7 Said, "Afterword" to the 1994 edition of *Orientalism*, 340.

8 Note that the Tunisian people were proud of their peaceful uprising against the repressive Ben Ali regime, yet their new leaders called on French legal scholars to help convene a transitional constituent assembly to

draft a new constitution (voted on in January 2014) based on the principles of the French Republic and its universalist premises. Legal scholars such as Robert Badinter have been troubled by this sort of foreign influence on the legal framework of a sovereign state, which sheds light on the persisting non-identity of nation and state in postcolonial countries. No wonder that in response, the political pendulum swings towards religious extremism.

9 In this regard, scholars such as Ranajit Guha, Gayatri Chakravorty Spivak, Edward Said, Abdul JanMohamed, Arif Dirlik, Dipesh Chakrabarty, Walter Mignolo, and Christopher Miller stand out for their thorough questioning of the Western academic construct and discourse on the postcolonial Other.

10 Heidegger, "The Age of the World Picture," in *The Question Concerning Technology*, 116.

11 Among writers and academics from the Maghreb, Kateb Yacine, Abdelkebir Khatibi, and Mohammed Arkoun have been the most persuasive at refuting presuppositions be they nationalistic, faith-based, or neocolonial.

12 Anne McClintock, "The Angel of Progress: Pitfalls of the Term 'Postcolonialism,'" *Social Text* 31–2 (1992), 86.

13 My reference to "historicism" here clearly follows in the footsteps of Chakrabarty, who in *Provincializing Europe* tackles the perception of historical time as a process of development leading up to Western modernity (74).

14 Achille Mbembe, "Provincializing France?," *Public Culture* 23, no. 1 (2011), 87.

15 For example, an important question to be raised in this regard is: What are the full intellectual and pedagogical implications of doing Maghrebi studies with little knowledge of the Arabic language and with no understanding of Islam on the theological or cultural level?

16 It is interesting to note that the French academic tradition (unlike the Anglo-Saxon one) does not distinguish between *humanités* and *sciences sociales*. This raises the problem of how to distinguish between a French cultural institution and the logic of the theories that sustain it.

17 Even Frantz Fanon, who was so important to the development of the postcolonial critique, misjudged the efficacy of socialist revolution for formerly colonized peoples. Witness how, from the 1960s to the 1980s, in terms of economic development as well as democratic expectations, Vietnam and Algeria both testified to the failure of centralized socialist systems.

18 One of the earliest questions about the recent democratic uprisings throughout the Maghreb and the Near East related to the place of Islam in these regions. It would be more sensible to attempt to understand a new brand of democracy that, for a change, does not serve or protect or further the interests of foreign nations.

19 Elie Kedourie, a noted British historian of Iraqi Jewish descent and founder of the journal *Middle Eastern Studies*, advanced defamatory and arguably racist positions vis-à-vis the cultures of the Arab sphere. For example,
in *Democracy and Arab Political Culture*, she wrote that "there is nothing in
the political traditions of the Arab world – which are the political traditions of Islam – which might make familiar, or indeed intelligible, the
organizing ideas of constitutional and representative government" (5).
It is not surprising that Kedourie got the attention of both American
neoconservatives and critics of Said's discourse on latent Orientalism.

20 Indian academics such as Ranajit Guha (in the 1960s) and Sumit Sarkar
(later on) have been at the forefront of the struggle to have the "subaltern"
voice heard, whether the voice be that of a scholar or a peasant.

21 We have seen, for example, how some French citizens of Maghrebi background claimed a sense of Frenchness superior to that of other "Arabs"
in voting for the far-right candidate in the latest presidential election.
Although precise statistics are difficult to obtain because polls based on
ethnicity are not allowed in France, the forthright and uninhibited nationalist positions adopted by some minorities demonstrate how nationalism
proliferates, paradoxically, in the face of growing ethnic heterogeneity
and greater European integration.

22 This is visible in post–Ben Ali Tunisia, where the Islam-based government
of Ennahda ("renaissance" in Arabic) has found itself confronted with the
sometimes violent opposition of the Salafist organizations; meanwhile,
the Westernized and secularized bourgeois class has been trying to figure
out what discourse to apply so as not to appear to be lackeys of France.

23 It is amazing how in the academic circles of France, the postcolonial nation
par excellence, they still wonder aloud about the place and purpose of postcolonial studies. For example, *Hérodote*, a French journal of geopolitics,
published a special issue (vol. 120, Spring 2006) on postcolonial studies
that asked one one key question – "Postcolonial studies, what for?" –
along with arguments that postulated about postcolonial discourse being
a historical provocation.

24 Anyone familiar with pan-Arab culture today knows how peoples of the
Near East look down on the cultures of the Maghreb, deeming them too
Gallicized to be genuinely "Arab." Meanwhile, some French have convinced themselves that their own identity is under siege and have taken
up extremist discourses and stances against their fellow citizens who share
with them the postcolonial condition.

25 France is not the only country that seems to have embarked on a nationalist political purge. Austria, Belgium, Denmark, Finland, Italy, and the

Netherlands have all held national elections in recent years in which the far-right parties have achieved big gains. So it is safe to say that issues of identity and racism actually do not cluster around purely national *topoi*, but rather around an exaggerated idea of the importance of the West itself.

26 See, for instance, the remarkable work of Jacques Berque on Orientalism and North Africa, or President de Gaulle's insight about the inevitablity of Algeria's independence.

27 In *Peau noire, masques blancs* (*Black Skin, White Masks*), Fanon addressed extensively the violence of the colonized on himself, caught between the demands of the capital and the imperial imagery at the centre.

2 The Orient in Question

1 In his *Reflections on Exile* (2000), published late in his life, Said seeks out the agency of the exilic condition while presiding over the autobiographical voice too often denied to the native.

2 Leyla Benhabib, *Another Cosmopolitanism* (Oxford: Oxford University Press, 2006), 45.

3 Varisco, *Reading Orientalism*, 106. Varisco draws this phrase from Jacques Waardenburg, an Orientalism scholar whom Said derides in his watershed esssay of 1979.

4 Jon B. Alterman, "This Revolution Isn't Being Televised," *New York Times*, 30 December 2011, A23. This is the same newspaper that took more than a year – see the editorial "The Times and Iraq," *New York Times* (26 May 2004) – to acknowledge that it had basically misled its readers in its reporting of the reasons for going to war with Iraq. The blame for this was laid on the war-mongering Bush administration, deceptive intelligence agencies, and money-greedy Iraqi defectors and informants, but at no point did the newspaper's editors question their own ethical failings in making sweeping generalizations about the ubiquitous presence of "Arab terrorists" in the wake of the attacks of 9/11.

5 Said, *Orientalism*, 56–7, 68.

6 Foucault comes to mind here with his concept of organization associated with knowledge, desire, and order. See his *Les mots et les choses*, 250.

7 Gilroy, *The Black Atlantic*, 7.

8 In 1539, Guillaume Postel, at twenty-nine years of age, became the first French scholar ever to hold a chair in Arabic studies.

9 In *Histoire de la folie à l'âge classique* (1961) and *Surveiller et punir* (1975), and even in *L'archéologie du savoir* (1969), Foucault elaborates on the formation, accumulation, and preservation of power (institutional and other) as if it

were an enduring universalist subject, while bypassing history and its multitude of conflicts and acts of resistance.

10 Hourani, *Islam in European Thought*, 8.

11 Baudet, in *Paradise on Earth*, 16–17, examines this particular example of the Western fascination with messianic figures.

12 See Kimble, *Geography in the Middle Ages*. In this study, published before the advent of postmodern theory, the author analyses the impact of Western myths and fantasies on the development of geography as a science and its relationship to contemporary political undertakings.

13 Barry, in "Renaissance Venice and Her 'Moors'" in *Venice and the Islamic World, 828–1797*, 146–73, does a remarkable job of examining the gradual disappearance of Turkish and Egyptian figures from paintings in Venice during the Renaissance.

14 Before the age of postmodernism and postcolonial studies, Helen Bacon showed that the principles of ancient heroism were ascribed evenly by the Greeks to themselves and to their enemies. See her *Barbarians in Greek Tragedy* (New Haven: Yale University Press, 1961), 12.

15 Said, *Orientalism*, 56.

16 Greek vase paintings of the fifth century BCE show Priam, the Trojan king, wearing Persian attire. See Keith De Vries, "The Nearly Other: The Attic Vision of Phrygians and Lydians," in Cohen, ed., *Not the Classical Ideal.*

17 Immanuel Kant, when elaborating on the sublime (transcendent subjectivity), referred to non-European peoples (mainly Africans) as "degenerate," "unnatural," "monstruous," "hideous," "despotic," "miserable," "grotesque," and "stupid." Kant, *Observations*, 113.

18 Herder, *Reflections*, 354.

19 Renan, *Qu'est-ce qu'une nation?* In this lecture at the Sorbonne, Ernest Renan brought together race, religion, language, and geography to define the identity of a nation. French Republicans failed to perceive the irony of espousing a concept that ran counter to the reality of the colonial enterprise.

20 Said, *Orientalism*, 39.

21 Miller, *The French Atlantic Triangle*, 62.

22 Contrary to common perceptions, most Enlightenment thinkers believed in God, even if it was only in relation to free will, the soul's immortality, or moral principles. What they rejected was the institution of the Church. In the second edition of *Critique of Pure Reason* (1781), Kant puts faith on par with knowledge; there is also the fact that, as his correspondence shows, he revered his deeply pious mother.

23 Renan, however great his academic competence, did not speak Arabic and was known for his blanket condemnation of Arab cultures as primitive,

sensuous, unimaginative, and so on. Notable as well was his deeply rooted anti-Semitism, even though he was highly regarded as a Hebrew scholar.

24 Renan, "De la part des peuples sémitiques dans l'histoire de la civilization," in *Oeuvres complètes*, vol. II.

25 Sir William Jones, in *The Sanscrit Language* (1786), was the first to point out similarities in the lexical roots and syntactical structures of Sanskrit, Greek, and Latin. His discovery took root among German philologists such as Johann G. Herder and Wilhelm von Humbolt, who injected it into their Romantic nationalist studies of folklore and their concept of racialized nations (by contrast, the French and American models of nationhood were based on a social contract and manifest destiny).

26 Jacques Derrida, borrowing from Hegel, analysed negativity as *différance*, something set against deterministic, teleological force. By dismantling the epistemology of the Orient/Other, Europe was reinventing itself. But as Derrida suggested, in the process Europe did not gravitate towards a source where it was capable of thinking. *L'écriture et la différence* (*Writing and Difference*), 82.

27 Said, *Orientalism*, 105.

28 Tocqueville, *Seconde lettre sur l'Algérie*, 8, 13, 21.

29 One such French philosopher of "progress" was Nicolas de Condorcet with his concept of a society perfectible through education and his views on the intricate relationship between science and consciousness. See his *Esquisse d'un tableau des progrès de l'esprit humain* (1793).

30 The decline of European nations as world powers serves as a clear reminder that they achieved their hegemony as a result of specific historical circumstances, not because of their innate superiority. Yet clearly, Europe has had a lasting impact on the rest of the world – an impact that has seen non-Western intellectuals honouring or criticizing Europe's legacy. A recent example of this has been the debate over merging British and *shariah* law (in more than eighty-five councils in 2012) – which would constitute true hybridity. In that debate, postcolonial scholars have taken the lead.

31 For Victor Hugo, Théophile Gautier, Prosper Mérimée, and Washington Irving, Spain was Europe's own site of exoticism, filled with essentialism but with little historical agency.

32 Blumenbach, *De l'unité du genre humain*.

33 By Royal Decree, Columbus was to receive a 10 per cent commission on all the wealth generated by trade and commerce in the new lands. Only after his dreams of riches faded (he never set foot on the American continent, and later found himself overtaken by other explorers) did he take up a spriritual quest and pledge to use whatever wealth he amassed to finance the "liberation" of Jerusalem from Islam before the second coming of

Christ (see Carol Delaney, *Columbus and the Quest for Jerusalem* [New York: Pree Press, 2011]).

34 Antonio Gramsci seems to have coined the term "subaltern." See his "History of the Subaltern Classes: Methodological Criteria," in *Selections from the Prison Notebooks*, ed. and trans. Quintin Hoare and Geoffrey Nowell Smith (New York: International Publishers, 1971). In the 1970s, Indian historian Ranajit Guha founded *Subaltern Studies*, a journal for the study of Indian and Asian historiographies from a Marxist perspective. More recently, Gayatri Chakravorty Spivak has been the most vocal advocate of the concept – for example, in *A Critique of Postcolonial Reason*, a collection of essays published between 1985 and 1995. The subaltern is the one person who can make possible new cultural practices through, in particular, "impertinent readings" of Western literary classics (336). More importantly, for Spivak the subaltern condition is informed by both patriarchy and imperialism. The female subaltern ends up a displaced figure, chasing modernization while supposedly being the custodian of tradition.

35 Said underscored this pattern of presence and absence in the Oriental that helps validate the ideational representation of the Arab and Muslim in latent Orientalism. See *Orientalism*, 208.

36 Note that the word "Moslim" was coined in English in 1613, while the word "mussulman" appeared in French in the sixteenth century. Before this time, Western writers and travellers referred to Muslims in ethnic terms or with derogatory expressions.

37 In his excellent essay on Bonaparte in Egypt, historian Juan Cole examines in great detail how the French revolutionary leader attempted to instrumentalize Islam in order to establish his legitimacy and subdue local authorities, to no avail. See *Napoléon's Egypt: Invading the Middle East* (New York: St Martin's Griffin, 2007).

38 Fanon, *The Wretched of the Earth*, 37.

39 *Harkis*, Algerians who enlisted in the French army during the Algerian War of Independence, found it impossible to perceive themselves as protonational subjects. For them, a French Algeria was the inescapable reality.

40 Henri Pirenne is one of the historians who introduced this idea, especially in his posthumously published *Mahomet et Charlemagne*, written in 1936. Basing his analyses mainly on socio-economic factors, he helped establish a doctrine grounded in racial and cultural superiority. The concepts of "dominant" and "subordinate" became the benchmarks in the golden age of colonialism that was the first half of the twentieth century.

41 The three main causes of the decline of Arab civilization were the *reconquista* in Spain (1085–1492); the sack of Baghdad by the Mongols in 1258; and, most importantly, the fact that there there had never been a true scientific

and cultural revolution in the Arab world, but merely a succession of extraordinary people who were not necessarily ethnic Arabs (al-Kindi, al-Farabi, Ibn Rush, Ibn Sina, al-Biruni, Ibn Khaldun, al-Razi, al-Khwarizmi, al-Idrissi, Ibn al-Haytham, etc.). Those people's work was forgotten, and their influence dried up after their deaths or after their patrons stopped supporting them. The purpose of science in the Arab world was mainly to understand and answer philosophical questions rather than to master nature or achieve intellectual advancement. Antirationalist posturing came to dominate intellectual inquiry in all aspects of Arab academic life. Even the printing press was absent from the Islamic world until its introduction in the Ottoman Empire in 1727 (267 years after it was introduced in Europe).

42 Said, *Culture and Imperialism*, 45.

43 In Camus's unfinished and posthumously published book, *Le premier homme*, his narrator describes the effects of the war on the city of Algiers, yet remains unable to put a name on it.

44 Albert Memmi (*Portrait du colonisé*) and Raymond Aron (*La Tragédie algérienne*), each with insights that are different from Sartre's or Fanon's historical materialism, clearly understand how colonialism holds the seeds of its own end.

45 Edward Said, Robert J.C. Young, Homi Bhabha, Gayatri Chakravorty Spivak, Ranajit Guha, Emily Apter, Christopher L. Miller, Abdul JanMohamed, Balachandra Rajan, Abdelkebir Khatibi, Ahmed Aijaz, Arif Dirlik, Charles Forsdick, and many other academics working in North America, in Europe, and in Morocco, Turkey, India, and Hong Kong, are on the forefront of the postcolonial critique.

46 Literary characters such as the Moors, El Cid, Caliban, Othello, and the narrator in *Don Quixote*, with all their "Arabic" foreignness, define the figurative image of medieval Spain and of the Italian peninsula during the Renaissance.

47 Sartre, an intellectual champion of the anticolonial struggle, called this paradigm *l'universel singulier*, in *Situations*, VIII.

48 In the last chapter I will elaborate on this thorny issue, with a discussion of the place of Islam in France today.

49 Muslim intellectuals (Abdelkarim Murad in Morocco, Messali Hadj in Algeria, Muhammad Iqbal in India, Sayid Qutb in Egypt, etc.) were trained in the West or were very familiar with it and saw through the prejudice and cultural limitations of Western models.

50 Beauvoir, *Le Deuxième Sexe*, 281. My translation.

51 A famous Indian squib about Europeans was: "The whites are overreaching, oversexed, and over here." The same line was recycled later when Britain was overrun with American soldiers during the Second World War.

52 In Proust's *Time Remembered,* Charlus's anti-Semitism represents a state of mind that was less controversial than subversive in prewar France. Ben Jelloun's study about Maghreban immigrants in France, *La plus haute des solitudes,* underscores the extent to which they are condemned to remain *figurants* (extras) in French society.

53 Freud, *Civilization and its Discontents,* 37–8.

54 For an introduction to these issues, see Miller, *Blank Darkness,* 15.

55 Those retaining French as their official language were Morocco, Tunisia, Mauritania, Mali, Niger, Chad, Senegal, Gambia, Burkina Faso, Côte d'Ivoire, Guinea, Benin, Togo, Cameroon, the Central Africa Republic, Gabon, Congo, the Democratic Republic of Congo, Djibouti, and Madagascar.

56 Again, the field of subaltern studies makes a strong case for awareness and resistance in the struggle against colonialism and representation.

57 Derrida, after addressing ideological and cultural subjectivity, using his concepts of grammatology or *différance,* ended up writing about his own subjectivity in *Le Monolinguisme de l'autre.* His main argument is that he realized that he was a citizen speaking an assumed language living in an assumed country.

58 Especially during the Song dynasty (tenth to the thirteenth centuries CE), with the revival of Confucianism and its world view.

59 Jean-Jacques Rousseau, *Discours sur l'origine et les fondements de l'inégalité* (Paris: Garnier-Flammarion, 1971) pt III, 193.

60 Etienne Balibar examines the predicament of self-referential identity in thecontext of proclaimed universalism in *Masses, Classes, Ideas.*

61 In short stories by Prosper Mérimée or in poems by Théophile Gautier, for example.

62 Montesquieu, *The Spirit of the Laws,* bk 16 (1751). He takes his cues from European missionary and diplomatic accounts of "East" India and China, and of the "seraglios" of Algiers.

63 Said's term; see *Orientalism,* 205.

64 The great colonial exhibition of 1931 in Paris, under the aegis of the "greater France," underscored in the most cruel fashion what exoticism boiled down to: the absolute strangeness of the Other.

65 A recent illustration of the legacy of this cultural superiority complex in relation to the Islamic sphere is provided in Curtis, *Orientalism and Islam,* a work in which the author inflicts old clichés on his readers (e.g., "The Islamic religion with its fatalistic doctrine of predestination and the resulting passive nature of the population in Oriental societies," 305), along with anti-Said ranting and not-so-hidden Islamophobic attacks, besides presenting an apology for faulty Orientalism.

66 Two examples cannot be overlooked. Grousset's *Histoire des croisades* was
    widely used to legitimize culturally the French presence throughout North
    Africa, especially in Algeria after the hundredth anniversary of the coun-
    try's colonization. And in *Orientalism*, Said refers to Norman Daniel's
    The Arabs and Medieval Europe (London: Longmans, Green & Co., 1975)
    as pathbreaking, while not being fully aware of the author's ideological
    goal of belittling Islam.
67 The martyrdom of Hussein (grandson of the Prophet Muhammad) in 680
    caused a foundational split between the two visions of Islam. Later on,
    after the ninth century, as a result of infighting between regional lordships
    and royal dynasties, the religious split between Sunnis and Shias evolved
    into an overt political struggle. For example, Harun al-Rashid, the famed
    king of *The Arabian Nights*, was a merciless foe of Shiism.
68 Events related by several Muslim historians and chroniclers, among them
    Norman Ya'qubi (?–897), *Les Pays*, trans. Gaston Wiet (Cairo: Institut
    Français d'Archeologie Orientale, 1937), and Norman Ahmad Bin Yahya
    Bin Jabir Al Biladuri (?–892), *Origins of the Islamic State* (Beirut: Khayats,
    1966).
69 Francesco Gabrieli, a scholar of Arab culture and Islam, published many
    books, including *Arab Historians and the Crusades*. In these works, the fall
    of Jerusalem is described from different angles and by different voices.
    All accounts concur regarding the atrocities that took place.
70 The seminal work on Jewish–Arab relations throughout history is Goitein,
    A Mediterranean Society. Gotein specifically tackles the fall of Jerusalem to
    the Franks in "Contemporary Letters."
71 Johan Galtung, "On the Dialectic between Crisis and Crisis Perception," in
    Europe at the Crossroads: Agendas of the Crisis, ed. Stefan A. Musto and Carl
    F. Pinkele (New York. Praeger, 1985), 11.
72 In defence of Camus's literary intention, it is fair to add that in Algeria
    until the late 1950s, the word "algérien" was the preferred term used to
    refer to those of European descent.
73 Both writers saw in the Orient a locus for homoeroticism and a terrain for
    projecting the discourse of their own victimhood as social outcasts. While
    Gide used the colonies as a mirror to tackle pedophilia head-on, Genet
    focused on the plight of the Palestinians and their minority discourse.
74 Kabbani, *Europe's Myths of Orient*, 5–6.
75 Before Antoine Galland translated *The Arabian Nights* from Arabic into
    French (published in 1717, two years after his death), he had translated the
    Koran (1704).
76 The early 1980s saw a famous dispute at the Sorbonne-Nouvelle between
    those who claimed an Orientalist scholarly tradition and those who

wanted to study Arabic and Arab cultures from a new approach free from the influence of the two academic institutions that had dominated Arab studies for nearly two centuries: the Institut de Langues Orientales and the Collège de France. Eventually the École Normale Supérieure established its own Department of Arab studies.

3 Orientalism and Postcolonial Studies

1 In the twentieth century, the Arabic word for "Orientalism" was *istishraq*; the more recent Arabic word for "Occidentalism" is *istighrab*, something that also connotes "to find something puzzling, weird."

2 Hulme, "Subversive Archipelagos," 3.

3 In *Semites and Anti-Semites*, Lewis addresses the political dimension of the Palestinians' right to self-determination with unfeigned contempt and simply considers Arab opposition to Zionism a pathology.

4 One year after the publication of *Orientalism*, Said wrote *The Question of Palestine*, in which he condemned both the incompetence of the Palestinian leadership and the Israeli and American lock on Palestinian self-determination and independence. To the chagrin of his academic opponents, more than thirty years later his argument still holds sway.

5 "I have found it useful here to employ Michel Foucault's notion of a discourse, as described by him in *The Archeology of Knowledge* ... to identify Orientalism." MacKenzie, *Orientalism*, 3.

6 Arran E. Gare, "Understanding Oriental Cultures," *Philosophy East and West* 45 (1995): 315.

7 In Algeria, Emir Abdel-Qadir led the revolt against the French from 1834 to 1843. In India, the rebellion of the last of the Mughal (Muslim) rulers took place from 1857 to 1859, first against the East India Company and then against British rule. In Sudan, Muhammad Ahmad proclaimed himself Mahdi (messianic redeemer) of the Islamic faith in a struggle against the Anglo-Ottoman coalition from 1881 to 1885.

8 Said, *Orientalism*, 32.

9 Ibid., 203.

10 Memmi, *Portrait du colonisé*, 116ff.

11 First Frantz Fanon, then Homi Bhabha, examined this particular point of the postcolonial critique. Fanon did so within a revolutionary frame, Bhabha as a project in postcolonial theory.

12 Jugurtha was a Berber military hero who fought against the Roman invaders of North Africa. Amrouche used his name for a collection of poems in French published in 1946. He claimed that war and poetry were part of the Maghrebi identity.

13 For Albert Camus, Algeria symbolized best what the Mediterranean stood for: a perfect meeting of East and West. See Camus, "La culture indigène, la nouvelle culture méditerranéenne" (1939) in *Essais*, 1324–5. Yet both in the 1930s, when he wrote articles decrying the abject poverty of the Algerian people, and in the 1950s, during the War of Independence, he remained unable to condemn the colonial system and its ideology.

14 Said, *Orientalism*, 201.

15 Spivak, "Explanation and Culture: Marginalia" in *In Other Worlds*, 108.

16 The 2003 Islamic headscarf affair symbolizes the national unease with the colonial legacy. In June 2007 the new government, under Nicolas Sarkozy, created for the first time in modern French history a ministry of "identity." In the fall of 2010, after much controversy, that ministry was eliminated.

17 MacKenzie, *Orientalism*, 210.

18 Throughout the second half of the nineteenth century, the Second and Third Republics in France strove to maintain a national cultural unity, mostly based on myths, language, and citizenship. Meanwhile, artists such as Flaubert, Baudelaire, Manet, and Courbet debunked, each in his own way, the country's material and fabricated cultural values.

19 Paul Valéry, *Oeuvres*, ed. Jean Hytier (Paris: Gallimard, 1960), 2:1557, quoted in Said, *Orientalism*, 251.

20 Ibid., 308; author's emphasis.

21 In the tradition of Montaigne, historicism grounds itself in hermeneutics. More recently, in North American academia, history as a discipline has cross-fertilized other sciences since reaching an ethical tipping point in the 1970s regarding the political implications of doing humanities. See for example, Stephen Greenblatt, "The Power of Forms," in David Richter, ed., *The Critical Tradition* (New York: Bedford St Martin's, 1988).

22 I take this idea from Aijaz Ahmad's *In Theory: Classes, Nations, Literatures* (London: Verso, 2008). "English will become, in effect, the language in which the knowledge of 'Indian Literature' is produced" (250). In a later chapter I develop the literary problematics of Maghreb writing in French.

23 Turkish historian Arif Dirlik, in "The Post-Colonial Aura," condemns both the mistaken Western practice of keeping politics and culture apart and Eastern intellectuals generally for selling out and turning into professional "minority" academics. He elaborates in on this theme in Dirlik, Bahl, and Gran, *History after the Three Worlds*.

24 Some the earliest and harshest criticisms of the postcolonial discourse are found in Ahmad, *In Theory*; Anne McClintock, "The Angel of Progress: Pitfalls of the Term 'Postcolonialism,'" *Social Text* 31–2 (1992): 84–98; and Benita Parry, "The Postcolonial: Conceptual Category or Chimera?," *Yearbook Of English Studies* 27 (1999): 3–21.

25 Spivak, *A Critique of Postcolonial Reason*, 142.
26 Cooper has shown how political forces (including trade unions) within the colonial *métropole*, as well as failed assimilation policies and supranational ideologies, have contributed to the demise of colonialism. See his *Decolonization and African Society*.
27 Said, *Orientalism*, 299.
28 Rushdie, *Imaginary Homelands*, 125.
29 Hélène Cixous, "Mon algériance," *Les Inrockuptibles* 20 (August 1997): 71–4. James Joyce made this same association with a dead past when writing about Ireland in *Dubliners* (1914). Note that Cixous wrote her doctoral dissertation on Joyce's work and his exile.
30 In her autobiography, *Les rêveries de la femme sauvage*, Cixous coins a highly ambivalent word: "inséparabe" (45) – as if she continues to struggle with an identity that is simultaneously individual (she feels herself to be French-German, not Algerian), collective (she describes her family life with hardly a word about her Jewish Arab father), and national.
31 Kwame Anthony Appiah criticized early on the masquerade of the nativist discourse in Western academia. See his "Out of Africa."
32 War veterans and faith-based activists were the real opponents of the war in Iraq.
33 Paul Gilroy drives the point home concerning this new dimension of the political and cultural commodification of the Other in *Against Race*.
34 Said, *Orientalism*, 301.
35 The Moroccan poet Abdellatif Laâbi translated Palestinian poetry from Arabic into French. But his work was rejected by all of the publishers he had collaborated with before. The collection was eventually published by a small, one-man house as *La poésie palestinienne contemporaine* (Paris: Éditions du Temps des Cerises, 2002).
36 Several examples come to mind, among them Tahar Ben Jelloun, whose ready-made Moroccan exoticism is tailored to French readers, and Malika Mokeddem, who recycles French metaphors of essentialized feminism as applied to the Arab or Muslim subaltern. Also noteworthy are Abdelwahab Meddeb and Malek Chebel, who take a supposedly scholarly anti-Islam stance in order to ingratiate themselves with those French intellectuals who trumpet secular and anti-Arab views, most notably in the wake of the 9/11 attacks but also in relation to the festering conflict in the Palestinian occupied territories. Later in this volume we examine why "house Muslims," especially in France, should not be taken at face value.
37 The following (among others) concern themselves with hegemonic post-coloniality, the inscriptive power of Western academia, and prevailing qualifications of Otherness: Ahmad, *In Theory*; Brennan, *At Home in the*

World; Mukherjee, "Whose Post-Colonialism"; Neil Larsen, "Imperialism, Colonialism, Postcolonialism," in *A Companion to Postcolonial Studies*, ed. Henry Schwartz and Sangeeta Ray (Oxford: Blackwell, 2000), 23–52; Parry, "Directions and Dead Ends"; and Mbembe, *De la postcolonie*.

38 Griffith, "Representation and Production," 23.

39 Morrison, *Playing in the Dark*, 17.

40 "There are institutes, centers, faculties, departments, all devoted to legitimizing and maintaining the authority of a handful of basic, basically unchanging ideas about Islam, the Orient, and the Arabs." Said, *Orientalism*, 302.

41 Witness, for example, the colonial overtones of the French political and media discourses *vis-à-vis* the ongoing postcolonial drama in the suburbs, and the deconstruction of (French) Muslims as the new dangerous social class. These sociocultural aspects will be fully examined in the final chapter of this volume.

42 This accusation is discussed and debunked by Derrida in *Specters of Marx*, 82.

43 Pierre Bourdieu coined this term in *The Rules of Art*, his critique of how art is consumed in twentieth-century France (336).

44 See Said, *Orientalism*, 304ff.

45 In *Nedjma*, Kateb plays with this issue of origin (Berber, Jewish, Arabic), only to bypass and exhaust the French colonial trauma best visible in the French language itself.

4 Unfinished (Literary) Business: Orientalism and the Maghreb

1 Postcolonial theory has spawned a multitude of subdisciplines over time. The point here is to underscore that the postcolonial writer is not simply commodified within a system of knowledge: he or she is also expected to assume the weight of a civilization, especially in terms of its history and language.

2 In *Empire*, Hardt and Negri bring forward the "liberatory" content of postcolonial studies. This actually reinforces the paradigm and strategies of rule (138). It is true that issues of "applicability" and self-reflexivity tend to trivialize readings, especially in an overloaded lexical field that includes "imperialism," "resistance," "power," "hegemony," "margins," and so on. For example, how are silenced voices expected to be retrieved and heard when postcolonial theory engages in self-consolidation?

3 "Disons en bref que, sur ce territoire linguistique de ladite 'francophonie,' je me place, moi, sur les frontières." Djebar, *Ces voix qui m'assiègent*, 27. My translation.

4 Henry Louis Gates, Jr, emphasizes that sense of "indenture" that culture and language can force on a historically dominated class of citizens in "'Writing,' 'Race,' and the Difference it Makes," in *"Race," Writing, and Difference*, 13; originally published in *Critical Enquiry* 12, no. 1 (Fall 1985), 1–20.

5 Said, *The World, the Text, and the Critic*, 223.

6 In *Maghreb pluriel*, Khatibi argues that hybridity and "in-between-ness" are valid concepts because these very notions predate French colonialism, having been equally applicable during the time of the Ottoman and Arab invasions.

7 In his analysis of the post-Renaissance world system, Marxist historian Immanuel Wallerstein was the first to address the idea of "border thinking" as a system, though not as a theory. See the introduction to his *The Modern World-System*.

8 In Heideggerian terminology, the difference between "knowledge" and "meaning," although subtle, is best explained not in terms of a quest for truth but rather as a mode of keeping truth alive, particularly through order (cultural, literary, ideological, faith-based, etc.) See chapter 5 of *Being and Time* (*Sein und Zeit*), in which Heidegger posits that meaning precedes language because man is himself a sign [*Sinn*].

9 One illustration is that of the Mutazilis, Muslim theologians of the ninth and tenth centuries who took Greek philosophy as a starting point for their speculative works in order to rationalize reality, including that of God's injunctions.

10 Said, "Shattered Myths," 410.

11 "Ma fiction est cette autobiographie qui s'esquisse." Djebar, *L'amour, la fantasia*, 244. My translation.

12 Boudjedra, *La Répudiation*; *L'Insolation*; *L'Escargot entêté*.

13 Note that one fundamental literary, if not philosophical, model for Kateb was Arthur Rimbaud, who applied all his talent to debunking Western archetypal discourses. The French poet eventually went into exile for more than ten years in eastern Africa, where, among many other activities, he learned and taught Arabic.

14 A highly influential critique of Orientalism is the Egyptian academic Anouar Abdel-Malek's "Orientalism in Crisis." This article, published during the early postcolonial era, underscored new forces to be reckoned with – nationalism and the desire for sovereignty, just as in the case of Kateb's Algeria.

15 Dirlik, "The Postcolonial Aura," 353.

16 The term "productive matrix" was coined in "The Commitment to Theory," an early article by Homi Bhabha in which he heaped praises on the rhetorical force of subaltern literature. Bhabha, "The Commitment to Theory," *New Formations* 5 (1988), 109–21.

17   Edward Said used these words to describe V.S. Naipaul's work in light of postcolonial theories. Said, "Intellectuals in the Post-Colonial World," 53.

18   The three Goncourt Prize–winning novels are Michel Tournier, *La Goutte d'or* (1986); Didier Van Cauwelaert, *Un Aller simple* (1994); and Jean-Christophe Rufin, *Katiba* (2010).

19   Can the endless debates on the "Arab Spring" signify anything other than the affirmation of the Western metropolis as democratic security in the same way that a bank customer would view his banking institution as "secure"?

20   This is exemplified in Djebar's *L'amour, la fantasia*, a novel in which the author hides her autobiographical voice behind those of Algerian women who live through a span of two centuries. Also, the poetry collections of Abdlelatif Laâbi, about his years in King Hassan II's prisons, claim to speak for all Moroccan political prisoners.

21   The rapid rise of francophone studies in North American academia tends to support the principle of hiring "black" or "Arab" faculty as genuine representatives, as opposed to all-purpose white professors who have no real "me" to return to, because they were never displaced in the first place.

22   In *Le Passé simple* (Paris: Gallimard, 1954), there is a power transfer from "le seigneur" to Chraïbi. In *Les Boucs* (Paris: Gallimard, 1955), the last chapter reveals the hero's identity, as if to emphasize his tragic fate. In *La Civilization, ma mère!* (Paris: Gallimard, 1972), the last chapter is an eye-opener for the father figure, whose life has become a lie.

23   Said, *The World, the Text, and the Critic*, 275.

24   In his highly literary *Of Grammatology*, Derrida rightly underscores the West's obsession with a metaphysics of truth and the subsequent disappearing act of the ideas of origin and representation.

25   During the colonial era, Algeria-born Europeans were referred to as *pieds-noirs*. Albert Camus probably exemplifies best what Algeria's future should have looked like: a commonwealth of cultures and peoples rather than an independent nation. In the 1980s, another *pied-noir* writer, Marie Cardinale, perceived her native land as in a game of absence/presence but without rethinking the nature of colonialism.

26   "Par l'acquisition du français, il devient possible de composer avec ceux qui détiennent le pouvoir. Cela procurerait aussi la maîtrise de la technique, voie d'accès à la reconnaissance et au confort. En tels rouages de symbolisation, la séduction était grande." Meddeb, "Le palimpseste du bilingue," 128. My translation.

27   Aijaz has written extensively on the linguistic double-bind of the postcolonial author and how literary criticism tends to overlap with neocolonial

ideologies. See his position vis-à-vis American academia in "Jameson's Rhetoric of Otherness.'"

28 This is a fundamental notion in Gilroy's *"There Ain't No Black in the Union Jack"* (see 155 in the reprint edition). In that book, Gilroy examines racial politics from the perspective of black people in contemporary England.

29 For example, Kateb, *Le Polygone étoilé*. Kateb gave up his writing career in the 1970s to become the director of a theatrical company, which staged plays across Algeria, mostly in Berber and in Arabic dialect. Another example is Mammeri, *La Colline oubliée*. Mammeri also taught Berber and edited a journal of Berber studies. Yet another example is Farès, *Mémoire de l'absent*. A psychoanalyst turned writer, Farès has focused part of his work on identity difference, with an emphasis on national languages.

30 A term originally from the literary world of Latin America from the 1930s to the 1970s, which included such figures as Jorge Icaza, Miguel Ángel Asturias, and José María Arguedas. The artistic intention of indigenism was to bring to the fore local traditions, dialects, and myths.

31 "C'est que nous sommes seuls vidés contrebattus / au pied du Murmurailles des lamentations véridiques / nous encerclant dessus dessous / avec la marque du désastre." Laâbi, "Oeil de talisman," in *Le règne de barbarie*, 55. My translation.

32 Said, *Orientalism*, 209.

33 Khatibi, *Amour bilingue*, 29. My translation.

34 This has become obvious in the taxonomy of bookstore shelving. In France, Maghreb literature in French is typically labelled "Middle Eastern and North African Literature," while in the Maghreb countries it has yet to become national literature.

35 "Renouons avec le désert, la montagne, le retrait hors cette histoire dont le cataclysme final risque de nous surprendre." Meddeb, *Talismano*, 189 (page citation is to the reprint edition). My translation.

36 In Arabic, "Maghreb" means where the sun sets, the Occident.

5 André Gide and Imperial Dystopia

1 By 1900 there were only two independent nations left in Africa: Morocco and Abyssinia (Liberia being a creation of the United States). These were the settings for the exotic images depicted in works by artists like Delacroix; they were also sanctuaries for writers like Rimbaud.

2 Between 1942 and 1944, Algiers was the capital of Free France and Dakar was the springboard for the Gaullist military reconquest of Metropolitan France.

3 Joseph Massad, a professor of modern Arab history, contends that gender issues (mostly homosexual) are made universal only through epistemic violence unleashed by a Western elite that purports to defend victims. The main, and defiant, argument revolves around the reification of the Arab subject, from the colonial era to the post-industrial age. See Massad, *Desiring Arabs*.

4 Voltaire, Hugo, and Zola, among others, all faced the task of mastering the uncharted waters of political engagement at a time when a burgeoning democracy was being widely heralded.

5 The abolition of slavery in 1848 was viewed as a giant step towards respect for human rights outside France. Yet although Tocqueville believed passionately in democracy and abolition, he also called for colonialism in Algeria.

6 Sociologist Lucien Lévy-Brühl contended that there were irreducible differences between the French and the colonized. In this way he exposed the ethical ambiguity of the colonial entreprise. In *Les Fonctions mentales dans les sociétés inférieures*, he called for races and ethnic groups to be ranked in terms of their capacity for reason and their attachment to "pre-logical" mysticism.

7 Victor Hugo, Gérard de Nerval, and Théophile Gautier turned to the Orient (e.g., the Ottoman Empire, Egypt, even southern Spain) for inspiration for their poetry. Alexandre Dumas in his novella *Quinze jours au Sinaï* (1830), based on a trip that his friend Adrien Dauzats took to Egypt, made a case for reconciling West and East. Flaubert, in his novel *L'Éducation sentimentale* (1869), presents Algeria as an unforgiving place of exile, very much in the Romantic line. The literary convention of the day posited that the Orient was enticing and free, as familiar but also threatening.

8 Native Jews from Algeria became French citizens by government decree in 1870; Muslim Algerians lived under the *indigènes* status throughout Algeria's 132-year colonial period.

9 Roland Barthes, *Le plaisir du texte* (Paris: Le Seuil, 1975).

10 For instance, in *L'Immoraliste*, Michel, the main character, lets his wife die while he is obsessed with a young Arab boy.

11 Gide borrowed the title character from Virgil's *Eclogues*. In one of the eclogues, the protagonist is Amyntas, a black shepherd. Incidently, this is one of the earliest instances in the Western canon of a celebration of homosexual love.

12 "[…] pas de compromis encore entre les civilisations de l'Orient et la nôtre qui paraît laide surtout quand elle veut réparer." Gide, *Amyntas*, 26 (page citation is to the reprint edition). My translation.

13 More than half a century earlier, Lamartine's journey to the Middle East was all a matter of spiritual syncretism: "Je répondis au gouverneur que, bien que je fusse né dans une autre religion que la sienne, je n'en adorais pas moins que lui la souveraine volonté d'Allah." (I informed the [Ottoman] governor that, although I was raised in a different religion from his, I did not worship less than he did himself the supreme will of Allah.) Lamartine, *Souvenirs*, 366. My translation.

14 "L'angoisse n'est qu'en nous; ce pays est au contraire très calme; mais cette question nous étreint: est-ce avant, est-ce après la vie?" Gide, *Amyntas*, 85. My translation.

15 "Oh! savoir, quand cette épaisse porte noire, devant cet Arabe, ouvrira, ce qui l'accueillera, derrière ... Je voudrais être cet Arabe, et que ce qui l'attend m'attendît." Gide, *Amyntas*, 111. My translation.

16 "In me division and trouble. But not revolt or ingratitude. Rather anxiety." Amrouche, "La culture peut être une mystification." My translation.

17 "L'étrangeté de l'Européen commence par son exil intérieur." Kristéva, *Étrangers à nous-mêmes*, 42. My translation.

18 In the winter of 1849, a full year before he began writing *Madame Bovary*, during his stay in a seedy Cairo hostelry, Flaubert met a French landlord who went by the name of Monsieur Bouvaret. For accounts of Flaubert's homosexual encounters, see his *Correspondance*, Tome I, 252, 571–3, 604–6.

19 In his novel *Histoire d'amour de la rose des sables* (1932), Montherlant replaces his own "story," which involved a pre-teenage boy in Algiers, with that of French military officer and a teenage girl in rural Morocco.

20 "Les Arabes s'accoutument à vous, on leur paraît moins étranger, et leur habitude, d'abord troublée, se réforme." Gide, *Amyntas*, 32. My translation.

21 Gide had married his cousin Madeleine, whom he called "the Orient of his life." He never consummated the marriage; however, he had a mistress and a daughter, Catherine, by that mistress.

22 Gide, *Journal 1939–1949*, 590–601.

23 One obvious example is Claire Duras's *Ourika* (1823). See the remarkable study "Duras and Her Ourika, 'The Ultimate House Slave,'" chapter 8 of Miller, *The French Atlantic Triangle*.

24 The Dreyfus affair fed the argument of what it meant to be French; the sentence for the officer wrongly accused of high treason was to be jailed overseas, in French Guiana.

25 "Près de nous, devant la misérable hutte où trois pauvres Arabes s'abritent, une femme couverte d'une loque safran lave une maigre fillette de cinq ans, toute nue, debout dans un chaudron noir [...] Que celui qui ne connaît pas ce pays imagine d'abord: rien." Gide, *Amyntas*, 58–9. My translation.

26 Ricoeur, *Histoire et vérité*, 292. My translation.

27 Jameson, *The Political Unconscious*, 198.

28 "J'ai dû m'écarter encore, pour cacher aux autres mes larmes. Dans la piété de ce peuple vaincu […] dans cette confiance désespérée en autre chose monte la désolation du désert." Gide, *Amyntas*, 142. My translation.

29 "Athman lit comme Bouvard et écrit comme Pécuchet. Il s'instruit de toutes ses forces et copie n'importe quoi." Gide, *Amyntas*, 36. My translation.

30 "Les hôtels sont pleins de voyageurs; mais ils tombent sous les lacs de guides charlatans, et paient très cher les cérémonies falsifiées qu'on leur joue." Gide, *Amyntas*, 46. My translation.

31 I contend here that Gide is pre-Foucauldian in his dramatic position on sex and social order. Nearly eighty years later, Foucault wrote: "The notion of 'sex' made it possible to group together, in an artificial unity, anatomical elements, biological functions, conducts, sensations, pleasures, and it enabled the use of this ficticious unity as a causal principle." Foucault, *The History of Sexuality*, vol. I, 154.

32 One of Césaire's arguments in *Discours sur le colonialisme* was that Nazism was the legacy of "the very humanist, very Christian, and very bourgeois" nineteenth century.

33 "Le sens moral, peut-être, dis-je, en m'efforçant de sourire – Oh simplement celui de la propriété." Gide, *L'Immoraliste*, 111 (page citation is to the reprint edition). My translation.

34 "J'oubliais ma fatigue et ma gêne. Je marchais dans une sorte d'extase, d'allegresse silencieuse, d'exaltation des sens et de la chair." Gide, *L'Immoraliste*, 50. My translation.

35 Jameson, "Cognitive Mapping," 349–50.

36 Edward Said notes the extent to which the French colonial endeavor was to erase native cultures by claiming that the stated goal for colonialism was no less than "the biological unity of mankind." Said, *Culture and Imperialism*, 184.

37 "Bachir suivait, bavard; fidèle et souple comme un chien." Gide, *L'Immoraliste*, 43. My translation.

38 "Je ne reconnais pas les enfants, mais les enfants me reconnaissent. Prévenus de mon arrivée tous accourent. Est-il possible que ce soient eux!" Gide, *L'Immoraliste*, 171–2. My translation.

39 Karl Marx, *Collected Works*, 12:132.

40 "Je m'assis au premier banc que je trouvai. J'espérai qu'un enfant surviendrait […] Celui qui vint bientôt ce fut un grand garçon de quatorze ans […] pas timide du tout, qui s'offrit de lui-même." Gide, *L'Immoraliste*, 44–5. My translation.

41 "Et je me comparais aux palimpsestes [...] Quel était-il ce texte occulté? Pour le lire ne fallait-il pas tout d'abord effacer les textes récents?" Gide, *L'Immoraliste*, 63. My translation.

42 Recall that Michel's homoerotic encounters are also construed as a wonderful opportunity for the children to be exposed to the benefits of European society. Michel always insists on how generous and benevolent he is.

43 Derrida, *The Monolinguism of the Other*, 40.

44 "Marceline est assise à demi sur son lit [...] ses draps, ses mains, sa chemise, sont innondés d'un flot de sang [...] Je cherche sur son visage transpirant une petite place où poser un affreux baiser." Gide, *L'Immoraliste*, 178. My translation.

45 Joseph Conrad, E.M. Forster, and André Gide all helped shape the canon of colonial literature, with its sense of commitment, its measure of humanism, and its complete misunderstanding of native identities and emergent resistance.

46 "Arrachez-moi d'ici à présent, et donnez-moi des raisons d'être. Moi je ne sais plus en trouver." Gide, *L'Immoraliste*, 180. My translation.

47 Along with his friend Paul Valéry, Gide was at the forefront of the Dreyfus affair in denouncing both anti-Semitism and nationalism.

48 See Sartre's introduction to Memmi, *The Colonizer and the Colonized*.

6 Fables of Maghreb Nationhood

1 The French Republic immediately embraced *ancien régime* characters such as Charlemagne and Joan of Arc, yet it is worth noting that Bastille Day became the French national holiday only in 1889, as if the nation had failed to construe itself in what historian Marc Bloch used to call "longue durée." No wonder that within such insecure parameters, the colonial empire was recalibrated in terms of the Other's citizenship and nationhood.

2 Joseph Arthur Gobineau was the most famous proponent of an ideology based on racial superiority. His *Essai sur l'inégalité des races humaines* became a bedside book for Nazis in the making. More striking is that during his three years (1855–8) as a French diplomat for Napoléon III in Persia (renamed Iran only in 1934), he continued to view the Orient as a fabled land. Gobineau's *Nouvelles asiatiques* is supposedly a tribute to Montesquieu's *Lettres persanes* (1721), but in fact it set out to undermine the Republic's democratic achievements.

3 The expression is from Bhabha, "Introduction: Narrating the Nation," in *Nation and Narration*, 1.

4 Morocco's King Abdel-Rahman did send troups to support the emir, but
after the French navy shelled Tangiers and Essaouira in 1844, he withdrew
all support from his fellow Muslim neighbour.

5 Bernard, *L'Algérie*, 76. Bernard was a Sorbonne professor who extensively
studied North Africa and its social fabric.

6 It is not that the colonial undertaking was based on the contradictory
premises of spreading French Republican principles while crushing peoples' right to self-determination; rather, the French political body was unable to grasp the limitations of its own imperial ideology enough to
rescind its claims to be an "enlightened" colonial power.

7 Between 1864 and 1895, 4,200 Algerians along with hundreds of Moroccans and Tunisians were sentenced to hard labour in New Caledonia.
Ouennaghi, *Algériens et Maghrébins en Nouvelle-Calédonie*, 81. Sources in
this work are drawn from French colonial archives. Note that the law on
political amnesty of 17 March 1880 did not apply to Algerian prisoners.

8 In the 1930s, fewer than fifty Algerian students were attending universities
in France; in the 1950s, around 400. Ageron, *Histoire de l'Algérie contemporaine*, 537.

9 An early encounter was Bonaparte's military and scientific expedition to
Egypt (July 1798–June 1801). This first massive French encounter with the
Arab/Muslim world was a precursor to the power play that would be
launched at the Orient in the coming century.

10 The primary purpose of the French colonial school system was to remove
native children from Islamic schools (*madrasas*). In Algeria, access to education in French was limited to the elementary grades; the goal here was
to provide low-skilled manpower for the colonial economy. In 1920, 8 per
cent of native children attended French schools; in 1961, only 15 per cent.
In 1953, three years before independence, 13 per cent of Muslim children
attended school in Morocco, and 11 per cent in Tunisia. These figures do
not reflect the widespread differences between the situations in the cities
and in the countryside, as well as the enormous gender gap.

11 Collot, *Les Institutions de l'Algérie*, 276.

12 "Destour" was actually borrowed from the Turkish language as a token of
close association with the Young Turks who were fighting Western med-
dling in Turkey's affairs after the Treaty of Versailles.

13 In his televised speech of 16 September 1959, President de Gaulle used for
the first time in French colonial history the taboo word "self-determination"
in relation to the Algerian people. He told his fellow Frenchmen: "Compte
tenu de toutes les données, algériennes, nationales et internationales, je
considère comme nécessaire que ce recours à l'autodétermination soit, dès

aujourd'hui, proclamé." Sources *Institut National de l'Audiovisuel*: http://
www.ina.fr/economie-et-societe/vie-economique/video/CAF88024409/
allocution-radiodiffusee-et-televisee-du-general-de-gaulle.fr.html. The
independence war had been both bloody and costly; furthermore, having
closely followed the end of British rule in India, de Gaulle was an early
adherent of the concept of the clash of civilizations. For him, the Muslim
world was incompatible with French ideals and culture, and the failure of
colonization was proof of this.

14 This idea is thoroughly analysed in Bourdieu and Passeron, *La Reproduction*
(see page 57), although they apply it to the struggle of the French social
classes, not to the colonial condition.

15 The term "Algérien" was reserved exclusively for Europeans born in
Algeria. Very soon after independence, this overhelming normative value
was shaken off, and Algerians claimed their own right to be a people.

16 The concept of the "third space" has emerged in postcolonial theory. It
relates mainly to the study of the conditions for asymmetrical social and
cultural relations among non-industrialized nations and their peoples in
a globalized world. The prominent scholars in the field include Edward T.
Hall, Homi K. Bhabha, Abdelkebir Khatibi, and Ulrich Beck.

17 "Bientôt vous célébrerez à Paris l'anniversaire du 14 juillet 1789. Nous
sommes avec vous par la pensée car nous sommes de ceux qui se souvien-
nent. Et de tels souvenirs entretiennent notre foi, et justifient notre es-
pérance." Kessel and Pirelli, *Le Peuple algérien et la guerre*, 68.

18 For example, while Algeria was exporting grains and other crops to the
French *métropole*, the natives suffered from famines in 1917 and 1920. In
The Plague (1947), Camus replaced the actual famine in western Algeria
with a plague; thus rats could be blamed instead of colonial institutions.

19 In July 1962, during the referendum on Algerian independence, most
French people knew little about the document's articles. They seemed
more interested in the Tour de France.

20 Cartier's *L'Algérie sans mensonge* was a scathing indictment of the gross
incompetence of colonial institutions, besides being a racist screed on how
Arabs were unassimilable.

21 See Aron, *La Tragédie algérienne*, a study originally commissioned by the
prime minister at the time, Guy Mollet.

22 A recurrent idea in Aron's *La Tragédie algérienne* was that to continue
the war would be more expensive than to pay to resettle the *pieds-noirs*
in France.

23 "La colonisation est le plus grand fait de l'Histoire. Est-il vrai qu'aujourd'hui
nous célébrions une apothéose qui soit proche d'une décadence? Jamais

chez nous l'élan de la pensée et son jaillissement n'ont été plus puissants qu'aujourd'hui." Reynaud, "Discours inaugural," 27. My translation.

24 This type of ideological proposition had its roots in the nineteenth century and endured until after the Second World War. See Saint-Germès, *Économie algérienne*, 34.

25 Senghor, *Anthologie de la nouvelle poésie nègre*.

26 In 1949, in *Les conditions de la renaissance*, Algerian intellectual Malek Bennabi coined the concept of "colonisabilité" – that is, Maghrebis had been colonized as a result of structural weaknesses across their territories and a loss of social "energy" (in part a consequence of their dogmatic understanding of Islam). With the end of the Second World War, the time was ripe for Maghrebis to overcome these cultural weaknesses and to wrench their identity and nationhood from their own condition.

27 The concepts of environmental determinism and vital space were developed by German geographer Friedrich Ratzel in the scholarly work *Die Erde und das Leben*. Twenty years later, while Germany was reeling from the aftermath of the First World War, Hitler appropriated this academic concept as the doctrine of "Lebensraum."

28 The Marçais brothers, William and Georges (and their sons Jean and Philippe), were a good example of the tremendous scholarly work carried on in Algeria and Morocco in the late nineteenth century and into the first half of the twentieth. But the linguistic and historical disciplines never progressed beyond their Orientalist origins. As could be anticipated, Arab history was sublimated by both its theological transcendance and a spiritual language!

29 Films produced during the interwar years must be considered in light of the aesthetics of Orientalism. Most of these productions were documentaries, whose function was to bring about an intellectual transition from objects of desire to objects of knowledge. For example, in *L'Homme du Niger* (1939), director Jacques de Baroncelli avoided all clichés based on the physical attributes of the native population; instead he presented a single African tribe, in today's Chad, as if it were an overseas "French village."

30 "Nous vivons les temps où la sauvegarde même de la vie nous impose d'élargir notre vision au-delà des horizons familiers." Sarraut, *Grandeur et servitude coloniales*, 27. My translation. He was so devoted to his job that he was twice appointed Minister of the Colonies.

31 In 1930 the budget for the military was slightly more than 2,000 million French francs; so the exhibition budget amounted to nearly 7 per cent of the national defence budget.

32 The expansion of the empire worldwide served as proof that France was not simply a nation but a great nation. The Berlin Conference (1885) had

already underscored this positivist feature by declaring that African peoples could not achieve sovereign status because they were uncivilized (never mind that it "civilized" nations that would soon begin two world wars).

33 Note that the doctors at the Algiers psychiatric hospital collaborated with the French military during the War of National Liberation in order to help them fathom how Arabs could abandon "laziness and mysticism" for radical politics and guerilla warfare.

34 The differences in political views within the liberation movement came to a head with the Melouza massacre of May 1957, when militants of the *Front de Libération Nationale* slaughtered three hundred members of the *Mouvement Nationaliste Algérien*.

35 For example, the Algerian Communist Party was founded in 1936 in Algiers by and for Europeans. Camus was a member for a short time in 1936 and 1937 (he was then twenty-three years old). After the war, he denied any association with the Communists so that he could apply for a US visa.

36 "Istiqlal" means "independence" in Arabic. After 1945 there were several such political parties throughout the Middle East and as far away as Indonesia.

37 To this day, it is a duty for Moroccans to consider their king the leader of the Muslim community and a descendant of the Prophet.

38 After independence was won at a high cost in casualties, the FLN made a point of calling the dead "martyrs" – a spiritually charged word (*shuhada*) in Arabic, even though the political party was very much a socialist one that was fully supported by the officially atheist Soviet Union.

39 "En Algérie, la société avait reçu plus de coups mortels que la nation, et cependant c'est cette dernière, et non la société qui devenait le but suprême, l'enjeu exclusif. C'était vraiment là une sorte de gageure, de défi, déterminés d'une manière indirecte par l'attitude de l'ennemi qui niait la nation puisqu'il n'avait pas de prises sur sa totalité spirituelle, sur les réserves clandestines de sa recouvrance." Lacheraf, *L'Algérie*, 323. My translation.

40 "Se peut-il que tant qu'il existe des étiquettes, je n'aie pas la mienne? Quelle est la mienne? Qu'on me dise qui je suis?" Feraoun, *Journal 1955–1962*, 70.

7 A View from *Diversité*: Writing and Nation

1 Articles 110 and 111 of the Ordinance of Villers-Cotterêts, signed by François I in August 1539, decreed French the official language of the state

(rather than Latin or regional languages). Yet until after the First World War, only half the French used it as their mother tongue.

2 "Les colonies," "l'empire français," "la plus grande France," "la France d'outre-mer." France became "l'hexagone" in 1962, after it had ceased to be a colonial power.

3 On this particular issue, see Hargreaves, "La littérature issue."

4 The word *Beur* is used here out of practicality. Unfortunately, the word, which had been coined by the late 1970s (it first appeared in the *Dictionnaire Le Robert* in 1980), has been picked up by the media and the body politic mostly with derogatory overtones, as a means to stigmatize people of the suburbs based on their ethnic background, religion, or economic status.

5 Rosello, *Declining the Stereotype*, 11.

6 In a now famous – and damning – interview with the Israeli newspaper *Haaretz* published on 18 November 2005, Finkielkraut showed his true xenophobic and basically anti-Republican colours.

7 A striking feature of the suburban riots of November 2005 was that people burned down their own schools, libraries, police stations, and stores – indeed, anything that signified economic inequality and institutional failure.

8 Nine *Beur* novels were published in 2005, seventeen in 2006, thirteen in 2007.

9 Hargreaves, "Une culture innommable?"

10 Especially in North America, academic conferences on *Beur* literature and culture are saturated with an elite discourse that embodies what could be called strategic essentialism, for it places politics before aesthetics. In American academe, *Beur* conferences have become feel-good circuses complete with Western "authorities" and *Beur* guest stars, who are disavowed in France by "ordinary" *Beur* because they cannot speak it authentically.

11 An example would be the Pasqua Laws (1993–8), which restricted the French citizenship of children of immigrants until they were sixteen, after which age they had to make a choice. This was a serious infringement on the fundamental Republican *jus solis*; it was also the first legal attack on postcolonial citizenry.

12 Technically speaking, Laroui is not a *Beur*. He was born and raised in Morocco, then migrated to the Netherlands. Somehow he has managed to ride the wave of *Beur* hype, especially among French postcolonial studies scholars in North America.

13 "Arrêtez tout! Je ne veux pas la maltraiter davantage. Qu'ici elle descende (hors du temps, hors de l'action) avec tous les egards. Je ne parlerai plus de Mina." Laroui, *De quel amour blessé!*, 134. My translation.

14 This literature by women writers (Maya Angelou, Rita Dove, Terry McMillan, Toni Morrison, Alice Walker, and others) tends to tackle issues pertaining to the subject himself or herself instead of pursuing the broader collective, militant narratives of male African American authors of the 1960s and 1970s.

15 Barthes, *Roland Barthes par Roland Barthes*, 6.

16 Belghoul, *Georgette!* An excellent novel (now out of print) that broke away from the predictable, or complacent, narrative frames of authors such as Azouz Begag.

17 For example, in the *département* of Seine-Saint-Denis (the poorest and most ethnically diverse in France), 30 per cent of people under age twenty-five are school dropouts; in Paris the number is around 13 per cent. See *Le Monde*, 1 March 2011.

18 The next chapter will examine to what extent *laïcité* in present-day France has become an exclusive doctrine.

19 "On est de la chair à chômage comme ils étaient de la chair à canon … Et les cv envoyés par centaines – pour rien! Et les entretiens d'embauche – pour rien! Et les candidatures spontanées – pour rien! Oualou. Et pire, les stages: le mensonge, le trucage légal, la parodie d'emploi, n'importe quoi – Oualouououou!" (Oualou: Arabic word for "nothing.") Smaïl, *Vivre me tue*, 69. The author (real name: Jack-Alain Léger) happens to be of 100 per cent Gallic background. He borrowed the *Beur* voice and style when it was trendy and marketable. This exercise in imposture set the tone for the ethnic mindset and prejudices that haunt "progressive" Parisian publishing salons.

20 For a deeper analysis of world literature in French today, see my article "Littérature-monde en français."

21 "En parlant je ne puis jamais gommer, effacer, annuler; tout ce que je puis faire, c'est dire 'j'annule, j'efface, je rectifie', bref de parler encore." Barthes, *Le Bruissement de la langue*, 93. My translation.

22 "J'me suis fait courser par les leurs. Les quoi? Les leurs. Les controleurs, quoi! Tu comprends pas le français?" Laroui, *De quel amour blessé*, 87. My translation.

23 This presumptuous and fossilized view of literature indicates the extent to which a fringe among the French establishment is unable not only to handle natural literary evolution but also to grasp the sustained momentum of postcolonial reality.

24 "Vivre – tu verras ma fille – c'est fabriquer de l'oubli et du mensonge." Imache, *Des nouvelles de Kora*, 118. My translation.

25 "J'irai à la gare ferroviaire pour m'engouffrer dans les entrailles de mon R, mon reu-reu, mon RER. Déguerpir chez mon spy et lui en dire long sur ma vie." Djaïdani, *Mon nerf*, 15. My translation.

26 The next chapter will show how literature has failed and has been re-
    placed by music and feature films in order to secure a reliable, genuine
    conversation with audiences, beyond the worn-out issue of *intégration*.
27 "En dehors du lointain Paris–X, autrement dit Nanterre, où j'allais en RER,
    toute ma vie jusqu'ici s'est déroulée dans un territoire borné, en gros, par
    La Fourche, La Chapelle, La République, La Trinité." Smaïl, *Vivre me tue*,
    22. My translation.
28 Tadjer, *Les ANI du Tassili*.
29 Rosello, "The "Beur Nation."
30 Riffaterre, "On the Complimentarity," 157.
31 "Si j'écrivais en arabe, il y aurait une espèce de continuité, mais en écriv-
    ant en français j'ai l'impression de piétiner sur mon heritage." Hargreaves,
    "An Interview with Farida Belghoul," 142.
32 For instance, Algiers was French before Nice, and Islam was visible in
    France more than a century ago; as for the *banlieue*, it was a place of soci-
    etal "threat" as early as the Industrial Revolution.
33 "Je suis français moi. Je suis dans mon pays. Tu me prends pour un Arabe,
    ou quoi?" Charef, *Le Thé au harem d'Archi Ahmed*, 140. My translation.
34 "Les références qui les [*Beur* authors] règlent appartiennent à la culture
    française et sont mises en jeu par la volonté de devenir français." Lachmet,
    "Une composante de l'underground français," 27. My translation.
35 "C'est en France que j'ai appris à être arabe / C'est en Algérie que j'ai
    appris à être immigrée." Boukhedenna. *Journal*, 5. My translation.
36 This is known in French as "avoir une gueule d'auteur plutôt que de fait
    divers."
37 See the latest novels by Tassadit Imache, *Des nouvelles de Kora*; Ahmed
    Kalouaz, *Avec tes mains*; and Rachid Djaïdani, *Viscéral*.
38 Issaad, *L'Enchaînement*.

8 The Challenge of Identities and the French Republic

 1 "Dans ces conditions, ce n'est pas pêcher par excès de polemique ou de
    méchanceté que de voir aussi, dans la soudaine promotion des post-
    colonial studies et dans la stigmatization de l'arriération française, des
    choses comme une stratégie de niche de la part de chercheurs en quête
    d'une part de marché académique; une forme de coquetterie à mi-chemin
    du snobisme américanophile et du masochisme hexagonal." Bayart,
    "En finir avec les études postcoloniales."
 2 In the twenty-first century, France boasts the largest Muslim, Jewish,
    African, and Chinese communities in the European Union. Muslims, mostly
    from the Maghreb, West Africa, and more recently Turkey, are 8 per cent

of the 65 million population. There are, of course, immense variations between nominal Muslims and observant ones.

3 One original position on this question of intellectual usurpation is Gayatri Chakravorty Spivak, "Who Claims Alterity?"

4 To a lesser degree, such a shift occurred between the second half of the nineteenth century and the First World War, when the French Republic turned its peasants into citizens, mainly by eradicating regional cultures.

5 In the second volume of the political memoirs of Jacques Chirac, the Conservative former president pays tribute to François Hollande, then head of the Socialist Party, for his unconditional support of the law banning religious symbols in French public schools, passed in March 2004. Chirac, *Le Temps presidential*, 603.

6 The leftist leaders Ségolène Royal, Arnaud Montebourg, Vincent Peillon, and Jean-Luc Mélenchon put the founding of a new Sixth Republic on their agendas and platforms during the presidential campaign of 2012.

7 Schor, "The Crisis of French Universalism," 48.

8 One recent glaring example was France's military intervention in Mali in January 2013 to save the African nation's "democratic institutions"; yet at the same time, France shrugged at a new Amnesty International report on bias and discrimination against French Muslims.

9 The goal set by the Minister of Immigration and National Identity in 2009 was to deport at least 29,000 illegal or undocumented people, some of them travellers transiting to other European destinations (source: www .franceinfo.fr, 14 December 2009). The cost to French taxpayers was between 15,000 and 20,000 euros per person deported.

10 Although immigration to France officially stopped in 1974, people are still migrating there, be they non-EU students, highly qualified guest workers, refugees, or those entering the country under the family reunification laws. Illegal immigration from western Africa and Southeast Asia remains important and constant, although reliable statistics do not exist.

11 Since 2001, applicants for passports and *cartes d'identité* have been required to demonstrate their French citizenship, often through a court certificate.

12 The "conversation on national identity" (October 2009–February 2010) that former president Nicolas Sarkozy expected ended in a political fiasco; from the start, it was deemed unhealthy in a democracy that boasted of being a land of immigrants. The government's proposals were eventually buried in a parliamentary commission.

13 This was a highly controversial endeavour, but it also proved to be a very successful one for far-right supporters. Let us remember that the only time in France's history when there was an actual Ministry of National Identity was during the Vichy regime.

14 Although the decision was made by a conservative government, the left-wing opposition proved unable or unwilling to ward off the threat of xenophobic radicalization. After three months, the debate died down because of the people's strong reactions and a grossly incompetent minister, Eric Besson, who made matters worse every time he tried to salvage his pet project.

15 In the 1980s, the *Front National*, the French far-right party, included in its platform the idea that "foreigners" were the root cause of unemployment because they were taking jobs away from the "real" French.

16 In 1968, around 30,000 people, originally from Portugal and North Africa, were living in the two largest slums outside Paris, in the east in Champigny and in the west in Nanterre. See Granotier, *Les Travailleurs immigrés en France*.

17 Novels of this period, by Maghrebi or French authors, all share that sense of existential inadequacy and metropolitan racism mimicking colonial rule, in the chosen context of immigration. See, for instance, Chraïbi's *Les Boucs* (1955); Etcherelli, *Élise ou la vraie vie* (1967); and Boudjedra, *Topographie idéale pour une agression caractérisée* (1975).

18 One argument often made by European people born in French Algeria is that along with independence came chaos, and that "Arabs could not manage without us, and are stuck with themselves." Many websites make nostalgic, derogatory claims of this sort; others (e.g, www.alger-roi.fr) spread outrageous sentiments about France's so-called extraordinary achievements in Algeria. Not surprisingly, these same European people, who bizarrely insist they are Algerians, tend to align with the far right.

19 According to the French social and economic (statistical and database) institute: www.insee.fr.

20 Algerian sociologist Abdelmalek Sayad pointed to this cultural and political paradox in the immigrant community in France in *La Double Absence*, 352.

21 Halbwachs, *Les Cadres sociaux de la mémoire*. Basically, for this French sociologist, what the individual remembers is determined by group association: workplace, family, religious values, sports clubs, and so on. For him, the subjective mind is actually structured by social arrangements.

22 The events were read through the lens of the Palestinian *intifada*, the Iraqi insurgency, or a new clash of civilizations, when actually, the fundamental identifier of this urban rage was a complete lack of any organizing leadership and stated agenda.

23 See one recent annual report: www.halde.fr/Publication-du-rapport-annuel-2009.html. During his last year in office, Sarkozy had the HALDE phased out.

24 Alain Finkielkraut especially likes to rehash his argument about humanism having ended when postcolonial immigration began in earnest after 1960. In *Qu'est-ce que la France?*, he embarks on a series of dialogues with fellow intellectuals, during which he denounces an education system that has failed to turn students into French citizens, or to preserve "humanités," as well as muticulturalism, which he sees as a threat to French universalism.

25 Note that besides Classical Arabic words (*algèbre, ambre, douanes, hasard, sucre,* etc.) that entered European languages as early as the Middle Ages, new words have entered the French language with the advent of the post-colonial condition: *baraka* (luck), *chouïa* (a little bit), *flouze* (money/dough), *kifkif* (the same), *toubib* (physician), *kiffer* (to like a lot), and so on. This sort of linguistic diglossia underscores power subdivisions within contemporary French popular culture. One last group is words associated with Islam: (*charia* (canonical law), *émir* (community leader), *zakat* (alms giving), *halal* (pure/licit), *ramadan* (month of fasting), and so forth; all of these have kept their high cultural register but remain open to misinterpretation. Among many recent studies, see Guemriche, *Dictionnaire*; and Walter, *Arabesques*.

26 The expression "colonial fracture" comes from the seminal work by French historians Bancel, Blanchard, and Lemaire, *La Fracture coloniale*.

27 "The West is attempting, and will continue to attempt, to sustain its pre-eminent position and defend its interests by defining its interest as the interests of the world community." Huntington, *The Clash of Civilizations*, 184. Everything else that resists the West's influence is prone to "indigenization" (pp. 99ff.), a paradigm shift leading to regression.

28 One favourite offhand formula by the "*Beur*" to depict their personal situation is: "Être assis le cul entre deux chaises" (To be sitting between two chairs).

29 The law of 15 March 2004 (Article L141-5-1 of the Education Code) bans all ostentatious religious signs from public schools. It was passed with 494 votes in favour, 36 against, and 31 abstentions. Unquestionably, those numbers reflect a nation that feels itself under siege. In its tradition of cozying up to the political powers-that-be, the *Grande Mosquée de Paris*, one of the leading Islamic authorities in France, asked Muslim students to go to school without wearing any visible signs of their faith. For the record, the law was denounced by the Pope and by Shirin Ebadi, the Iranian Nobel Peace Prize winner, a noted militant for women's rights in her country.

30 Scott, *The Politics of the Veil*, 90–1.

31 One example is a political science scholar at the University of Toronto who explained how a law that forbids people from acting in accordance with their religious duties and freedom of conscience jeopardizes France's democratic tradition. Carens, "Démocratie, multiculturalisme et hijab."

32 A few authors in France, largely because they are biased or have been misinformed, support a prohibition on religious signs. See, for example, Djavann, *Bas les voiles*; Djitli and Troubac, *Lettre ouverte à ma fille*; Fourest, *La Tentation obscurantiste*; and Dubreuil, *Sous le voile*. Then there are authors who either examine the issue on rational grounds or support the right to wear religious symbols in public. See McGoldrick. *Human Rights and Religion*; Gole, *The Forbidden Modern*; Joppke, *The Veil*; Scott. *The Politics of the Veil*; Nordmann, ed., *Le Foulard islamique en questions*; and Bowen, *Can Islam Be French?*

33 "Le rêve d'une totale domestication de la société algérienne à l'aide des femmes dévoilées et complices de l'occupant, n'a pas cessé de hanter les responsables politiques de la colonisation." Fanon, *L'An V de la révolution algérienne*, 20. My translation.

34 This was one of the core claims of *Ni Putes Ni Soumises* (literally, "Neither Whores nor Submissive"), an organization founded out of the blue in March 2003, with the blessing of the government, at a time when the Islamic head scarf was being hotly debated. Despite wide access to the mainstream media and the support of political leaders, the organization has failed to gain any credibility on the ground. Yet its political umbrella and financial sponsors have overshadowed genuine feminist and social action. In just its first year, the organization received 300,000 euros in funding from the government, while other grassroots associations, long established in the *banlieues*, were financially struggling.

35 Guénif-Souilamas and Macé, *Les Féministes et le garçon arabe*.

36 In 2010, the unemployment rate for people under thirty who live in some of the working-class *banlieues* north and east of Paris, as well as in Lyon, Marseille, Toulouse, and Lille, was 43 per cent (the national rate hovers at 10 per cent). This amounts to a Third World situation at the doors of wealthy European cities. The *Observatoire National des Zones Urbaines*, a national agency that gathers statistics on suburban areas, in 2010 reported that 50 per cent of the people in some working-class *banlieues* were living below the national poverty line, which stood at 8,700 euros/year per person. The national average was 7 per cent. Before joining any serious debate about secularism in France, remember that joblessness and economic decay are now the greatest obstacles to social integration. Visit http://www.statistiques-locales.insee.fr and http://www.ladocumentationfrancaise.fr/rapports-publics/084000718/. The information also appeared in *Le Monde*, on 15 December 2010.

37 France became a signatory to the European Convention on Human Rights on 4 November 1950. Article 9–1 of the convention states: "Everyone has

the right to freedom of thought, conscience and religion. This right includes freedom to change one's religion or belief, and freedom either alone or in community with others, in private or in public to manifest one's religion or belief, in worship, teaching, practice, and observance." Article 9–2 continues by stating that limitations can be applied in cases when: "[limitations] prescribed by law, are necessary in a democratic society, in the interest of public safety, for the protection of public order, health or morals, or the protection of the rights and freedom of others." Visit http:// conventions.coe.int/Treaty/Commun/QueVoulezVous.asp?NT= 005&CL=ENG. This language raises the following questions: How do French Muslim students who wear head scarves and who seek a French education deserve these limitations? Why are they deemed a threat to French democracy?

38 The first three notable cases were in September 1989, six months into the Rushdie affair and just before the fall of the Berlin Wall (November), two events that brought political Islam to the forefront just as twentieth-century Western ideologies were coming to an end.

39 This is the highest administrative court in the nation, yet its rulings do not have the force of law.

40 Lower courts across the country ruled in every single case brought before them that students were allowed to wear their scarves in school. Only a bill passed into law by the National Assembly in March 2004 was able to overturn those rulings.

41 Deltombe, *L'Islam imaginaire*, shows how ingredients taken from world events (in Iran, Iraq, Palestine, Algeria, Sudan, Afghanistan) from the 1980s to the early twenty-first century were conveniently added to the national anti-Islamic propaganda mix.

42 Magazine covers showed women completely veiled (Afghan style) and the French flag in the background with a question mark regarding the future of the republic. News shows presented riots in the French suburbs and the war in Iraq back to back. Politicians willingly praised secular, assimilated *immigrés* and blamed the rest, who were portrayed as representing a national threat. Political discourse often used coded expressions to refer to that "other" France. At times, blatantly derogatory language was used when referring to people in the *banlieues*. The frenzy has continued unabated, yet there has been no legal prosecution of the people guilty of this race-baiting.

43 The expression "house Muslims" derives from "house Negroes," the slaves who worked in close contact with the plantation masters, in their homes. They enjoyed basic material comforts and sometimes received an

elementary education, eventually becoming condescending to the "field Negroes." This same psychological kowtowing to the West and eagerness to receive approval and validation can be seen among house Muslims today.

44 It is called the *Fédération des Femmes du Québec*; 90 per cent of its members are Catholic.

45 Benhabib, *La Vie à contre-Coran*. There is play on the words "contre-courant/ contre-Coran," to go against the tide. This would lead readers to believe she is a genuine advocate for freedom, even though everything about her argument smacks of neoconservatism and anti-Islamic prejudice.

46 This has been the main position of the Socialist Party, as well as a key political line among most Maghrebi intellectuals who live in France (e.g., Abdelwahab Meddeb, Tahar Ben Jelloun, and Malek Chebel), who tend to miss the neocolonial fault line of the assimilationist discourse.

47 Elizabeth Badinter, Pierre-André Taguieff, and Alain Finkielkraut have been at the forefront of this discourse. The real nature of their semiotic and political manoeuvres is easily exposed. See, for example, the seminal essay by Lentin and Titley, *The Crises of Multiculturalism*.

48 Françoise Gaspard argues that France resorts to flawed science and historical discourse in order to mask its own insecurities and to stigmatize everyone who seems to enjoy a secure, stable identity. Based on surveys and investigations in the *banlieues*, her work reveals that researchers had never in their investigations run into supporters of radical Islam or associations based on it. Gaspard, *Le Foulard et la République*.

49 "Exclure les filles de l'école publique n'est-ce pas adopter une mesure de nature sexiste puisqu'elle conduit à romper l'égalité entre les garcons et les filles face à l'obligation scolaire?" Gaspard, *Le Foulard et la République*, 210. My translation.

50 The word *féminisme* was coined in 1881 by the French women's rights activist Hubertine Auclert in her monthly review *La Citoyenne*. She also travelled to Algeria (1888–92) and wrote a collection of articles, *Les femmes arabes*, in which she advocated in the strongest terms equality of rights for colonized women and mandatory access to free education.

51 There are many scholars of Islamic feminism, in the West as well as in countries from the Maghreb and all the way to Pakistan, who hold a variety of viewpoints on the issues. For example, Algerian sociologist Marnia Lazreg acknowledges the hegemonic tendencies rooted in Western academe that bear on Muslim woman as a subject of discourse, while still questioning the assumptions of Islam as culture. Her *Questioning the Veil* is an interesting case study, although predicated on the debatable premise

that the veil is "an issue" to begin with. Margo Badran, a true scholar of Islamic feminism, draws on the politics of control and liberation by Muslims themselves, who borrow from their own scholarly legacy to rebuke imported Western hegemonic ideas on the position of women. Her groundbreaking work was *Feminists, Islam, and Nation: Gender and the Making of Modern Egypt* (Princeton: Princeton University Press, 1995).

52 Roudinesco, *La laïcité à l'école*, 2:53.

53 In 1905 the word *laïcité* itself was fairly recent; it was coined only in 1871 (in the French newspaper *La Patrie*) and made it into the *Dictionnaire Larousse* in 1873.

54 Note that the law on the separation of Church and State was modified nine times between 1905 and 2005, mostly so as to meet the standards of international treaties and conventions, but also to fine-tune details regarding the salaries of religious leaders and rents of state-run places of worship.

55 In 1895 the *Comité de l'Afrique française* began to collect funds to build a mosque in Paris, a project that gathered momentum after the tremendous sacrifices of the French Colonial Army during the First World War.

56 See Patrick Weil, who was originally against any ban, then changed his argument in view of social violence in the *banlieues* wrongly associated with radical Islam. In his "Lever le voile," he strongly advocates a ban on Islamic symbols, more in an effort to reconcile France with itself than to uphold Muslim citizens' rights. Historian Gérard Noiriel, in *A quoi sert l'identité nationale?*, acknowledges that the secular arguments are dated and that both the Islamic faith and postcolonial identity have been exploited within the shifting paradigms of national identity. Sociologist Vincent Geisser, in *La Nouvelle Islamophobie*, examines the mechanisms of exclusion and hatred towards Islam in France by pointing to academics and journalists who, in his view, have opened the way for politicians to implement anti-Muslim policies.

Epilogue: Elusive Convergence?

1 In the winter of 2011, the world witnessed how "our good friends," Tunisia's Ben Ali and Egypt's Hosni Mubarak, became overnight pariah dictators.

2 Louis Althusser, "Ideology and Ideological State Apparatuses," in *Lenin and Philosophy*," 162.

Bibliography

[Anon.] *Le Livre d'or de l'Exposition coloniale internationale de Paris*. Paris: Honoré Champion, 1931.

Abdel-Malek, Anouar. "Orientalism in Crisis." *Diogenes* 44 (Winter 1963): 104–12.

Ageron, Charles-Robert. *Histoire de l'Algérie contemporaine*. Paris: Presses Universitaires de France, 1977.

Aijaz, Ahmad. *In Theory: Classes, Nations, Literatures*. New York: Verso, 1994.

– "Jameson's Rhetoric of Otherness and the 'National Allegory.'" *Social Text* 17 (Fall 1987): 3–25.

Althusser, Louis. *Lenin and Philosophy* (1968). New York: Monthly Review Press, 1971.

Amrouche, Jean. "La culture peut être une mystification." *La Vie intellectuelle* 8–9 (August–September 1952): 82–5.

– *L'éternel Jugurtha*. Paris: L'Arche, 1946.

Appadurai, Arjun. *Modernity at Large: Cultural Dimensions of Globalization*. Minneapolis: University of Minnesota Press, 1996.

Appiah, Kwame Anthony. *In My Father's House: Africa in the Philosophy of Culture*. New York: Oxford University Press, 1992.

– "Out of Africa: Topology of Nativism." In *The Bounds of Race: Perspectives on Hegemony and Resistance*, edited by Dominick LaCapra, 134–63. Ithaca: Cornell University Press, 1991.

Apter, Emily. *Continental Drift: From National Characters to Virtual Subjects*. Chicago: University of Chicago Press, 1999.

Arkoun, Mohammed. *Essais sur la pensée islamique*. Paris: Maisonneuve & Larose, 1973.

– *Humanisme et Islam: Combats et propositions*. Paris: Vrin, 2005.

Aron, Raymond. *La Tragédie algérienne*. Paris: Plon, 1957.

Auclert, Hubertine. *Les Femmes arabes*. Paris: Société d'Éditions Littéraires, 1900.

Badran, Margo. *Feminists, Islam, and Nation: Gender and the Making of Modern Egypt*. Princeton: Princeton University Press, 1995.

Balibar, Étienne. *Masses, Classes, Ideas: Studies on Politics and Philosophy before and after Marx* (1994). New York and London: Routledge, 1994.

– *Race, Nation, Classe*. Paris: La Découverte, 1988.

Bancel, Nicolas, Pascal Blanchard, and Sandrine Lemaire. *La Fracture coloniale: La Société française au prisme de l'héritage colonial*. Paris: La Découverte, 2005.

Barry, Michael. *Venice and the Islamic World, 828–1797*. New Haven: Yale University Press, 2007.

Barthes, Roland. *Le Bruissement de la langue*. Paris: Le Seuil, 1984.

– *Roland Barthes par Roland Barthes*. Paris: Le Seuil, 1975.

Baubérot, Jean. *L'Intégrisme républicain contre la laïcité*. La Tour d'Aigues: Aube, 2006.

– *Laïcité 1905–2005*. Paris: Le Seuil, 2004.

– Baudet, Henri. *Paradise on Earth: Some Thoughts on European Images of Non-European Man*. New Haven: Yale University Press, 1965.

Bayart, Jean-François. "En finir avec les études postcoloniales." *Le Débat* 154 (March–April 2009): 119–40.

Beauvoir, Simone de. *Le Deuxième Sexe*. Paris: Gallimard, 1949.

– *Djamila Boupacha*. Paris: Gallimard, 1962.

Belghoul, Farida. *Georgette!* Paris: Bernard Barrault Editions, 1986.

Benhabib, Djemila. *La Vie à contre-Coran: Une Femme témoigne sur les islamistes*. Montréal: VLB, 2009.

Ben Jelloun, Tahar. *L'Enfant de sable*. 1985.

– *La plus haute des solitudes*. Paris: Le Seuil, 1977.

Bennabi, Malek. *Les conditions de la renaissance*. Alger: Éditions de la renaissance enahda, 1949.

Bernard, Augustin. *L'Algérie*. Paris: Librairie F. Alcan, 1929.

Bernheimer, Charles, ed. *Comparative Literature in the Age of Multiculturalism*. Baltimore: Johns Hopkins University Press, 1995.

Berque, Jacques. *Dépossession du monde*. Paris: Le Seuil, 1964.

– *L'Islam au temps du monde*. Paris: Sinbad, 1984.

Bhabha, Homi K. "The Commitment to Theory," *New Formations* 5 (1988): 109–21.

– *Edward Said: Continuing the Conversation*. Chicago: University of Chicago Press, 2005.

– *The Location of Culture*. New York: Routledge, 1994.

– ed. *Nation and Narration*. London and New York: Routledge, 1990.

Blumenbach, Johann Friedrich. *De l'unité du genre humain, et de ses variétés.* Translated from the Latin by Frédéric Chardel. Paris: Allut, 1804.

Bouazar, Dounia. *L'Islam des banlieues.* Paris: La Découverte, 2001.

Boudjedra, Rachid. *L'Escargot.* Paris: Denoël, 1977.

– *L'Insolation.* Paris: Denoël, 1972.

– *La Répudiation.* Paris: Denoël, 1969.

– *Topographie idéale pour une agression caractérisée.* Paris: Denoël, 1975.

Boukhedenna, Sakinna. *Journal: Nationalité immigrée.* Paris: L'Harmattan, 1987.

Bourdieu, Pierre. *The Rules of Art.* Cambridge: Polity, 1996.

– *Sociologie de l'Algérie.* Paris: Presses Universitaires de France, 1958.

Bourdieu, Pierre, and Jean-Claude Passeron. *La Reproduction: Éléments pour un système d'enseignement.* Paris: Éditions de Minuit, 1971.

Bourget, Carine. *The Star, the Cross, and the Crescent: Religions and Conflicts in Francophone Literature from the Arab World.* Lanham: Lexington Press, 2010.

Bowen, John R. *Can Islam Be French?* Princeton: Princeton University Press, 2010.

– *Why the French Don't Like Headscarves.* Princeton, NJ: Princeton University Press, 2007.

Brennan, Timothy. *At Home in the World: Cosmopolitanism Now.* Cambridge, MA: Harvard University Press, 1997.

Camus, Albert. *Essais.* Paris: Gallimard, 1965.

– *L'exil et le royaume.* Paris: Gallimard, 1957.

– *Le premier homme.* Paris: Gallimard, 1994.

Carens, Joseph H. "Démocratie, multiculturalisme et hijab." *Esprit* 311 (January 2005): 54–61.

Cartier, Raymond. *L'Algérie sans mensonge.* Paris: Hachette, 1960.

Cauwelaert, Didier van. *Un Aller simple.* Paris: Albin Michel, 1995.

Césaire, Aimé. *Discours sur le colonialisme.* Paris: Présence Africaine, 1955.

Charef, Mehdi. *Le Thé au harem d'Archi Ahmed.* Paris: Mercure de France, 1983.

Chakrabarty, Dipesh. *Provincializing Europe: Postcolonial Thought and Historical Difference.* Princeton: Princeton University Press, 2007.

Chirac, Jacques. *Le Temps presidentiel.* Paris: Robert Lafont, 2011.

Chraïbi, Driss. *Les Boucs.* Paris: Gallimard, 1955.

– *La Civilisation, ma mere!* Paris: Gallimard, 1972.

– *Le Passé simple.* Paris: Gallimard, 1954.

Cixous, Hélène. *Les rêveries de la femme sauvage.* Paris: Galilée, 2000.

Cohen, Beth, ed. *Not the Classical Ideal: Athens and the Construction of the Other in Greek Art.* Leiden: Brill, 2000.

Collot, Claude. *Les Institutions de l'Algérie durant la période coloniale (1830–1962).* Paris: Éditions du CNRS, 1987.

Condorcet, Nicolas de. *Esquisse d'un tableau des progrès de l'esprit humain* (1793). Paris: Vrin, 1970.

Cooper, Frederick. *Decolonisation and African Society: The Labour Question in French and British Africa*. Cambridge: Cambridge University Press, 1996.

Curtis, Michael. *Orientalism and Islam: European Thinkers on Oriental Despotism in the Middle East and India*. Cambridge: Cambridge University Press, 2009.

Deltombe, Thomas. *L'Islam imaginaire: La Construction médiatique de l'islamophobie en France, 1975–2005*. Paris: La Découverte, 2005.

Derrida, Jacques. *La dissémination*. Paris: Le Seuil, 1972.

– *L'écriture et la différence*. Paris: Le Seuil, 1967. Translated by Alan Bass as *Writing and Difference*. Chicago: University of Chicago Press, 1980.

– *Of Grammatology*. 1967.

– *Le monolinguisme de l'autre*. Paris: Galilée, 1996. Translated by Patrick Mensah as *The Monolinguism of the Other, or The Prosthesis of Origin*. Stanford: Stanford University Press, 1998.

– *Specters of Marx*. New York: Routledge, 1994.

Dib, Mohammed. *Le Sommeil d'Eve* (1989). Paris: Éditions de la différence, 2003.

Dirlik, Arif. "The Postcolonial Aura: Third World Criticism in the Age of Global Capitalism." *Critical Enquiry* 20, no. 2 (Winter 1994): 328–56.

– *The Postcolonial Aura: Third World Criticism in the Age of Global Capitalism*. Boulder: Westview Press, 1997.

Dirlik, Arif, Vinay Bahl, and Peter Gran, eds. *History after the Three Worlds*. Lanham: Lexington, 2000.

Djaïdani, Rachid. *Mon nerf*. Paris: Le Seuil, 2004.

– *Viscéral*. Paris: Le Seuil, 2007.

Djavann, Chahdortt. *Bas les voiles*. Paris: Gallimard, 2006.

Djebar, Assia. *L'amour, la fantasia*. Paris: J.C. Lattès, 1985.

– *Ces voix qui m'assiègent … en marge de ma francophonie*. Paris: Albin Michel, 1999.

Djitli, Leila, and Sophie Troubac. *Lettre ouverte à ma fille qui veut porter le voile*. Paris: La Martinière, 2004.

Donadey, Anne, and Adlai Murdoch, eds. *Postcolonial Theory and Francophone Literary Studies*. Gainesville: University Press of Florida, 2005.

Dubreuil, Sophie. *Sous le voile*. Paris: Le Seuil, 2005.

Etcherelli, Claire. *Élise ou la vraie vie*. Paris: Éditions Denoël, 1967.

Fanon, Frantz. *L'An V de la révolution algérienne*. Paris: Maspéro, 1959.

– *Les damnés de la terre*. Paris: Maspéro, 1961. Translated by Richard Philcox as *The Wretched of the Earth*. New York Grove Press, 1963.

– *Peau noire, masques blancs*. Paris: Le Seuil, 1952.

- Farès, Nabile. *Mémoire de l'absent.* Paris: Le Seuil, 1974.
Fassin. Éric. *De la question sociale à la question raciale?* Paris: La Découverte, 2006.
Feraoun, Mouloud. *Journal, 1955–1962.* Paris: Le Seuil, 1962.
Finkielkraut, Alain. *Qu'est-ce que la France?* Paris: Stock, 2007.
- Interview published in supplement to *Haaretz*, 18 November 2005.
Flaubert, Gustave. *Correspondance,* Tome I: *Janvier 1830–Mai 1851.* Edited by Jean Bruneau. Paris: Gallimard–La Pléiade, 1973.
- *L'éducation sentimentale* (1869). Paris: Gallimard, 1965.
Forsdick, Charles, ed. *Francophone Postcolonial Studies.* London: Arnold Publishers, 2003.
Foucault, Michel. *L'archéologie du savoir.* Paris: Gallimard, 1969.
- *Histoire de la folie à l'âge classique.* Paris: Gallimard, 1961.
- *The History of Sexuality*, vol. I: *The Will to Power.* Translated by Robert Hurley. New York: Vintage, 1990.
- *Les mots et les choses.* Paris: Gallimard, 1966.
- *Surveiller et punir.* Paris: Gallimard, 1975.
Fourest, Caroline. *La Tentation obscurantiste.* Paris: Grasset, 2005.
Freud, Sigmund. *Civilization and Its Discontents.* London: W.W. Norton, 1960.
Gabrieli, Francesco. *Arab Historians and the Crusades.* Translated by E.J. Costello. Berkeley: University of California Press, 1969.
Gafaïti, Hafid, ed. *Cultures transnationales de France.* Paris: L'Harmattan, 2001.
Gaspard, Françoise. *Le Foulard et la République.* Paris: La Découverte, 1995.
Gates, Henri Louis, Jr, and Kwame Anthony Appiah, eds. *"Race," Writing, and Difference.* Chicago: University of Chicago Press, 1986.
Geisser, Vincent. *La Nouvelle Islamophobie.* Paris: La Découverte, 2003.
Gide, André. *Amyntas.* Paris: Mercure de France, 1906; Paris: Gallimard/ Poche, 1993.
- *L'Immoraliste.* Paris: Mercure de France, 1902; Paris: Mercure de France, 1991.
- *Journal I: 1887–1925.* Paris: Gallimard/Pléiade, 1996.
- *Journal 1939–1949.* Paris: Gallimard-La Pléiade, 1993.
Gilroy, Paul. *After Empire: Multiculture or Postcolonial Melancholia.* London: Routledge, 2004.
- *Against Race: Imagining Political Culture beyond the Colour Line.* Cambridge, MA: Harvard University Press, 2000.
- *The Black Atlantic: Modernity and Double Consciousness.* Cambridge, MA: Harvard University Press, 1992.
- *"There Ain't No Black in the Union Jack": The Cultural Politics of Race and Nation.* London: Hutchinson, 1987; Chicago: University of Chicago Press, 1991.
Glissant, Édouard. *Poétique de la relation.* Paris: Gallimard, 1990.

Gobineau, Joseph Arthur. *The Inequality of Human Races*. Translated by Adrian Collins. London: Heinemann, 1915; originally published as *Essai sur l'inégalité des races humaines*, 4 vols. Paris: Firmin Didot Frères, 1853–5.

– *Nouvelles asiatiques*. Paris: Didier et Cie, 1876.

Gole, Nilufer. *The Forbidden Modern: Civilization and Veiling*. Ann Arbor: University of Michigan Press, 1996.

Goitein, S.D. "Contemporary Letters on the Capture of Jerusalem by the Crusaders." *Journal of Jewish Studies* 3, no. 4 (1952): 162–77.

– *A Mediterranean Society: The Jewish Communities of the Arab World as Portrayed in the Cairo Geniza*. 5 vols. Berkeley: University of California Press, 1967–93.

– Gramsci, Antonio. *The Prison Notebooks*. New York: Columbia University Press, 2007.

Granotier, Bernard. *Les Travailleurs immigrés en France*. Paris: Maspero, 1970.

Griffith, Gareth. "Representation and Production: Issues of Control in Post-Colonial Cultures." In *Interrogating Postcolonialism: Theory, Text, and Context*, edited by Harish Trivedi and Meenakshi Mukherjee. Simla: Indian Institute of Advanced Studies, 1996.

Grousset, René. *Histoire des croisades et du royaume franc de Jérusalem*. Paris: Plon, 1934–6.

Guemriche, Salah. *Dictionnaire des mots français d'origine arabe*. Paris: Le Seuil, 2007.

Guénif-Souilamas, Nacira, and Éric Macé. *Les Féministes et le garçon arabe*. La Tour d'Aigues: Éditions l'Aube, 2004.

Guha, Ranajit. *Elementary Aspects of Peasant Insurgency in Colonial India*. Durham: Duke University Press, 1999.

Halbwachs, Maurice. *Les Cadres sociaux de la mémoire*. Paris: Alcan, 1925.

Hardt, Michael, and Antonio Negri. *Empire*. Cambridge, MA: Harvard University Press, 2000.

Hargreaves, Alec. "Une culture innommable?" In *Cultures transnationales de France*, edited by Hafid Gafaïti, 27–36. Paris: L'Harmattan, 2001.

– "An Interview with Farida Belghoul." In *Immigration and Identity in Beur Fiction: Voices from the North African Community in France*. New York: Berg, 1991.

– *Immigration and Identity in Beur Novels*. New York: Berg, 1991.

– *Immigration, "Race," and Ethnicity in Contemporary France*. London: Routledge, 1995.

– "La littérature issue de l'immigration maghrébine en France: recensement et évolution du corpus narratif." *Expressions maghrébines* 7, no. 1 (Summer 2008): 193–213.

– *Multi-Ethnic France*. London: Taylor & Francis, 2007.

Heidegger, Martin. *The Question Concerning Technology and Other Essays*. Translated by William Lovitt. New York: Harper & Row, 1977.

Herder, Johann G. *Reflections on the Philosophy of the History of Mankind*. Chicago: University of Chicago Press, 1968.

Hourani, Albert. *Islam in European Thought*. Cambridge: Cambridge University Press, 1991.

Hulme, Peter. "Subversive Archipelagos: Colonial Discourse and the Break-Up of Continental Theory." *Dispositio* 14 (1989).

Huntington, Samuel. *The Clash of Civilizations and the Remaking of the World Order*. New York: Simon & Shuster, 1996.

Imache, Tassidit. *Des nouvelles de Kora*. Arles: Actes Sud, 2009.

Irwin, Robert. *For Lust of Knowing: Orientalism and Its Enemies*. London: Penguin Books, 2006.

Issaad, Ramdane. *L'Enchaînement*. Paris: Flammarion, 1995.

Jameson, Fredric. "Cognitive Mapping." In *Marxism and the Interpretation of Culture*, edited by Cary Nelson and Lawrence Grossberg, 347–57. London: Macmillan, 1988.

– *The Political Unconscious*. Ithaca: Cornell University Press, 1981.

– *Postmodernism, or, the Logic of Late Capitalism*. Durham: Duke University Press, 1991.

JanMohamed, Abdul. *Reconsidering Social Identification: Race, Gender, Class, and Caste*. New Delhi: Routledge, 2011.

Joppke, Christian. *The Veil: Mirror of Identity*. Cambridge: Polity, 2009.

Kabbani, Rana. *Europe's Myths of Orient*. Bloomington: Indiana University Press, 1986.

Kadri, Aissa, ed. *Parcours d'intellectuels maghrébins*. Paris: Karthala, 1996.

Kalouaz, Ahmed. *Avec tes mains*. Arles, Rouergue, 2009.

Kant, Immanuel. *Observations on the Feeling of the Beautiful and Sublime*. Translated by J.T. Goldthwait. Berkeley: University of California Press, 1960.

Kateb, Yacine. *Nedjma*. Paris: Le Seuil, 1956.

– *Le Polygone étoilé*. Paris: Le Seuil, 1966.

Kedourie, Elie. *Democracy and Arab Political Culture*. Washington, D.C.: Washington Institute for Near East, 1992.

Keller, Richard C. *Colonial Madness*. Chicago: University of Chicago Press, 2007.

Kepel, Gilles. *Banlieue de la république*. Paris: Gallimard, 2012.

Kessel, Patrick, and Giovanni Pirelli. *Le Peuple algérien et la guerre: Lettres et témoignages 1954–1962*. Paris: Maspéro, 1963.

Khalidi, Rashid, ed. *The Origins of Arab Nationalism*. New York: Columbia University Press, 1991.

Khatibi, Abdelkebir. *Amour bilingue*. Montpellier: Fata Morgana, 1983.

- ed. *Du bilinguisme*. Paris: Denoël, 1985.
- *Maghreb pluriel*. Paris: Denoël, 1983.
- *La Mémoire tatouée*. 1971.
Khosrokhavar, Farhad. *L'Islam des jeunes*. Paris: Flammarion, 1997.
Kimble, George. *Geography in the Middle Ages*. London: Methuen, 1938.
Kopf, David. *British Orientalism and the Bengal Renaissance*. Berkeley: University of California Press, 1969.
Kristéva, Julia. *Étrangers à nous-mêmes*. Paris: Gallimard, 1991.
Laâbi, Abdellatif. *Le Règne de barbarie*. Rabat: Barbare/Compte d'auteur, 1976.
LaCapra, Dominick, ed. *The Bounds of Race: Perspectives on Hegemony and Resistance*. Ithaca: Cornell University Press, 1991.
Lacheraf, Mostefa. *L'Algérie: nation et société*. Algiers: SNED, 1978.
Lachmet, Djanet. "Une Composante de l'underground français." *Actualités de l'émigration* 80, 11 March 1986.
Lamartine, Alphonse de. *Souvenirs, impressions, pensées et paysages pendant un voyage en Orient (1832–1833), ou Notes d'un voyageur*. Paris: Gosselin, 1845.
Laronde, Michel. *Autour du roman beur*. Paris: L'Harmattan, 1993.
Laroui, Fouad. *De quel amour blessé*. Paris: Julliard, 1998.
Laroussi, Farid. "Littérature-monde en français: mélancolie ou illusion?" *International Journal of Francophone Studies* 12, nos. 2–3 (Winter 2009): 417–24.
Lazreg, Marnia. *Questioning the Veil: Open Letters to Muslim Women*. Princeton: Princeton University Press, 2009.
Lentin, Alana, and Gavan Titley. *The Crises of Multiculturalism: Racism in a Neoliberal Age*. London: Zed, 2011.
Lévy-Brühl, Lucien. *Les Fonctions mentales dans les sociétés inférieures*. Paris: Presses Universitaires de France, 1910.
Lewis, Bernard. *The Arabs in History*. Oxford: Hutchinson and Co., 1950.
- *Faith and Power: Religions and Politics in the Middle East*. Oxford: Oxford University Press, 2010.
- *Semites and Anti-Semites*. New York: W.W. Norton, 1986.
MacKenzie, John. *Orientalism: History, Theory, and the Arts*. Manchester: Manchester University Press, 1995.
Mammeri, Mouloud. *La Colline oubliée*. Paris: Plon, 1952.
Marçais, Georges. *La Berbérie musulmane et l'Orient au moyen âge*. Paris: Éditions Montaigne, 1946.
Marx, Karl. *Collected Works*, vol. 12. London: Lawrence & Wishart, 1979.
Massad, Joseph. *Desiring Arabs*. Chicago: University of Chicago Press, 2007.
Mbembe, Achille. *De la postcolonie: Essai sur l'imagination politique dans l'Afrique contemporaine*. Paris: Khartala, 2000.
McGoldrick, David. *Human Rights and Religion: The Islamic Headscarf Debate in Europe*. Oxford: Oxford University Press, 2006.

Meddeb, Abdelwahab. "Le palimpseste du bilingue." In *Du bilinguisme*, edited by Abdelkebir Khatibi, 125–40. Paris: Denoël, 1985,
- *Talismano*. Paris: Sindbad, 1987.
Memmi, Albert. *Portrait du colonisé, précédé du portrait du colonisateur*. Paris: Éditions Buchet/Chastel, 1957; Paris: Gallimard, 1985. Translated by Howard Greenfield as *The Colonizer and the Colonized*. London: Souvenir Press, 1974.
Miller, Christopher, L. *Blank Darkness: Africanist Discours in French*. Chicago: University of Chicago Press, 1986.
- *The French Atlantic Triangle: Literature and Culture of the Slave Trade*. Durham: Duke University Press, 2008.
Mokeddem, Malika. *L'Interdite*. Paris: Grasset, 1993.
Montherlant, Henry de. *Histoire d'amour de la rose des sables*. Paris: Éditions des Deux-Rives, 1951.
Morrison, Toni. *Playing in the Dark: Whiteness and the Literary Imagination*. Cambridge, MA: Harvard University Press, 1992.
Mukherjee, Arun P. "Whose Post-Colonialism and Whose Postmodernism?" *World Literature Written in English* 30, no. 2 (1990): 1–9.
Noiriel, Gérard. *A quoi sert l'identité nationale?* Paris: Grasset, 2008.
Nordmann, Charlotte, ed. *Le Foulard islamique en questions*. Paris: Éditions Amsterdam, 2004.
Norman, Daniel. *Arabs and Medieval Europe*. London: Longman, 1975.
Ouennaghi, Mélica. *Algériens et Maghrébins en Nouvelle-Calédonie: Anthropologie historique de la communauté arabo-berbère de 1864 à nos jours*. Algiers: Éditions Casbah, 2008.
Parry, Benita. "Directions and Dead Ends in Postcolonial Studies." In *Relocating Postcolonialism*, edited by David Theo Goldberg and Ato Quayson, 66–81. Oxford: Blackwell, 2002.
Pirenne, Henri. *Mahomet et Charlemagne*. Paris: Presses Universitaires de France, 2005.
Ramadan, Tariq. *To Be a European Muslim*. Markfield: Islamic Foundation, 1999.
- *Islam, the West, and the Challenge of Modernity*. Markfield: Islamic Foundation, 2001.
Ratzel, Friedrich. *Die Erde und das Leben*. 2 vols. Leipzig & Vienna: Bibliographisches Institut, 1901–2.
Renan, Ernest. *Oeuvres complètes*, vol. II. Paris: Calmann-Lévy, 1948.
- *Qu'est-ce qu'une nation?* Whitefish: Kessinger Publishing, [1882]2010.
Reynaud, Paul. "Discours inaugural de l'exposition coloniale, 6 mai 1931." In *Le Livre d'or de l'Exposition coloniale internationale de Paris*. Paris: Honoré Champion, 1931.
Ricoeur, Paul. *Histoire et vérité*. Paris: Le Seuil, 1955.

Riffaterre, Michael. "On the Complimentarity of Comparative Literature and Cultural Studies." In *Comparative Literature in the Age of Multiculturalism*, edited by Charles Bernheimer. Baltimore: Johns Hopkins University Press, 1995.

Rodinson, Maxime. *Islam et capitalisme*. Paris: Le Seuil, 1966.

Rosello, Mireille. "The "Beur Nation": Toward a Theory of Departenance." *Research in African Literatures* 24, no. 3 (Fall 1993): 13.

– *Declining the Stereotype: Ethnicity and Representation in French Cultures*. Hanover: University Press of New England, 1998.

– *France and the Maghreb: Performative Encounters*. Gainesville: University Press of Florida, 2005.

Roudinesco, Elisabeth. In *La laïcité à l'école: Un Principe à réaffirmer*. Edited by Jean-Louis Debré. Paris: Éditions de l'Assemblée Nationale, 2003.

Roy, Olivier. *L'Échec de l'islam politique*. Paris: Le Seuil, 1992.

Rufin, Jean-Christophe. *Katiba*. Paris: Gallimard, 2011.

Ruhe, Ernstpeter, ed. *Les Enfants de l'immigration*. Würzburg: Königshausen & Neumann, 1999.

Rushdie, Salman. *Imaginary Homelands: Essays and Criticism, 1981–1991*. London: Granta, 1991.

Said, Edward. *Culture and Imperialism*. New York: Vintage, 1994.

– "Intellectuals in the Post-Colonial World," *Salmagundi* 70–1 (1986): 44–80.

– *Orientalism*. New York: Verso, 1978; London: Pantheon, 1978.

– *The Question of Palestine*. London: Taylor & Francis, 1980.

– "Shattered Myths." In *Middle East Crucible: Studies on the Arab–Israeli War of October, 1973*. AAUG Monograph Series no. 6. Edited by Naseer H. Aruri. Wilmette: Medina University Press International, 1975.

– *The World, the Text, and the Critic*. Cambridge, MA: Harvard University Press, 1983.

Saint-Germès, Joseph. *Économie algérienne*. Algiers: La Maison des Livres, 1950.

Sarraut, Albert. *Grandeur et servitude coloniales*. Paris: Éditions du Sagittaire, 1932.

Sartre, Jean-Paul. *Situations, VIII*. Paris: Gallimard, 1972.

Sayad, Abdelmalek. *La Double Absence: Des Illusions de l'émigré aux souffrances de l'immigré*. Paris: Le Seuil, 1999.

Schor, Naomi. "The Crisis of French Universalism." *Yale French Studies* 100 (2001): 43–64.

Scott, Joan Wallach. *The Politics of the Veil*. Princeton: Princeton University Press, 2007.

Senghour, Léopold Sédar. *Anthologie de la nouvelle poésie nègre et malgache de langue française*. Paris: Presses Universitaires de France, 1948.

Smaïl, Paul [pseud. of Jack-Alain Léger]. *Vivre me tue*. Paris: Balland/J'ai lu, 1998.

Sorel, Georges. *Réflexions sur la violence*. CreateSpace Independent Publishing Platform, [1908] 2014.

Spivak, Gayatri Chakravorty. *A Critique of Postcolonial Reason: Toward a History of the Vanishing Present*. Cambridge, MA: Harvard University Press, 1999.

– *In Other Worlds: Essays in Cultural Politics*. New York: Routledge, 1988.

– "Who Claims Alterity?" In *Remaking History*, edited by Barbara Kruger and Phil Mariani, 269–93. Seattle: Bay Press, 1989.

Tadjer, Akli. *Les ANI du Tassili*. Paris: Le Seuil, 1984.

Tocqueville, Alexis de. *Seconde lettre sur l'Algérie*. Paris: Éditions des Mille et Une Nuits, 2003.

Tournier, Michel. *La Goutte d'or*. Paris: Gallimard, 1986.

Varisco, Daniel M. *Reading Orientalism: Said and the Unsaid*. Seattle: University of Washington Press, 2007.

Vialar, Baron Antoine Étienne Augustin de. *Première lettre à M. le Maréchal Bugeaud, duc d'Isly, gouverneur-général de l'Algérie*. Alger: A. Bourget, 1846.

Wallerstein, Immanuel. *The Modern World-System: Capitalist Agriculture and the Origin of the European World-Economy in the Sixteenth Century*. New York: Academic Press, 1974.

Walter, Henriette. *Arabesques: L'Aventure de la langue arabe en Occident*. Paris: Laffont, 2006.

Weil, Patrick. *Etre français: Les quatre pilliers de la nationalité*. La Tour d'Aigues: Aube, 2011.

– "Lever le voile." *Esprit* 311 (January 2005): 45–53.

– *La République et sa diversité: immigration, intégration, discriminations*. Paris: Le Seuil, 2005.

Index

Abdelkader, Emir, 42, 108, 112
Adorno, Theodor W., 20
Aeschylus, 25
aesthetics, 5, 6, 17, 32, 53, 60–1, 69–70, 72, 74–5, 79, 82, 90, 92, 93, 95, 98, 101, 106, 123, 128–9, 132, 135, 136, 141, 142, 156, 172, 196n29, 198n10
Africa, 27, 33, 44, 46, 47, 63, 65–6, 68, 72, 90–2, 95, 100, 113, 116, 155, 157–8, 177n17, 181n55, 187n13, 189n1, 196n29, 197n32, 199n14, 200n2, 201n8, 201n10. *See also* Maghreb; North Africa
Ahmad, Aijaz, 55–6, 184n22
Algeria, 10, 11, 13, 15, 18, 32, 34, 35, 38, 42–4, 49, 52, 56–9, 61, 64–6, 70, 73–6, 78, 80, 82, 84–7, 90, 92–101, 104–5, 107–15, 117–19, 121–3, 137, 141, 146, 147, 151, 155, 156, 159, 162, 165, 166, 168, 171, 173n1, 174n17, 176n26, 179n39, 180n49, 182n66, 182n72, 183n7, 184n13, 187n14, 188n25, 189n29, 190n5, 190n7, 190n8, 194n7, 194n8, 194n10, 194n13, 195n15, 195n18, 195n19, 196n28, 197n35, 202n18, 205n41, 206n50

alienation, 20, 31, 38, 40, 43, 46, 85, 92, 103, 105, 113, 116, 136, 139, 148, 155–8, 170
Americas, 27, 28, 33, 36, 49, 91
Amrouche, Jean, 43, 57, 94, 183n12, 191n16
Anderson, Benedict, 143
Appadurai, Arjun, 71
Appiah, Kwame Anthony, 12, 185n31
Apter, Emily, 21, 180n45
Arab Human Development Reports, 9
Arab Spring, 5, 22, 159, 188n19
assimilation, 13, 25, 38, 44, 46, 64, 88, 91, 93, 97, 102, 110, 112, 116, 120, 127, 129, 131, 138, 147, 151, 162, 163, 185n26, 205n42, 206n46
authenticity, 19, 26, 31, 33, 38, 43, 46, 47, 85, 100, 115, 122, 131, 144, 198n10

Badinter, Élisabeth, 163, 206n47
Bahrain, 9
Balandier, George, 11
banlieue, 127–8, 130–3, 135–6, 140–8, 159, 161–2, 169, 200n32, 204n34, 204n36, 205n42, 206n48, 207n56